China Beyond Deng

China Beyond Deng
Reform in the PRC

by
Gu Zhibin

McFarland & Company, Inc., Publishers
Jefferson, North Carolina, and London

British Library Cataloguing-in-Publication data are available

Library of Congress Cataloguing-in-Publication Data

Gu, Zhibin.
    China beyond Deng : reform in the PRC / by Gu Zhibin.
      p.   cm.
    Includes bibliographical references and index.
    ISBN 0-89950-583-X (lib. bdg. : 50# alk. paper) ∞
    1. China—Politics and government—1976- 2. China—Economic
policy—1976- 3. China—Forecasting. I. Title.
DS779.26.G8 1991
951.05—dc20   90-53497
                                      CIP

Manufactured in the United States of America

McFarland & Company, Inc., Publishers
  Box 611, Jefferson, North Carolina 28640

CONTENTS

PREFACE

The aim of this book is to investigate the various possible future courses of China's political and economic affairs. Focus will be on the next five to ten years.

The Russian writer Tolstoy has wisely written that happy families are all the same, while in unhappy families each member has his or her own story.

In the Chinese mind, the mother country is like a big family. His family is often under the shadow of misfortunes. Yet, his misfortunes are very different from those of the others. To understand the sorrows of the others is not easy, nor is it easy to understand one's own family. Up to this date, China is mysterious not only to the outsiders, but also to the Chinese themselves.

It is much more difficult to understand China than to understand America, for America is an "open" society. Though no society is entirely open, much more information about American life is available to inquisitive people who may have an interest in looking for it. People, native or foreign, can wonder around in almost any part of the United States as they please. But China is a different story. Her land has been isolated from the rest of the world for centuries and her life is kept a secret from foreign eyes. This creates almost impenetrable limitations for outsiders attempting to understand Chinese life. Especially due to the political upheavals of the last 41 years and earlier, China's minds, young and old, have daily suffered the unspeakable pain of a life trapped in a man-made "cage." This cage has held captive all the free and lively imaginations that are so unique, and so often taken for granted in most other countries.

China has paid a dear price for her self-imposed isolation. Not to mention other things, all China's reforms in the past have ended in bloodshed. China's latest reform, during the 1980s, was finally drowned in bloodshed in China's capital city, Beijing. Like all the reformers in China's previous history, China's current generation of reformers have met with bullets, state persecution, or the choice of life in exile.

In the wider sway of China's history, the history of the numerous old dynastic governments has been like a mediocre writer who could only write so many books; therefore, new volumes are repetitiously copied from his first book. China's history has been characterized by the deadly cycle of powerful autocratic government followed by chaos and civil war. China has not found a way to break away from this cycle. Even her very best minds have not managed to produce alternative paths for China throughout her long history. Again and again, many of her best sons and daughters have ended up as the victims of brave attempts at reform. Nonetheless, China has had the fortune to rise up firmly again and again from the chaos and civil disarray following the collapse of each old government.

China now lives in a radically different world. The progress of the outside world has forced China to begin to modify her social structure, to begin to reform her way of life, to seek new directions, and above all, to seek to become a great modern society. Yet, her slow attempts at reform miscarried in the early part of her modern history. The failures of China's modernization at the turn of this century paved the way for violent movements, and the Communist Revolution was the beneficiary of this trend.

However, the Communist government has not created a new China. Communist political and economic systems built directly upon China's past autocratic traditions. The only real difference between past and present is that the Communist government has pushed China's autocratic tradition to the extreme.

Communist China has run into deadly troubles during the last 41 years. Like China's previous autocratic governments, the Communist party created an excessive concentration of power and economic monopoly that led to endless inner conflicts within its bureaucratic establishment. China's peace and progress were hindered. Even the Communist reform of the 1980s did not enable the Communist authorities to decisively resolve China's crises. Finally, in June 1989, China's great reform abruptly ended in bloodshed.

China's most urgent problem remains her modernization — the creation of modern political and economic institutions. Today, China is part of the world community like never before in its long history. Choices for China too are much wider than ever before. China's own rich experiences and culture compare well with those of the rest of the world, but China continues to lag behind the progress achieved in so many places elsewhere in the modern world. China needs to become a truly modern society, both pluralistic and progress-minded.

Before China can embrace her better alternatives, she could run into a period of pain and suffering in the near future. China's failed Communist reform is now pushing China in this direction.

Future events in China over the next five to ten years are difficult to predict with certainty. On the one hand, China will not be able to escape the powerful influences of her long history and enduring culture. After all, all fundamental changes must be accepted by the Chinese people. On the other hand, fundamental changes in Chinese society have already commenced, especially in the last ten years or so. Many of these changes are irreversible. In fact, though China's reform in the 1980s has suffered serious setbacks since June 1989, reform ideas and actions are still visible everywhere, in all corners of China. In particular, China's door has been kept open to the outside world since June 1989. These facts indicate that no repressive political force in China is strong enough to completely undo the reform movement.

In this book I will try to present China in the truest light possible. I will attempt to reveal the nature of current struggles in China. Many things described here may be unpleasant to contemplate, but those are the things the future China must change without hesitation. I believe a better future is in store for China. China's better future will come when she finds a way to unburden herself of this heavy load of accumulated problems. In short, I must present China to the reader in the truest light I see.

The understanding of the true China today by scholars and researchers is greatly facilitated by the sudden explosion of information on China in the 1980s. Like never before, China's new reality has forced all people in China to reexamine China's past. In fact, almost all Chinese, from the bureaucrats, productive-enterprise directors, and teachers to the blue-collar workers, students, farmers, street vendors, and even soldiers, have begun to be critical of their own lives as well as the existing system in China. China's people are prepared to rediscover themselves as well as the outside world. This is a tremendous force for China's better future. Never in China's history have so many people been searching for an alternative life for themselves as well as for their nation. This new courage of the people by itself will determine that nobody will be able to stop China from entering a creative and productive age. A new China must come to life.

The "China Question" must be viewed in a global context. China and the outside world comprise the international community. China's on-going struggles for a better future must be viewed as her way to become a part of the world, pluralistic, and progress-minded. More and more people are coming to understand that the hope for global peace and global progress must include China. Moreover, progress and peace in China will be one of the achievements of a better world. I believe that China will be able to share more responsibility for creating a more enjoyable life on earth for all. The current struggles of the Chinese people will definitely move China closer toward this goal. A reformed, democratic, and prosperous China will expand the sphere of human activity on a scale that is well beyond ordinary imagination.

This book will focus on China's next five to ten years. It is my view that the decade of the 1990s will be of crucial importance for China's future. All the competing forces in China will have a showdown in this new decade. The outcome of this showdown will be a different China, for better or for worse. I believe that China will have superb chances to depart from the Communist way of life and to embrace a multiparty and pluralistic society. In this book I will investigate all these possibilities.

This book benefits from the fact that I, the author, am a citizen of China, who was brought up and educated there. I have had extensive personal experiences in contemporary Chinese society. I view China not as an outsider, but as an insider.

This book is a product of firsthand experiences plus intense and sometimes painful reflections. I have gone a long way and many times have walked in dark tunnels where things "go bump in the night." In the process of witnessing China's reform, many of my old concepts have had to be abandoned and numerous new ideas have replaced them. I have seen some light, though still dim, at the end of the tunnel. It is my main purpose here to share my thoughts with all those people who wish to know how a better China will help to create a better world and how the outside world can help to promote a better China.

In addition to drawing on my personal experiences, I have used numerous books and articles, many of which are cited in the bibliography. I have read extensively in many of the major journals, newspapers, magazines, and books published in China. I regret that I am able to collate only a very small portion of this new information here in this book. Needless to say, much greater effort will be needed to really digest the massive growth of information on China characteristic of China in the 1980s. Here only a tiny step can be taken in this direction.

Also, I found that the published works of China's leading politicians—such as Mao Zedong, Deng Xiaoping, Chen Yun, and Liu Shaoqi—were extremely useful. Unlike other Chinese writers living in China, these men did not have restraints imposed on them in expressing their views and thoughts. Of course, many of their speeches and writings are still unpublished or unavailable. We have tried to search for the most original works by these politicians.

I am most privileged to have received help from numerous friends. Deep gratitude is extended to everyone who aided me. Some scholars and reformers from China have assisted in this project. They have shared their experiences, insights and research ideas with this author. Without their help, this book could not have been finished. But for some reason, at this time, I cannot thank them name by name. However, this author can thank several other helpers as follows.

Dr. Li Weimin of Dallas, Texas, was the first friend who learned of my project. He has helped throughout this project to fight for a better understanding of today's China. Mr. John D. and Mrs. Elizabeth Hearn Hemenway of Washington, D.C., have been most helpful. Their enthusiasm, extraordinary kindness, and generous help made a significant contribution to the quality and content of this book. Their painstaking efforts to improve the numerous drafts of this book deserve my deepest thanks. Gratitude and appreciation must also go to many other friends, especially Dr. Chen Ping of Austin, Texas, for warm attention and encouragement. Of course, I alone am to be held responsible for all the remaining defects of the book.

As for myself, I have had varied interests. But many of these interests are tied to the "China Question." My research areas include mathematics, in which I received my formal training, and extend to philosophy and intellectual history. I have studied and taught in the United States since 1981 but have followed China's unfolding events closely and kept in close contact with numerous intellectuals in China.

Note on Sources

All quotations of Mao Zedong dated from the period 1957–58 are taken from *The Secret Speeches of Chairman Mao: From the Hundred Flowers to the Great Leap Forward.* The rest can be found in Mao's *Little Red Book* and his five-volume *Selected Works,* or as specified in the text. What appears within brackets [. . .] was added either by the original translators or by the present author in hope of increasing a clear understanding.

All quotations of the other Communist leaders — Deng Xiaoping, Chen Yun, and Liu Shaoqi — are taken from their official *Selected Works.*

For the official version of China's economic reform, see Gao Shangquan and others, *Current China's Economic Reform* (Beijing: China's Press for Social Science, 1984). Also see Ma Hong and others, *Contemporary China's Economy* (Beijing: China Press for Social Science, 1987). Both books are published in the Contemporary China Book Series.

The quotations of other people are taken from the references listed in the Bibliography. Notes are given at the end of each chapter.

INTRODUCTION:
CHINA BEYOND DENG,
PEACE OR CHAOS?

The Communist party has dominated China since 1949. During these more than forty years China has experienced a kind of peace and unity. However, China has also endured endless disasters, tremendous power struggles, widespread famines, frequent civil unrest and chaos, mass purges, and endless political campaigns. Needless to say, almost all these miseries were man-made.

Amidst these man-made tragedies, the Communist leadership has pursued spectacular reform over the past ten years under the leadership of Communist strongman Deng Xiaoping. But these reforms have only gone halfway and have hardly resolved the fundamental problems of Chinese Communist system. Old crises have not been resolved, and many new crises have been spawned. The most serious new crises concern widespread government corruption and inflation.

The 1989 democratic movement indicated the grave trouble characteristic of China's existing Communist system. For the first time in the Communist history, tens of millions of Chinese from all walks of life have directly demanded changes in the Communist rule. Tragically, this popular movement was suppressed with bloodshed in China's capital, Beijing, on June 4, 1989.

As soon as the news spread that guns had been fired into the peaceful crowds, many Chinese immediately sensed the arrival of a new chaotic and violent era. This ability to perceive impending doom is oddly characteristic of the Chinese people, and is perhaps a product of the cycle of war and peace that has occurred over the several millennia of Chinese civilization.

China's four decades of "peace" have been maintained at the sacrifice of tens of millions of lives. Even before the Chinese people could

1

recover from the tremendous man-made tragedies, they wondered whether China would again be drawn into the bitter sea of anarchy and chaos.

This volume shall recount a number of social, political, and economic elements that could throw China into that bitter sea. My purpose here is (1) to present this picture as realistically as possible and (2) to analyze the possibility of minimizing or even avoiding future disasters.

In particular, it is my view that China's problems will have to be resolved by the Chinese people themselves. China's better future will not depend upon paratroopers dropped on Tiananmen Square sent from Taiwan or some other country. A clear focus on the nature of China's crisis and the role played by various social forces within China makes this evident.

WHY DOES THE COMMUNIST LEADERSHIP SEEK REFORM?

Many intellectuals are born reformers and almost always demand reform. To them, change must be constant because things should and can become better. Many Communist power holders are different. At times, the Communists may talk about reform, and at other times do nothing about it. The Maoists even regard reform as "revisionistic" and a "bourgois occupation." Naturally, the Communists are human beings and human beings are different. In a way, Deng Xiaoping is as different from Mao Zedong as Soviet strongman Gorbachev is different from Stalin. When Deng talks seriously about reform, he has some definite benefits to gain from this talk or some unbearable troubles to dump. These "benefits" and "troubles" are what one must try to fully understand. Only then can one comprehend what the Beijing authorities would like to gain and what they would not like to lose. After all, these internal motivations of the Beijing authority have predetermined to a great extent the outcome of the reform in the decade of the 1980s in China.

However, the conspiratorial nature of the Communist authorities seems to demand a special imperative to conceal their true motives and desires. Some ten years have passed since the Communist authorities initiated its reform, but many of us are still confused about the nature of that reform. In particular, the bloodshed in Beijing in 1989 demands from us some clarification of this riddle.

A Puzzle about Deng's Reform

Deng's reform is dominated by this fact: the central leadership now passes down significant decision-making authority to the lower bureaucrats and even to entrepreneurs. Naturally, once the latter have been given opportunities, they immediately become the tough competitors of the central authority that yielded power to them. Competition becomes troublesome to the supremacy of the Beijing government that has permitted competition; yet it is Beijing that has chosen this kind of new life for itself. Here is the puzzle!

Certain human characteristics are universal. Almost all politicians seek to hold as much power and influence as humanly possible. The Communist authorities are naturally just as reluctant as any other power to yield even a little of their authority. The bloodbath on Tiananmen Square resulted from this fact. It took three decades of violent war for the Communists to gain power in China. Since 1949, there have been many tremendous power struggles within the Communist authority. Why did the Communist strongman Deng Xiaoping suddenly choose a reform path that would yield considerable power to the lower bureaucrats? After all, Deng was the de facto government head.

This question can be answered only by looking at the larger picture and the circumstances surrounding Deng's historical decision. In particular, we must discover what factors led Deng to this choice. Only in this way can we gain some understanding of what these leaders expected to gain and to avoid.

Deng's reform slogans are revealing. Deng wanted to bring the chaotic China of the late 1960s and 1970s into a new era of stability, and push the poorly managed Communist bureaucracy into high gear. He wanted to preserve the Communist framework in China and, at the same time, to create a new foundation for the troubled Communist empire. But what has caused these troubles for the Communist empire? Is Deng's decentralization policy actually a realistic way to save the trembling Communist empire in China?

We must enter the secret tower of Communist order. Inside this vast tower the situation is striking: all kinds of internal conflicts, centered on the centralized bureaucratic system, bring endless troubles for the Communist central government to resolve. These troubles can hardly be curbed without radical changes. But how? There were numerous options open for the Communist power holders. But it was Deng who singlemindedly picked the decentralization program as a permanent way out.

Power Succession and Legitimacy

The instability of Communist China, especially in the late 1960s and the 1970s, has been caused by constant power struggles within the Communist leadership. Deng's reform sought to provide a strong and stable cadre. But this was not an easy job for the Beijing authorities. Actually, Communist party attempts to resolve this issue were not without bitter struggles and even civil war throughout Mao's era. Even Deng Xiaoping has followed a very circuitous path to become China's ruler today.

Throughout her long history, China has been ruled by a succession of powerful autocratic governments. The present Communist leadership continues this tradition. With this type of government, the stability of the whole society depends solely on the stability of the high ruling court. The stability of the high court, in turn, depends most often and singlehandedly on a supreme leader. A weak ruler means a weak government, and therefore political unrest and chaos. China's Communist government could hardly change this fact. After all, Communist practices in China today rely on this Chinese tradition of keeping a strongman at the helm.

The Chinese Communist government today is not an institution in the modern sense. It has set up a constitution for the nation, a set of regulations for the Communist party, but China has not been governed according to these written words for even a single day. Rather, the top leadership exploits these written rules or doctrines only when they are instrumental in its power games. In fact, it is hardly an exaggeration to say that power is the only thing that the Communist leaders actually cling to relentlessly. As far as China's palace struggles are concerned, Mao Zedong was correct to a great extent in his recognition that political power comes from the barrel of a gun. Both the old dynastic rulers and the Communist leaders have all manipulated power for their own ends. After all, China has no history of independent political forces to challenge the absolute political authority of the central government, whether imperial or Communist.

In Europe there have been powerful aristocrats as well as rich merchants, among other forces, to provide "checks" and "balances" of the royal power. But China has not had such powerful independent forces throughout her long history. In Communist China today, even private properties have been taken away by the state. There is no clearly defined property ownership law. The conditions for the birth of any independent forces are practically absent. Every citizen has to rely solely on the political authority to survive.

The old autocratic governments had many problems, and

modern China's Communist government has been unable to avoid many of these same troubles. After all, the Chinese Communist government is woven from the same political threads as the old dynasties: Chinese society itself.

Among China's traditional troubles, the biggest one was the problem of power succession and establishing legitimacy. The old rulers experienced much trouble in the orderly transfer of power even within the royal family system. Though the power succession was traditionally accomplished within the royal family, with power usually passing from the father to the eldest son, no absolute rules governed the choice of heirs. After all, the emperor had enormous power in his own hands. An emperor could have many sons, or no son at all, or perhaps sons with different mothers. For various reasons, the emperor might not like his eldest son to be his heir. The eldest son might not be fit mentally or physically or politically. Or an emperor might favor some particular palace woman, other than the empress, and wish to have her son claim the throne. Or the palace eunuchs, the powerful ministers, and the provincial leaders might conspire to elevate their particular royal personage to the throne. In this way, the choice of heir became the balance of various political divisions within the bureaucratic establishment. Therefore, China's history has had endless palace intrigues and power struggles. These inner conflicts have caused hundreds of instances of chaos, anarchy, and civil war in the past.

Today's China is ruled not by a family but by a political party: the Communist party. The Communist power succession takes place within the party hierarchy rather than within the imperial family. But this party hierarchy has hardly resolved the troubles surrounding power succession and political legitimacy.

Communist leader Mao Zedong held more power than any imperial ruler could have dreamed of holding. His very power added to his troubles in choosing an heir. The older he became, the more panic-stricken he and his potential "heirs" became. From the late 1950s until his death in 1976, Mao successively chose four heirs. But none of these potential heirs had lasting good fortune.

Mao's first choice went to his long-time aide, Liu Shaoqi. By 1959, after the grand failure of the Great Leap Forward, Mao was forced to resign as head of state. Liu was chosen for this job and made Mao's official successor. But this choice clashed with Mao's own ambitions. The public explanation was that Mao believed that Liu had departed from Mao's class struggle line and politics-over-economy policies. In truth, Mao turned against Liu because he favored incentives and introduced some market factors such as the "free markets" for the farmers to sell vegetables and other sideline products. Mao was outraged by Liu's actions, which he later denounced as "revisionist." Of course, many of Mao's true motives were successfully concealed by Mao. It took Mao several years to enlist enough allies to dump Liu together with those elements of the Communist bureaucratic establishment that supported Liu's changes. Mao finally succeeded only by plunging China's population into civil war. This Maoist "Cultural Revolution" caused the deaths of hundreds of thousands of innocent people in the course of ten years of factional fighting and state persecution of all perceived "enemies." Already weak Communist laws and regulations were completely destroyed in the process.

As a reward for his help, Mao chose his "Cultural Revolution" crusade partner Lin Biao, who had been defense minister since 1959, as his second heir. The next step in the succession game turned out to be more shocking. Lin, according to Mao, tried for several years to get rid of Mao in order to claim the Communist throne a little sooner. To Mao it appeared that Lin Biao had helped him to dump contenders for Mao's power only in hope of advancing his own position. Although Lin Biao succeeded in becoming the second most powerful Communist, Mao imagined that Lin could not wait for his death. Lin Biao was already in his mid–60s, and perhaps did not want to grow too old to rule while he waited for Mao's death. Palace intrigues sharpened, but Mao acted faster than Lin. As a result, Lin was killed, according to the "official" version, in an airplane "accident," while attempting to flee to Moscow, in September 1971.

Now Mao had to find a third heir to replace Lin Biao. This time, again as a reward, the prize went to his youthful helper, Wang Hongwen, a Red Guard[1] from a Shanghai factory and – as would be claimed in a later denunciation – a member of "the Gang of Four" led by Mao's wife, Jiang Qing. Yet, Mao apparently did not have a minute of peace by this time. Somehow, Mao felt that the Gang of Four had more interest in gaining supreme power than in continuing Mao's cult of personality. Mao believed that these gang members were in hot pursuit of the supreme power. Mao, of course, could come up with this or that reason to dump anybody as he saw fit. As a result, before he died, Mao panicked to such a degree that he hurriedly began to promote his fourth heir, Hua Guofeng, a colorless bureaucrat. A few weeks after Mao's death, his wife, together with the rest of the Gang of Four, were imprisoned by Hua. Yet Hua's power was short-lived. In few years, Hua, together with his followers, had to move out of the Beijing palaces to make way for a new group of leaders led by Deng Xiaoping and Chen Yun.

These decades of Communist power struggles pushed China into misery and despair. China's people had hardly a single peaceful year. Hundreds and thousands of people were killed directly in the course of bitter power struggles and millions perished indirectly as a result of political chaos. Most significantly, the myth of the infallibility of the Communist party was extinguished as a result of these power struggles. All China wished for new and strong leadership to end these troubles, but this outcome would take several years to accomplish.

In the present stage of reform, the power struggles have become more complex, though reform is supposed to bring stability to the Communist power structure and today more is known publicly about its members and its workings. The new star is Deng Xiaoping. It is Deng who has responded to the call of history to provide new leadership and a new direction for China.

However, Deng's rise to supremacy over China was not easy. Deng's power within the Communist party could hardly match that of superman Mao. Following Mao's death in 1976, several leading personalities in the party could match Deng's seniority as well as challenge his experience. In fact, some cadres such as Chen Yun were far more senior than Deng. Chen Yun had been a senior cadre in the top leadership for a couple of decades before Deng was called to join the central authorities in the 1950s. Nonetheless, within the last 15 years or so, Deng has firmly established himself as the head of the second generation of the leadership of Communist China. His consolidation of power has been surprising, especially considering how much hunger for power the old cadres have demonstrated in the last 41 years. But close analysis reveals that Deng's rise to power was a natural consequence of this reform era.

It is Deng's reform programs that have made Deng the supreme leader in China today. He has done many things to make him outshine the other cadres, especially in the late 1970s and the early 1980s during the early stages of China's reform. Undoubtedly, Deng's rapid rise to supremacy was determined by his single-mindedness in turning Communist China in a dramatically different direction. His effort to open China's door to the outside world made him almost immediately an international superstar; his slogan, "to get rich is glorious," warmed Chinese souls that had suffered poverty and hardship for several decades; his call to treat intellectuals as friends, instead of enemies, made the intellectuals feel that they had found a new god to worship; and his determination to let the lower bureaucrats have more power excited the entire bureaucracy. In these and other ways, this clever and calculating politician gained worldwide popularity and a mandate from the Chinese people, thus enabling him to claim the Communist throne and to continue to hold it today.

Deng's strongman leadership has proved to be more effective at keeping China stable than at any time during the previous some two decades. This has not meant that Deng has completely avoided Communist power struggles. In fact, Deng's popularity and power cannot guarantee his supremacy forever, nor can it alone guarantee China's unity and stability. Over the last 15 years or so, he has been able to establish a reform-minded central leadership and he has found useful aides such as Hu Yaobang and Zhao Ziyang. Many of his ideas have been put into practice by Hu, Zhao, and other aides during the 1980s. However, good things do not always last forever. Deng's power declined much faster than his rise to the pinnacle.

In the second half of the 1980s, Deng's two powerful successors, Hu and Zhao, were ousted from the leadership. More ominously, the talentless bureaucrat Li Peng was able to take over the all-important premier seat from Zhao in 1988. During his tenure, Li Peng turned tens of millions of potential friends into bitter foes and greatly reduced China's wealth within the last two years. Indeed, over the last few years, the hard-line doctrinaires led by Chen Yun have invaded Deng's "sacred territories" step by step. By 1989, Deng had to rely on his power contenders to crush the democratic movement. Now he is engaged again, at age 86, in making perhaps his last fight with contenders for his power.

What instrument will Deng employ now? He has lost his reform hero status in China and elsewhere since 1989; his cult of personality has evaporated; his former mainstay, the bureaucracy, is now pursuing its own interests; and his remaining loyalists are looking around for a younger master. What magic does he still have? Sadly, in these intense power struggles, China's unity and peace are in grave trouble. As Frenchman Charles de Gaulle said, "old age is a shipwreck." In this impending shipwreck under "Captain Deng" the only question remaining is: will the crew and cargo be lost on the Chinese ship of state guided by Deng?

Economic Monopoly Versus Total Mess

In essence, Deng's reform in the 1980s aimed at shedding the burden of the Communist central authority. The Communist government retreated significantly from its previous policy of maintaining tight control over China's economic life. Actually, wherever the Communist government retreated, economic progress occurred.

However, to reach this level of determination has taken the Beijing leadership several decades. Moreover, this kind of reform based on decentralization is only one of the many options currently available to the Communist authority. In fact, heated debates on possible recentralization in Beijing are still underway within the Communist power structure.

What was the economic system in Communist China prior to Deng's reform? This system was no more nor less than the Communist government itself. It was the only economic force — and all other forces were practically nonexistent. The nation's whole wealth, means of production, and labor were controlled by the vast Communist bureaucracy. All economic decisions were made by the bureaucrats alone. Everyone else — the workers, the farmers, the businessmen, and the enterprise directors and managers — did what they were told, got only what they were offered, lived on what was provided them.

This centralized economy is a product of the Communist Revolution. Through the central plan, the centralized bureaucracy controls the economic life of the nation. Though this system was relatively easy to create and add to, it is difficult to change. By 1957, the Communist economic system was firmly established. This new economic order means that all China's economic life is controlled by the vast Communist bureaucracy. In particular, this system empowers just a few leaders as the sole managers of all the economic affairs of the nation — at least in principle. Even if some leaders, including Mao Zedong and Deng Xiaoping, have had no knowledge about economics, even the workings of a specific industry, they have the power to make critical decisions. In fact, this vast bureaucratic system has become so inhuman that many cadres have no desire to handle the various economic issues in their particular counties, cities, and provinces, but they are not allowed to dump their load. Such an act would constitute a criminal offense. In essence, the system mandates that Communist officials supervise and interfere with all aspects of the economic activities of Chinese society.

With power comes responsibility. The centralized socialist economy put all power in the hands of the vast bureaucracy, and with it, the responsibility for China's economic success. But before the Communist government could celebrate its impressive victory in the so-called socialist transformation, the bureaucrats' administrative nightmare had begun.

Although by 1957 the Communist bureaucracy was in firm control of the wealth of Chinese society and all means of production, the real troubles had just begun. The whole Chinese population's food, shelter, clothing, education, hospitalization, and millions of other things became the responsibility of this bureaucracy. These burdens now became a more divisive issue than the Communist authorities could ever have dreamed of. To understand the problems of this overextended centralized bureaucracy, an American needs only to imagine the headaches suffered by Washington politicians if the livelihood of every American citizen, including birth, education, housing, hospitalization, food, employment and millions of other things were to be planned and provided by the Washington bureaucracy alone.

China is the world's biggest underdeveloped country. Supplying food to the most populous country on earth, whose population surpassed one billion in the 1980s, constitutes an overwhelming problem for the Communist bureaucracy and one with which they cannot possibly cope. Arable land in China is scarce; with less than 1.5 tillable muo (one muo is one-sixth acre) per capita. Virtually all arable land is already under intense cultivation. Any natural disaster would deprive many of China's people of enough food for survival. Furthermore, this scarce arable land must not only feed China's vast multitudes, but also must provide raw materials for the industrial sector, and produce some agricultural exports necessary for earning foreign currency to finance key industrial imports. Of course, the Communist system is hardly able to resolve these problems.

It is easy to understand why the Communist bureaucracy has experimented with various farming policies during the last four decades, changing from traditional household-based farming to collectives to highly bureaucratic communes, then back to household-based farming again during the current reform era. The purpose of these efforts has been to find a way to produce more food. Over the past forty years the Communist bureaucracy has not stopped its direct interference with rural life for a single day. If the bureaucracy demands the growth of more wheat, rice, and other cereal products, then there will not be enough land to grow vegetables or cotton or oil-plants. These dilemmas are well beyond the comprehension of most people. Finally, the Beijing authorities seem to have realized that the solution to their problems might be simply to leave farming to the farmers. This change is the core of the rural reform in the last ten years.

Nonetheless, all problems, big or small, simple or complex, have to be resolved within the Communist bureaucracy. There are additional burdens to the bureaucracy. Since all former "free markets" and family-owned small stores have been taken over by the state, state-owned stores have also become troublesome. They are usually half-stocked and offer poor-quality services. These problems also have to be dealt with by the bureaucracy.

Since free choice of employment is not allowed in China, the government must find jobs for each citizen, or simply ship the urban people to the country and ban the peasants from entering the cities.

To isolate China from world markets, the Communist authorities had to call upon the nation to "struggle hard" and "stand on its own feet." Economic knowledge of the outside world has been unavailable to the Chinese people. Mutual trade and exchanges in the global markets did not take place during the Maoist era.

Under this centralized system in Communist China, the manufacturing enterprises have virtually no power over production. In Mao's era, all decisions that would be handled by company and managers in Western countries were handled in China by government officials or cadres at the top. The Communist bureaucracy alone allotted money for investment, planned the amount of production, assigned workers and managers to each firm, and distributed the resulting products. The government took any profits or absorbed any losses of the enterprises. For example, a television factory in Shanghai is given a certain amount of money and the necessary materials to produce a specified number of television sets within a specified time. The factories cannot even buy a single piece of equipment or build a toilet without prior approval from the government officials in Beijing.

This rigid centralized control has gone so far as to deny almost all decision-making authority to the millions of provincial and local officials. All provincial and local heads are appointed by the central government. Careers are determined solely on how diligently they take orders from the top. Initiative and independent spirit in these lower bureaucrats could bring immediate trouble to their lives. So even when top directives are obviously wrong, lower officials choose not to stand up and oppose them. In the Great Leap Forward during the late 1950s, the central directives concerning steel and grain quotas were obviously ridiculous and impossible to carry out, but the lower officials did not dare to voice this reality. Instead, many officials faked their production reports and claimed big victories of all kinds. Today, to meet often impossibly high targets for production, enterprise directors and managers count large numbers of defective products while making up the official reports. Such practices are so widespread that the Beijing leadership has been unable to alter them.

Complete control over the production enterprises by the government has many deadly effects on the government. Even when state-owned enterprises could not run at a profit, the government could not close them for fear of causing unemployment, thus damaging political stability. Because the central government skims off all the profits of these enterprises, it also has to assume responsibility for all the losses. In China, it is very common for an enterprise that is not making profits to keep going for several decades, all the time losing money.

All such responsibilities would be very difficult to handle even for the ablest and most flexible governments in the world. Thus, it is no great wonder that all kinds of problems — political, economic, social — are turned into conflicts within the Communist authority. They cause endless troubles to the central government.

The other side of story is even more dismal. Once this centralized system was firmly established, there was and is no easy way to end it. Though China's wealth is controlled by this vast bureaucracy, there is hardly any individual responsibility or accountability within the system. Hardly anybody is certain who is in charge of what and who is responsible for what. The lower bureaucrats say that the higher bureaucrats should be responsible since the latter hold the decision-making authority. But the higher bureaucrats blame the lower bureaucrats for failing to carry out their assigned tasks under the central plan. It must be surprising to many Western people to learn that top leaders, even Mao Zedong and Deng Xiaoping, were and are powerless to move this bureaucratic machine. The rigidity of the centralized economy is the biggest problem for the central bureaucracy. This fact is crucial to the understanding of the root causes as well as the problems for the reform in the 1980s.

Since the time when China's centralized system was established (with help from Soviet planning experts) in the mid–1950s, the

Beijing leadership has experienced vast troubles with its centralized bureaucracy. Mao Zedong could not convince himself that the unitary central plan could fit Communist China. Even the number one central planner, Chen Yun, has constantly expressed doubts about this centralized system. Chen Yun constantly stresses the need for some market elements to make up the deficiencies of central planning, though he feels that market elements must take second place to the centralized system in China.

Since the mid–1950s, the Beijing leadership has tried one way and another to make corrections in the rigidity of the centralized economy. Mao's Great Leap Forward was actually envisioned as a way to partly do away with central planning. Mao simply transferred much decision-making authority and responsibility into the hands of the provincial and local officials. Even the commune-level bureaucrats were offered much more administrative power. Yet that program ended in terrible failure with dreadful consequences such as nationwide famine and economic chaos. The number one heir to Mao at this time, Liu Shaoqi, tried desperately to reintroduce incentives and other market elements to stimulate farm and industrial production. But Liu's experiments ended with the Maoist Cultural Revolution. During the Cultural Revolution, lower-level power abuses increased dramatically, and power was reasserted later by the central authorities.

China's centralized economy has been in complete chaos for the last four decades. The biggest problem, ironically, is the lack of a unified central plan. Endless power struggles within the bureaucracy have prevented the creation of a unified vision for the Chinese economy. After all, Communist authority was established only after several decades of guerrilla warfare. There are so many factions in the government, so many powerful and ambitious regional and local leaders to satisfy, and numerous army generals demanding a lion's share. In short, there are too many claims for attention and power. The central government has to meet all these demands, in an optimal effort to maintain its unity and stability. Therefore, economic development assumes a lesser priority. In fact, long-term economic planning is probably the last thing that this vast bureaucratic body considers.

Little wonder then that maintaining security and stability, not promoting affluence, is the first goal of the central bureaucracy in meeting the needs of the nation. The Beijing authorities have to focus almost exclusively on the political unity and reliability of the bureaucracy, to the detriment of economic development. It has no choice. After all, economic interests are directly tied to various political divisions of the government. China's economic life is constantly sacrificed to the political strife of the vast bureaucracy. And meanwhile no one has ever lost his job for waste on a grand scale.

In particular, once a brand of the economy is chosen to receive priority attention, immediately every central ministry and every province attempts to relate itself to that particular priority. They then demand the same priority attention. When the central government decided to make agriculture its priority, the various industrial ministries cited Mao's slogan, "the ultimate direction for agriculture is mechanization." (Mao invented enough slogans for everyone to use and for all occasions.) Thus all the ministries for industry justified their claim to a share in what began as an agricultural priority. The energy, transportation, and service-oriented ministries also found ways to claim a share of agriculture's priority. As a result, the government's decision to grant priority to agriculture becomes meaningless because "priority" is enjoyed by every branch of the economy.

Even in this reform era, when coastal development strategies centered on intense international trade and exports were emphasized, all the ministries and provinces competed for raw materials, labor, energy, and transportation. These other sectors of the economy demanded adequate investment from the central government. As a result, central government investment was scattered. Yet, the raw material, energy, and transportation sectors have remained a bottleneck for the coastal economy and beyond.

When academics talk about China's realities, they are hard-pressed to find adequate explanations for the strange practices, the irrational policies, and the grave damages inflicted by the government on the Chinese economy. The question is, indeed, quite troublesome: mistakes are unavoidable under all governments, but why does the Chinese government keep repeating the same mistakes over and over again? Moreover, past mistakes have been critically examined and condemned publicly by the central government itself. For example, the central government has historically been unable to stop building new factories even when it clearly sees a threatening shortage of money and raw materials. As a result, many new projects have to be abandoned when only halfway finished. Such waste has consumed tens of billions of yuans. Yet such mistakes have been made continually for several decades and still occur. The simple truth is that every ranking bureaucrat wants to secure as much money and other resources for his own ministry as he can, and selfishly disregards the needs of all other ministries. All the property of the society is effectively controlled by the bureaucracy; hardly anyone or any institution wants to protect this system. Rather, all the bureaucratic institutions in charge of China's economic life want to secure as much advantage as possible from this system. No individual or institution within the system or outside it can seem to stop such waste.

At present a huge quantity of fairly modern, electrically operated equipment, worth $6 billion yuan, together with 20 million tons of steel, sit idle in storage facilities in state-owned factories.[2] This waste is equivalent to the total sum of investments the central government can offer for a whole year. Yet no cadre has lost his job because of this.

The central government has emphasized the importance of agriculture for decades, but China's agriculture has never had sufficient investment to promote appropriate development. In the last few years the central government has also emphasized education, but it lacks the resources to invest in education. In short, there is not enough money to go around for everybody. Agriculture and education can wait because they pose no immediate threat to the existing bureaucratic system. After all, the central government can easily handle China's farmers and intellectuals, but the powerful provincial and local leaders, the army generals, and the directors of large-scale state-owned enterprises are a different kettle of fish.

Despite all these tremendous inner conflicts, it took several decades for the Beijing authorities to reach the level of determination required to dump the central plan. This finally happened — at least to some degree — in Deng's era. Explosive inner conflicts had reached a point where there were no short-term solutions. That is also the reason why Deng Xiaoping believes that the current reform to do away with the centralized economy is a great revolution. Even Chen Yun, the biggest central planner, indicates that the current effort to "revive" China's economy is much more significant than the 1956 Communist "socialist transformation" when central planning was initiated.

So far, the best idea of Deng's reform is what is called "sanctioned decentralization." Provincial and local officials are offered more decision-making authority. Even the individual entrepreneurs are allowed to pursue their private interests. In short, the Communist central authority has taken a series of retreats from previously held positions.

Deng's decentralization programs resolved some of the problems of the rigid centralized system of the Maoist era. In essence, however, decentralization is no reform. It does not create any new economic system. Well defined property ownership does not exist today anymore today than it did in Mao's time. Rather, it is merely a way for the central bureaucracy to dump its responsibilities and troubles. Above all, Deng's reform has not aimed at creating a market economy, independent of bureaucratic control. The Communist bureaucracy remains the dominating force in China's economic life. This Communist bureaucracy still has the power to control directly and to interfere in the people's economic activities. China's new problems such as government corruption and inflation in the decade of the 1980s are fundamentally tied to this reality.

Finally, we must point out that China's old dynastic governments also ran into problems similar to the problems of the Communist bureaucracy. In fact, the problems facing the old governments were centered on efforts to put as much of economic life of the nation under the complete control of the government. The old governments all tried to control as much of economic life as they could. But central control always turned out to be too much of a burden. As happened repeatedly, the old governments tried to dump their burden by sanctioned decentralization. Yet deadly consequences invariably followed. Decentralization ushered in power erosion at the level of local government. Erosion at the local level then led to chaos and disintegration within the centralized bureaucracy, and then to national chaos. China's reality today parallels China's dynastic past in precisely this sense.

Social Elements in the Early Reform Stages

Most politicians are realists. Unlike Hamlet, they do not ponder the question "to be or not to be." Their actions represent more their own interest than that of God or the common weal. After all, the leaders who represent their fellow men's interest believe that they can accomplish as much, if not more, as those who formally claimed to represent God. Actually, a little personal gain can push many politicians into obsession, though that in turn may jeopardize their long-term interest.

Mao Zedong was precisely such a politician. His uncontrollable zeal for absolute power drove him in a lifelong mad pursuit. His intense jealousy of such able aides as Liu Shaoqi and Deng Xiaoping and his inability to manage the Communist bureaucracy drove him to mobilize China's entire population in the so-called Cultural Revolution, a civil war by another name, to regain his personal power. The myth of the infallibility of the Communist party, together with Mao's own personality cult, was lost in the process. This is also the case with Deng Xiaoping. His obsession with absolute power pushed him to mastermind the massacre of June 1989. This action will deprive him of the status of great statesmanship in history books. To understand this point is to be a step closer toward understanding China's reality today.

The Beijing authorities had various options and they might have chosen to pursue a different kind of reform than that which has dominated the Chinese scene in the 1980s. Various political divisions within the Communist power centers held difficult ideas. The Communist authorities could well change things within the Communist system. After all, even the colorless Hua Guofeng managed to attain and hold China's rulership for some years after Mao's death. That Deng could successfully launch his reform programs has had a rather involved historical background.

Chinese society was deeply enmeshed in the Maoist "Continued Revolution." By the end of Maoist Cultural Revolution in 1976, the then-existing Communist system was despised by almost all the people. This included millions of cadres, including Deng Xiaoping and Chen Yun, the two most powerful Communists in the reform era. The last thing the Communist authorities wanted is for China's people to recognize their failures. By the late 1970s, however, China's people realized that the Communist economy *was* a total failure.

China faced a tragic situation throughout the Cultural Revolution from 1966 to 1976 and even beyond this period of social disruption. The biggest agricultural country of the world, China suffered grave shortages of food, vegetables, cooking oil, laundry soap, and other absolute essentials for survival. The shops had half-empty shelves. The people could find little food beyond government-issued coupons and other essentials were also scarce. China's people clearly saw that this tragedy was caused by the Communist system. Increased abuses of power and official erosion galvanized the people into demanding less control and more openness within their society.

In a completely new dimension for China's people, China's

narrow opening up since the mid–1970s has brought much new information about the progress of the outside world. Extensive media coverage — though still censored by Western standards — brought new inspirations to tens of millions of people in China. Progress, not only in Western nations and Japan, but also in the Chinese societies of Taiwan and Hong Kong, and in the Chinese culture–based societies such as South Korea and Singapore, have opened the eyes and the minds of the Chinese people like never before.

Needless to say, Maoist class struggle was rapidly dying out. China's people, at least the majority of them, had followed Maoist class struggle for several decades. Though tens of millions people had fallen victim to the numerous civil unrests, famines, mass purges, and general chaos, the Maoist revolutionary promises had not been fulfilled. There had been great failures in the economy, in political stability, and in social progress. Nothing resulted from Maoist class struggles except common poverty, starvation, unemployment, spouse separation, massive purges and killing, and public despair.

It became unbearable for the Communist power holders, and even more for the Chinese people, to see that Taiwan and Hong Kong were achieving economic miracles over the same period when Communist China was failing miserably. What was Taiwan in the eyes of the mainland Communist power holders? Taiwan was no more than a tiny island that had been controlled by the badly defeated Kuomintang after it fled the Communist victory in 1949. Those Kuomintang cadres were going to be captured someday and put on trial for being the enemies of the people. Since 1949 the Beijing authorities had been telling the Chinese people that the people in Taiwan were suffering under the Kuomintang and that they dreamed of the day when the Beijing power would "liberate" them. Yet reality showed otherwise: living standards of the Taiwan Chinese were far better than their counterparts on the mainland. The Chinese believe that Hong Kong is Chinese soil, but that it has fallen shamefully into British hands as a colony for some one hundred years. To make Hong Kong part of China once again is one of China's greatest dreams. However, China's people have learned that even under British control, Hong Kong has enjoyed an economic miracle similar to Taiwan. These facts demonstrated, among other things, that even when operating under "oppressive" colonial conditions, Chinese could enjoy a better life outside China than in a so-called perfect "socialist" society.

Following Mao's death in 1976, more and more overseas

Chinese and other foreigners began visiting China. It was most striking to mainland Chinese that their overseas cousins could return to
their homeland with so many goodies that their mainland relatives
could not even imagine owning. Chinese people had never dreamed
of owning a car and a house, but their cousins in Taiwan, Hong
Kong, and the United States did possess such things. This was a
striking discovery: the Chinese people in Taiwan and Hong Kong
were producing modern electronics, computers, highways, cars,
and houses, while the Chinese in China were producing mass
purges, class enemies, empty slogans, prisons, and labor camps.
How perverse the Communist system had become! This simple
reality has become the most powerful inspiration for China's people
to desire to change the Communist system.

No one is able to stop the new dream of the Chinese people.
Once China's people learned something about the outside world,
they undertook to totally discover that world with a determination
that was absent during Mao's era and even for many centuries earlier.
Never in China's history have her people been more interested in
discovering the outside world. The "open door" practices in the
decade of the 1980s reflect this popular inspiration. In fact, it has
become the number one task for China's people to discover the outside world as well as their own life in the 1980s.

All things considered, departure from the Maoist lines was inevitable. Even veteran leaders such as Deng Xiaoping and Chen Yun
suffered terribly under Mao's tyranny during the Cultural Revolution. Hardly anybody at any social level could tolerate the existing
Communist system. Reform was in the minds of all China's people,
much as it was in the Soviet Union after the death of Stalin in 1953.

The Communist bureaucratic body played a most significant
role in pushing the reform movement at this stage. There were numerous personnel changes in the bureaucratic system in the late
1970s and early 1980s. The Maoist politicians, the Red Guards, the
troublemakers, the political peddlers, the opportunists, and the
class-struggle specialists, who sat on all China and dominated during Mao's era, especially during the Cultural Revolution, were
largely ousted by this time. Veteran cadres who had suffered under
Mao's regime were restored to their old or similar positions. These
old cadres, now in their 60s and 70s, suddenly regained youthful
strength and vigor and openly demanded a complete change in the
Soviet, Stalinist-type centralized economy and political system. In
fact, any word suggestive of absolute central authority smelled

rotten to millions of cadres. After all, this Communist system had made them the victims of oppression for some ten years. Communist China had built hundreds and hundreds of prisons and labor camps supposedly for "counterrevolutionaries," but millions of veteran cadres, the revolutionary heroes, were locked up in those prisons for a number of years during the Cultural Revolution. No wonder that once these men were freed from imprisonment, these aging cadres would suddenly gain youthful energy and agitate to dump Maoist practices. Naturally, in this early stage of reform, the strongest voice against the Maoist order came from these old Communist warriors. Numerous official study groups were sent to the Communist states in the Eastern European Bloc and beyond. Successful experiments with less central control and a more flexible economic life in such Communist states as Hungary and Yugoslavia excited the entire bureaucratic body in China. Many of China's veteran cadres were eager to try anything that was not Maoist.

Also during this period, new faces from the technically trained professionals and intellectuals were rapidly entering the bureaucratic system. To these new officials, as to millions of disillusioned veteran cadres, the central authority repeatedly made countless great mistakes, and therefore lost its moral supremacy. With the influx of this new blood, the bureaucracy was less inhibited by the thinking of the older veteran cadres. Each person, not just the powerful veteran cadres, would now have the right to question the policies of the central authority. Each person, upon entering office, hoped one way or another to gain a greater share of power from the central government. In short, hardly any cadre was as likely to follow the directives from Beijing as blindly as in the Maoist era. After all, millions of cadres believed that their fellows' blind obedience to the central authority had caused their persecution and suffering for so many years.

At this stage, the central authority lost much of its long-held moral supremacy and the absolute prestige of inherent legitimacy. Every bureaucrat, including the enterprise directors and managers, felt freer to demand less central control and more power sharing. This was a very significant factor promoting Deng's reform. Because this demand came from within the bureaucracy, it was much more powerful than voices in the streets. After all, Communist authority rests upon its vast bureaucracy. To the Beijing authorities, to unify the Communist bureaucracy is to unify Communist China. The significance of the bureaucracy, and its dissatisfaction with the central authority, joined to become the key factor that led to reform in China.

In fact, due to its repeated failures, the Communist central authority gradually lost confidence in its ability to govern with an iron hand as previously. Many central leaders finally became disillusioned with rigid central planning. By the late 1970s the situation reached an explosive stage. Income for the central government had fallen terribly short. Yet demands from all directions—provincial and local governments, the army, the large state-owned enterprises—were higher than ever. The central government would not allow the various government units, especially the provincial and the local governments, to manage their own revenues prior to reform. So the central government had to have enough money for everyone. Yet by this time the central government had little money in hand to go around. The political stability of the bureaucratic system was in grave danger. The most obvious way to reduce this bureaucratic tension was to let the provincial and local governments look after their independent revenues and share more burdens, and to let the productive enterprises share more responsibility. Yet this idea was not yet fashionable when Mao died.

Other crises faced the central authority. Let us mention one or two cases that have attracted much attention from the international media. Since the mid-1960s the central government has had increasing problems supplying jobs in sufficient numbers to absorb high school graduates from the urban areas. Indeed, due to the failure of the Great Leap Forward, about 20 million city dwellers were sent down to the rural areas in the early 1960s. Also, throughout the Cultural Revolution (1966–76), tens of millions of high school graduates from urban regions were sent down to rural regions. By the late 1970s, the harsh manual work and the backward rural life had finally driven many millions of these disillusioned high school graduates to demand a return to urban areas. This situation was deadly troublesome for the Communist bureaucracy. In Beijing, Shanghai, and other major cities unrest fueled numerous demonstrations. The government could not find the money to supply jobs for these dissatisfied people. In the 1980s, it is very natural to see the benefits of private initiatives that enable youths to find jobs for themselves. Yet in the mid–1970s, such a solution did not surface.

Also, in 1978–79, during the crucial time of the numerous Communist conferences that would give rise to Deng's reform, tens of thousands of victimized peasants gathered and slept in Beijing's streets. These angry crowds were demanding the end to man-made tragedy: hunger, forced family separations, official corruption, and state repression. In fact, it was at this time that the public voiced most strongly its demand that the people have freedom and be allowed to take more initiatives. The absolute image of the legitimacy of Communist authority was completely gone in the eyes of hundreds of millions of Chinese people. After all, it was this Communist authority that had pushed China into chaos and despair. A new leader was needed to lead the people to confront the crises.

At this time, China's intellectuals and educated people were raising their voices to demand fundamental changes within the Communist system. The major demands centered on enterprise freedom, separation of the party from the administration, greater private initiative, and less government control. It is not surprising that the reform slogan became "Give more authority to the enterprises and individuals!" By the late 1970s a small but determined number of democratic activists were actually calling loudly to introduce a multiparty system and a market economy. Wei Jingsheng and his fellow democratic activists tried to establish an organized opposition to the Communist party at this stage.[3]

However, the background of Chinese society was much more complicated at this stage. Most noticeably, despite all the popular enthusiasm for change, very few people in China knew precisely what changes they would like to see introduced, though they could list many current realities they did not want anymore. Therefore, there was an urgent need for a new leader to surface and to articulate exciting reform programs calculated to cure the frustrations of the people. Mao's fourth and final heir, Hua Guofeng, proved only capable of pursuing Maoist policies after Mao's death and the fall of Gang of Four. So he was found to fail and to step down soon.

The newly restored Beijing leadership under Deng Xaioping and Chen Yun was divided on policy. In particular, this new leadership did not quite know what to do to resolve the crises. Hua Guofeng's vision for another "great leap forward" in 1977–78 ground to a halt as he yielded power to Deng Xiaoping and Chen Yun. By the late 1970s, by which time Deng and Chen had returned to the top levels of leadership and had successfully consolidated their power, they already had made up their minds to depart completely from the previous Maoist practices of class struggle and mass mobilizations.

Now, as the real holders of power, Deng, Chen Yun, and other aging leaders were faced with deciding between various competing policies. Almost all these leaders in the reform era opposed Mao's economic policies. But they did not know what to introduce to replace Maoist policies. As realists, Deng and his colleagues turned their ears to the public voices, within the bureaucracy and beyond. The provincial and local bureaucrats, as well as enterprise directors and managers, had been crying for more power sharing. It was natural for Deng to choose a policy of decentralization in order to gain wide support.

In this reform era, Chen Yun has led the opinion group for the so-called central planners. He had been very wary of Deng Xiaoping's sanctioned decentralization as a way out of the troubles Communist centralism had created for the socialist planned economy. Chen Yun and his colleagues looked at China's economy from an engineer's point of view: they tried to decide what can be done, and what cannot be done if Communist supremacy is to continue.

To continue Communist supremacy, Chen Yun and his followers believe in continued Communist domination over China's economic life. Therefore, to "perfect" the existing centralized system rather than to disperse it is the ultimate goal of these central planners. To them, the Communist system in China cannot afford to have a weak central power. They have insisted that the absolute control of the economy by the central government is essential to the maintenance of the Communist political monopoly. The central planners see no other choices possible.

Yet Deng Xiaoping has been critical of Chen Yun's containment policy. Complete control of the economy by the government was, to Deng and his followers, the very cause of the fundamental disasters that characterized the first 30 years of Communist rule. After all, tight control had been very troublesome to the top leadership. How could the leaders just give orders and not let the people have some incentives? Deng viewed the troublesome problems of the centralized economy as the direct result of "controlling too much" and "too much central power."

It must be said that Chen Yun and his followers have a number of persuasive arguments against Deng's decentralization-based reform programs. Chen can easily point out that even in Mao's era, all the attempts at decentralization ushered in economic chaos and political instability. Both the Great Leap Forward and the Cultural Revolution were instances in which a decrease in central power led to wild abuses of power and chaotic economic life at the local level. Furthermore, it was only through tough, austere recentralization programs that the nation recovered from the chaos and failures of these two experiments. Reading Chen Yun's published speeches and writings, one can sense that, at the bargaining table, Chen Yun easily and convincingly pointed out to Deng that another decentralization-based reform would not work since similar attempts had failed terribly several times already. If another decentralization would probably fail, why try it in the first place? "Don't you, Deng Xiaoping," Chen Yun asks, "want to uphold the Communist supremacy over China? Why, then, do you wish to yield the Communist central power if it is bound to cause trouble? Once the bird escapes the cage, how can you make it go back?" Chen asked.

However, Deng Xiaoping and his followers were unconvinced by Chen Yun's arguments. Reading Deng's speeches and writings, we can see that Deng is firmly convinced that the ultimate way for the central authority to rid itself of its worst problems is to push for complete decentralization. To Deng, the Communist authorities would be terribly foolish to continue to handle all the affairs and thus all the troubles of Chinese society. Deng might have asked, "How could you, Chen Yun, be sure that the central authority would be able to handle all these crises alone? Have not the decades-long mischiefs of the central authority been enough for you, Chen Yun? How could you allow the millions of lower officials to sit idle and do nothing, while blaming the central authority for all failures? Shouldn't all the officials be held responsible for something? Above all, with millions of officials already quite disillusioned with the central power, how could you make them believe in you again without offering them some incentives? Then, if you could not keep the bureaucratic body together, in what way would you talk about the Communist supremacy over China?"

Therefore, in Deng's mind, the reform program based on decentralization and an incentive-responsibility system must be installed once and for all. Only then, Deng asserts, can the Chinese society operate on a rational basis. Even if there will be more serious problems in the future, everybody, not just the central authority, will share the responsibility for them equally. Once this system of individual responsibility becomes fully established, the Communist authority only needs to "work with half effort, while double work is accomplished." Thus Deng has pushed his program at full speed.

How then did Deng Xiaoping gain the upper hand over Chen

Yun and his followers? After all, both Deng and Chen have many strong reasons for their different opinions.

Answers are readily apparent. Deng received popular support from all the lower bureaucrats in the Communist party and government. This should be no surprise: every bureaucrat, in every ministry, in every country in the world would like to get more power. Therefore, Deng enjoyed great popularity with the provincial and local cadres. Most Central Committee members are from the provinces rather than from Beijing. In this way, the Party Conference easily adopted the Deng's reform policies in December 1978 and thereafter.

One most interesting event concerns the 13th Party Congress held in October 1987. In that meeting, though the reform-minded cadres lost many key positions in the government, the reform slogans were still upheld in the party documents. Yet, soon after, Zhao Ziyang lost his premier seat and Chen Yun's followers took numerous key positions, including the premiership. All the events since have resulted directly from these personnel changes.

Over the decade of the 1980s, Chen Yun has had strong support in the capital from the central planners. Beijing is not just China's capital but also the capital for central planners. Therefore, Deng Xiaoping has had to recruit many of his top aides from outside the capital. By 1980, Deng immediately formed his reform cabinet by moving into the capital Zhao Ziyang of Sichuan Province and Wan Li of Anhui Province, among other provincial leaders.

Since late 1986, most of Deng's top aides have been defeated by the central planners. If Deng should want to pursue his reform again, he would have to assemble a new cabinet by drawing members from the provincial and local leaders. Actually, he has been moving in this direction. The new party chief, Jiang Zemin of Shanghai, and the new Politburo standing member, Li Ruihuan of Tianjin, have been called into the capital since the June 1989 bloodshed.

Beginning in the late 1970s, Deng gained overwhelming support from almost the entire Chinese population. After all, Deng publicly offered a slogan that the people should try to get rich: "Getting rich is no crime in Maoist terms, but glorious." Deng's reform programs won worldwide admiration. In the eyes of the lovers of the free-market economy, Deng became the campaigner for the cause of free markets — the great reformer for a brave new world. Even many socialist theorists thought that Deng wanted to depart from the bureaucratic economy. It was partly because of all this international praise that Deng and the other aging leaders, in front of the eyes of the world, carried out the bloody crackdown in Beijing in June 1989. Now Deng is again trying hard to gain back the image of a great reformer as well as the image of a creator of a brave new world.

The bloodshed in June 1989 in Beijing has awakened most people. More people now see clearly that all the Beijing leaders, and in particular Deng Xiaoping, have lost in their political crusade. Naturally, Deng is the biggest loser of all.

However, China is no longer either the Maoist or the Dengist China. China's reform in the decade of the 1980s has progressed remarkably. Many of the reform results are irreversible. In particular, the new social forces that were produced by the reform will have to grow. We will turn to these issues in the following chapters.

Notes for Chapter 1

1. Red Guards are sometimes limited to the Maoist student rebels in some literature. Here we consider the Red Guards in a more general sense, which includes all the Maoist rebels, or the so-called troublemakers, who took part in the power struggles of the Maoist Cultural Revolution.

2. Lin Wenyi and Jia Lurang, "On the Law of Supply and Demand and Its Role in Socialist Economy," *Economic Research* 1 (1981).

3. Wei Jingsheng was the leader of the Beijing Spring Movement in 1978–80. That movement raised the question of democratic alternatives for China. Wei and his fellow comrades tried to form China's first independent political opposition. But the movement was crushed and many democratic activists including Wei were put in prison by Deng's administration by 1980. Wei remains in prison to this date. For more information, see Wei Jingsheng and others, *A Selection of Poetry and Essays from the Beijing Spring Movement — The Fate of the "Democratic Wall"* (Hong Kong: Ping Ming Press, 1979); and *Say Yes to Yourself, Say Yes to Democracy — A Declaration of Human Rights of the Mainland Youths* (Taipei: Associate Press, 1979). Some English translations can be found in Gregor Benton, ed., *Wild Lilies, Poisonous Weeds: Dissident Voices from the People's Republic of China* (London: Pluto Press, 1982).

2

REFORMS AND NEW
SOCIAL FORCES

If one short sentence could summarize the results of China's reform, it would be: The reform has created many new social forces.

Prior to the reform movement, under the tight centralized economy, the Communist central bureaucracy was the most powerful force in determining China's economic life. By 1990, China's economic life was no longer determined by the central government alone. The old centralized economy no longer dominates the market.

If we imagine economic life as a basketball court, then today in this basketball court the Beijing government is only one of the teams playing there. In fact, it has now gained many competitors—the provincial and local governments, the productive enterprises, and the entrepreneurs. Most interestingly, almost all of these teams are playing against the Beijing government team. Whenever the Beijing team loses, progress is made in China.

Since 1979, the cage imprisoning China has been slowly opened. China's economic dynamics have shifted. The central authority has rapidly declined in its power and domination. China has changed faces. All social groups have been engaged in the hot pursuit of their own economic interests and benefits. Many dramatic results have occurred within a short span of some ten years.

All the socioeconomic groups in Chinese society are competing in a new field, mainly with the central government, for space and influence. The farmers have gained incentives to return to a traditional rural life. The Communist bureaucracy has made a major retreat from the rural areas. Also, small-scale entrepreneurs have emerged in both the rural and urban areas in hot pursuit of prosperity.

The productive enterprises now have clear economic interests of their own. They want to have more independence from the bureaucracy. Increasingly, they *are* becoming more independent.

The provincial and local governments are the biggest winners of the reform so far. They have demanded more power from the central government openly and successfully. An enormous transfer of power has taken place over the last ten years. Provincial and local officials have had direct incentives and received much benefit from the reform. The reform results in the 1980s have been actively tied to the performance of the provincial and local governments.

In a broad sense, China's various socioeconomic groups are also competing with each other for more independence and influence in society. The central government has become merely one competitor among many. All these things have created a new environment as well as new social forces for a completely new system in China: a market economy based on fair competition as well as well-defined property ownership law.

Though China's reform has suffered a serious setback since June 1989, China's new social forces are still in existence. To be sure, these new forces will increase their influence and power in China's future. It is safe to say that a new China will eventually be built by these new forces.

Current Reform Is Fundamentally Different from Previous Reform Attempts

All the previous reform attempts, or more precisely, adjustments, in the Maoist era were carried out only within the Communist system. There were numerous adjustments prior to 1978, but all of them were in the nature of "kicking the ball around." Broadly speaking, both Mao's Great Leap Forward in 1958–60 and Deng Xiaoping's brief reform attempt in 1974–75 were of this nature. But Deng's reform has broken with the previous cycles of very limited adjustments.

China's reform in the decades of the 1980s started with a fundamental different premise. The key difference is that Deng's reform focuses on breaking up the centralized system and finding some definite alternatives once and for all. Ultimately, Deng would like to relieve the heavy load on the central government by giving more power to the lower bureaucrats and even to the entrepreneurs. It is precisely in this manner that Deng's reform has gone out beyond the usual limit of the Communist reform attempts.

China's current reform also differs from previous reforms in several other significant ways. First, Deng's economic reform takes place within a global context with his so-called open door policy. That is, China's economic life is now linked to global markets and for the first time since 1949 China intends to become part of global economic life. It is a truly revolutionary step for China to accept this new principle in her search of modernization. The previous Communist reforms all tried to keep China isolated and away from the outside world. This new openness in the decade of the 1980s is a most significant policy shift.

The last thing the Maoist government wanted the Chinese people to know was that the Communist government had not succeeded in creating a miracle. Once Deng's administration opened China's door to the outside world, the very first thing confronting China's people was the realization that there has been no miracle in Communist China. With knowledge of the outside world has come new inspiration for China's people to struggle for a better life. The economic miracles in Taiwan, Hong Kong, and other regions in the outside world have convinced China's people that they do not need to rely on Mao's class struggle and purges to make progress in China.

China's people have gained fresh confidence about their ability to establish a new system in China. China's people are now determined to rediscover the world. This new determination could be as significant to China as the Renaissance was to Europe. In fact, the intensity of the Chinese inspiration to build a modern China has far exceeded European inspiration during that restless age. China's intense struggles in the decade of the 1980s can only be understood in this light. In a way, China is like America in the 18th century, when she stood on the threshold of an entirely new age. Indeed, what the Chinese people have been doing since the late 1970s is completely new to themselves as well as to the outside world.

China's reform came after great Communist failures, especially the Maoist Cultural Revolution. Since the Cultural Revolution had involved almost every citizen in China, its tragic lessons were particularly revealing to the Chinese people. China's people saw that they were trapped by the deadly consequences — economic chaos, political unrest, and social disintegration — caused by ten years of bitter political struggle. Only after the deaths of millions of people in the Maoist class struggles of the previous several decades could the frustration and anger of China's people reach the level at which they were ready to turn against the Communist system. Now China's people are determined to bring a new life to China.

However, China's current reform has walked a twisting path. China's economic reform has immediately raised the issue of establishing a complete new economic order to replace Communist central planning. In the process of reform, the failure of central planning has been revealed to millions of people. This, in turn, has offered courage to China's people to completely dump the central planning system.

From 1980 on, the reform issues related to the basic conflicts between the market economy and the centralized economy were raised and intensely debated. Also, many people, from Deng Xiaoping on down to the people on streets, have been talking about new relations between the government and the productive enterprises. These debates reflect the fact that the people are now trying to escape the existing Communist framework. Few people are working to repair the numerous big flaws in the existing system. Most people now want to search for new directions, new paths, new systems. Somehow, the popular mentality in China by 1980 had reached the critical stage: people believed that whatever existed in the Communist system was bad, and whatever is new is good. However, this change in the popular mentality has not really hastened the establishment of a new system in China. In fact, the idea of completely replacing the bureaucratic authority by the market economy did not enter the Chinese mind until very recently. Even China's intellectuals did not realize the urgent need for China to establish modern institutions and the market system until the late 1980s. However, a strong desire for a complete change of the old centralized economic life has greatly expanded the vision and courage of the people. This, in turn, has speeded the decline of the existing Communist system.

Two important viewpoints in the Beijing leadership have gradually emerged. One faction of the cadres feel that whatever the government is unable to handle successfully should be handled by the people outside the government. The second faction consists of those cadres who feel that whatever the markets cannot do correctly and with optimal results should be handled by the government.

The debates between these two groups have given rise, one way or another, to many new opportunities for the Chinese population. Through this process, more and more people understand that Communist central planning has little to do with China's economic development; indeed, many now recognize that the central planning system is the economic source for the endless Communist power struggles. In particular, the legitimacy of the authority for a centralized economy is broken. The ugly contents of the central planning system have been revealed to the public. This knowledge of the Communist government's inner working has helped to speed the rapid decline of the centralized system by discrediting it.

Today, China's people no longer look at the centralized economy as something "sacred," an attitude which had been carefully and skillfully maintained by the Communist authorities for 30 years. Now more people, including intellectuals, lower cadres, businessmen, educated professionals, and enterprise managers, openly question the positions of the government. Unlike in the past, the Beijing leaders can no longer hide their true motives and avoid the effects of popular opinion. In Mao's era, it was very different. Anybody who questioned the "sacred central plan" committed a criminal offense. Now, China's people can talk openly about the rights and wrongs of the government. This change could have explosive consequences. One thing leads to another and eventually it leads the people to ask the most basic question: on what basis does government legitimacy and authority rest?

In the decade of the 1980s China's people can openly discuss whether the government should interfere with China's economic activities. If it should, then how much? Should the government tell the people what to do, even if the people know better than the government and knowledgeable people believe that the government's intended course is incorrect? What rights does the government have to stop people from getting what they desire? Should the government take over the profits of the enterprises? Who is really responsible for an effective economy that fulfills the needs and desires of the Chinese people?

In this reform era, the government wants to adjust its relations with the productive enterprises. This change will mean that the enterprises will no longer be merely tools in the hands of the bureaucracy. The enterprises now have their own identity, their own interests, their own demands, and their own needs. The workers, the farmers, and the individual businessmen can pursue their own interests, interests that might not be identical with those of the Beijing authorities. In this way, the reform movement has been directly involved at the grassroots level and has enjoyed the support of the various government organizations as well. The basic production units have become the most important social foundation for all the changes to follow.

The "sacred cow," the image of the centralized economy, has

been killed, and by the hands of the Beijing authorities themselves; the absolute authority of the government has thus become nothing but a "paper tiger." In this way, the provincial and local officials, the enterprise directors and managers, the individual businessmen, and the farmers have all stepped up onto the stage of the reform. "While gods and ghosts are still fast asleep, millions of events have taken place" — China's reform in the 1980s has again verified this old Chinese saying.

The results of China's reform during the 1980s are very impressive by any objective measure. It is our view that China has made threefold progress. First, China has entered the world markets and its economic life is now linked to that of the outside world. Second, China has undergone dramatic changes in its internal economic system; central planning is now considered virtually obsolete as a way to command the economic life of modern China. Third, and probably the most important manifestation of progress, China's reform has produced new social forces. In short, China's reform movement has opened a wide field for Chinese society to introduce new players into a new economic system based on a clearly defined property ownership law. More and more people have now realized that only with a well-defined property ownership law will China become a truly great modern society.

The Present Reform Has Started at the Weakest Points, Not at the Crucial Points

"Many things we desired so much never come; many other things we never dreamed about occur." This has been China's history for the last ten years and it is especially true of China's rural reform.

Since its beginning in 1979, the reform movement in China has lacked one thing: theory, or what some would call "vision." Nobody, from Deng Xiaoping on down to the people on the streets, dreamed that so many opportunities would show up in this reform age. Hardly anyone was prepared to offer suggestions or insightful comments. During the three years prior to 1979 all of China was caught up in dramatic events that took place one after another. Premier Zhou Enlai died in January 1976; three months later, on April 5, tens of thousands of people filled Tiananmen Square to denounce Mao's class struggle, only to be shot at by military forces under Mao's control. Deng Xiaoping, although a popular reformer, was ousted from a leadership role in the same month. Mao Zedong died in September 1976. Mao's wife and three other members of what came to be called "the Gang of Four" were put in prison a few weeks later after a palace coup led by Mao's successor, Hua Guofeng. In 1977 Deng Xiaoping was back on the political stage. In 1978 Deng, addressing a populace eager for reform, promised reform. With Deng's assurance, China's universities again started to admit competent students whose admittance was based on the uniform national entrance examination. A new era had begun.

Near the turn of the decade, Deng's government sent a few official study groups to Hungary and Yugoslavia, among other countries, for a few weeks. There they toured the cities, factories, and farms. Upon their return, these groups made lengthy reports. Their audience was as delighted with their tales of these foreign lands as the "proletarian Europeans"[1] had been with Marco Polo's China tales. These reports and lectures prompted the people to request that similar reform steps be taken in China.

Reporting on another trip abroad, the *People's Daily* newspaper journalists wrote of their shock when the American store clerk said, "Thank you for shopping," the kind of statement unheard in Communist China for more than 30 years. Chinese charm and courtesy in marketplaces such as New York and San Francisco's Chinatowns, were ruined in China by Communist state ownership. China's stores had been run with a "devil-may-care" attitude for several decades. These journalists wired home delightful stories of this kind. Such tiny stories stirred up the nation in a way that is only understandable to China's people (and perhaps to the Soviets and their little brothers).

Deng Xiaoping did not need a theory or vision to start his reform, nor did the Chinese people. Moreover, the actual reform did not follow a predetermined pattern. Its path was rather like that of a stranger who has walked in the desert without compass for a few days. Surprisingly, somewhat like a fire that starts from spontaneous combustion, China's reform started at the weakest points of government control: the rural areas. Reform on the farms followed three decades of disasters in agriculture.

Never in China's history had an emperor extended so much control over the farmers as the Communist rulers did. The Communist rulers effectively controlled every village, every household, and every individual for more than 30 years. The Communists told villagers what to do, what to wear, what to think, what and where to buy and sell. Nor had an emperor ever squeezed the same volume of agricultural products from individual farmers as Mao Zedong did.

However, never had an emperor been responsible for so many disasters in rural China as Mao Zedong. In the words of Liu Shaoqi, the "three bad years" (1959–62) following Mao's disastrous Great Leap Forward were caused mainly by bad government policies.[2] Those three years had produced record-breaking famine. According to the official *China Statistics Book 1987*, China's population dropped by 10,000,000 people in 1960 and 3,480,000 more in 1961. Liu Shaoqi had to partially abolish the Maoist commune system and return to a less communal system like the previous collectives. Farmers were even allowed to keep some private plots and traditional rural free markets were allowed to operate once again. Nonetheless, Liu's rural policies ended bitterly when Mao initiated his infamous Cultural Revolution to dump Liu and his followers.

The most important fact about China's present rural reform is that the Communist authorities have retreated a gigantic step from the former Communist system. Letting the farmers till the land on their own is a return to China's traditional way of rural life. Yet the most important question needs to be answered: why would the Communist power holders make this impressive retreat? Change in China began long before similar events in the Soviet Union or Eastern Europe.

The Beijing authorities allowed rural reform to start in the late 1970s and early 1980s, because agriculture was not a primary concern of the vast majority of bureaucratic branches and ministries. The agricultural sector was not highly regarded by ambitious central officials since agriculture investment by the central government had always been small compared to investment in heavy industry. There is only one agricultural ministry, but more than a dozen industrial ministries. Most bureaucrats in the central government were involved with industrial investments. After all, more food production was good for everybody, so why would anyone object to any policy that assuredly was going to produce more food?

One persistent Chinese tradition is "to save face"; even in Communist China one strives to keep one's reputation sound in public. This can be a very good thing. However, sometimes this tradition is misused by Chinese politicians. Lin Yutang, in his classic book *My Country and My People*, observes that China's politicians have done more harm by trying to save "face" than simply by being shameless. This is what has happened with the Communist authorities. Mao Zedong and his colleagues wasted many good words trying to argue the sacredness of the Communist commune system. Thus, it was extremely difficult, for the leaders to publicly back away from the commune system. In the 1960s head of state Liu Shaoqi did try to make the commune system less rigid, but he could not institute sweeping reforms. But even Liu's care and restraint could not save him from Mao's anger; Liu and his supporters were crushed by Mao during the Cultural Revolution. Most Beijing leaders still remember that tragic lesson even today: they forget the details of how Liu tried to reform the commune system, but they do not forget that his reform efforts angered Mao and led to his death. Consequently, most bureaucrats believed that it would be much safer to keep some distance from the hot commune issue. After all, to the Beijing authorities, China's farmers had suffered for several decades, and they could continue to suffer a little longer. No one could imagine an armed uprising by tens of millions of illiterate and voiceless farmers.

However, the farmers themselves were *not* willing to suffer a little longer. They finally stood up on their own initiative to complain about the poverty and misery caused by the Maoist commune system. A wave of protest started with a county in the poor inland province of Anhui, in the late 1970s. Production teams were disbanded and the farmers divided among themselves the commune land together with the farm equipment and animals. By themselves they made the decision to return to traditional private farming again. Gratefully, the county-level officials supported this action. This time the central government did not attempt to crush the farmers for their independent action, as had happened so many times before, especially after the disastrous Great Leap Forward.[3] After all, that was the time when the palace intrigues were at their worst; who had time and energy to worry about the starving farmers in a remote rural area. Soon many other counties in Anhui (under Wan Li) and also in Sichuan (under Zhao Ziyang) and in other provinces took similar steps. By the time Deng Xiaoping consolidated his power for the third time in 1981, agricultural production in Anhui and Sichuan already had expanded greatly.[4] Such an agricultural revolution was bound to grow and expand. While the farmers themselves were really responsible for this agricultural revolution, Deng Xiaoping reaped the credit in the Western world.

The Communist authorities could retreat from the old farm

policy due to the fact that an easing of bureaucratic control in rural areas would not result in the collapse of the Communist bureaucracy. It is the Communist bureaucracy that makes up the Communist power. Allowing the farmers to grow crops on their own plots had little serious consequences for the inner workings of the Communist bureaucracy. Though it was viewed as a painful retreat — especially for the Maoists and the central planners — the Communist authorities had also dumped a terrible burden from their shoulders. Now the Beijing authorities would be able to deal with more serious problems and concentrate on the state-owned enterprises and the internal conflicts of the bureaucracy.

Rural progress in the various provinces has made a strong impression on the minds of China's people from the reform-minded party chief Hu Yaobang on down. After several decades of tragic rural experiments, the best agricultural solution turned out to be simple: just leave the farmers alone. Though nobody came up with a new theory or grand vision for agriculture, the people could easily compare private initiative with the Maoist commune system. The Chinese people are particularly good at making comparisons.

Actually, the comparison was a striking one. In 1977 and 1978, under Hua Guofeng's administration, another Great Leap Forward was planned: by 1985, the Communist government would produce 60 million tons of steel, 250 million tons of raw oil, and 400 billion kilograms of food. When this plan was passed by the central authorities, the high-ranking officials were confident that all the targets could be achieved, except, perhaps, for the agricultural target. The high-ranking officials were actually quite worried about the rural situation. However, as events turned out in 1979, the overambitious industrial targets produced a terrible budget shortfall. By 1980, this new Great Leap Forward had to be abandoned abruptly.[5] However, with little government investment, agriculture made impressive progress during the same period. This agricultural miracle was the result of the new land rental practices in rural China.

Therefore, there was nothing to lose and a whole world of glory to gain for Deng's administration by legalizing the rural revolution, as finally happened in 1982. Yet the Beijing authorities would only let the farmers rent their plots for five years at a time in the beginning of the reform, although they later extended the period to 15 years. So far, the Beijing authorities still do not want to consider privatization of land. Perhaps when China's farmers stand up to make privatization happen by extending the 15-year leases into leases for life with rights for successors, the Beijing leadership will jump in to claim the credit.

China's farmers have fed the nation for several thousand years, yet most history books record little about their lives. Most facets of farm life had to wait until this century and the curiosity of foreigners, such as Joseph Needham, John Fairbank, and William Hinton, before they were studied and written about. The great debate known as the *Salt and Iron Debate*, which took place more than 2,000 years ago in the high court of the great Han Dynasty, on the relations between the government and the people, is largely neglected today even by reform-minded scholars in China. In that historical debate, China's leading officials and scholars met as equals, argued extensively, and tried to determine the best government policies for relations with the Chinese people. The most wide-ranging policy debates in Communist China today can hardly match that historical debate in spirit, or scope of knowledge, or intellectual depth, though the problems facing China today would appear to be far more complex than those of 2,000 years ago.

In essence, throughout rural reform, the government has done only one thing: it has relaxed the heavy hand of bureaucracy that was inhibiting the natural productivity of China's farmers. China's rural people have basically returned to their traditional way of life. This change alone stimulated rapid growth and progress in the rural regions.

Chinese rural reform represents a return to the traditional farming system that the Communist party destroyed several decades ago. In China, farming was based on individual families for several thousand years. The Communist government had destroyed this system completely. From Mao's age to this date, land had been claimed as the property of the collective body of the communes, which are themselves branches of the government. The peasants became something like low-wage laborers in the commune system. Some critics have gone so far as to label the commune system as a modern form of slavery. Much poverty and misery resulted from this system. In fact, some of China's leading agricultural researchers believe that China's reform has produced a double liberation for the farmers: farmers are finally liberated from the hand of the Communist bureaucracy and the land once again belongs to those who till it.[6]

China's rural reform has a long way to go before it approaches Western standards. In fact, so far, China's agricultural reform has not created any new system in China's rural areas. Reform is simply a retreat from the Communist system to the traditional system that existed before the Communist takeover. However, there has been some impressive progress in the countryside since 1978. The individual peasant families rent plots of lands according to their interests and ability. These families pay a fixed rental fee, agree to grow the particular crops assigned by the government, and agree to sell their produce to the government at the end of the season at a specified price. The new system allows the farmers to sell their excessive production in the free market at unregulated prices. The freedom to sell surplus production has been the driving engine for the rapid growth in agriculture.

Other results also derive from the rural reform. The progress in the rural areas has produced many incentives for the farmers, despite the fact that the government has invested very little in agriculture. State investment in agriculture dropped sharply in the 1980s. Farmers themselves provide most farm investment. The farmers have been able to invest more in the farms and small businesses, due to their progress with the new household rental system.

Growth in farmers' incomes has been impressive in many regions nationwide. The farmers now can use their new money for a wide range of investment activities. The newly created wealth of individuals and locally owned enterprises has inspired further investments. These investment activities have resulted in rapid growth for rural business enterprises. Many counties have had an average annual economic growth rate approaching 40 percent, and some have even reached 100 percent. These township and rural enterprises have also gained much independence. In fact, the central government can no longer rely on its old policies to interfere with the new rural enterprises.

Another significant change is the increase in mobility of the farming population. Prior to reform, four-fifths of China's population was tied to farming. Individual farmers were bound completely to a particular commune. The ten-year-old reform has changed this situation somewhat. Individual farmers are no longer completely bound to their place of birth. They can move with relative ease to different rural regions, and, though with much less ease, even to the urban regions. Over the last ten years, there has been an impressive migration of the farming population, especially those engaged in the service, construction, and transportation sectors. Over the last ten years, more than 80 million farmers have stopped tilling the fields and switched to working in various community and private enterprises.

The most important change in the rural reform is the new mentality that has been born out of reform. China's farmers have finally realized that they can depend on themselves, and that alone they can pursue their own interests. Nobody else can provide a good life for them. This new mentality has stimulated tens of millions of Chinese farmers to invest their own energy and talents to create an improved life. This trend can only grow. In the future, this new mentality will motivate hundreds of millions of farmers to want a direct voice in the government. So far, this has not happened. Once it does, China will take a most significant step toward creating a truly progressive modern society.

Naturally, any reform is contagious. Rural success has pushed the urban reform. Changes in the cities such as appearance of street markets, private craftsmanship, and street vendors have been stimulated by the rural reform. Of course, the urban reform has its own story to tell. The housemaids, the tailors, the privately owned restaurants and clubs were all created in direct response to the urban consumer needs, which cannot be supplied by the government alone. In this way, more than 20 million people have started small businesses in the last few years.

Since rural development is not directly tied to the interests of the various bureaucratic ministries and agencies, it has been relatively easy for the central government to let such changes move ahead. However, the bureaucratic reform centered on the relations between the central and the provincial and local governments, as well as enterprise reform, are much more complex. The enterprise reform would involve labor markets, the investment system, the price-setting system, the production processes, and distribution, among other things. These things would certainly involve the main interests of the government ministries and agencies at all levels. Therefore, such changes impact upon the very nature of the Communist bureaucratic framework.

Of course, Deng's reform has focused on preserving the Communist infrastructure so far. Under the Communist system, the Communist bureaucracy is given all the rights to control directly all aspects of activities in society. In the bureaucratic and enterprise reform of the 1980s, such issues have moved to the center of the main battle for China's people.

The Actual Results of Reform: The Conflicts in the Old Communist System Have Expanded Logarithmically

Relations between the government and productive enterprises have become very complex. The underlying problem is that these state-owned factories are an integral part of the bureaucratic establishment. The enterprises had no independence during the Mao era. At the same time, the government depended on these enterprises for most of their revenue. However, up to 25 percent of these factories regularly lost money, and many continue to lose money even today. Mismanagement inevitably occurs when all aspects of productive enterprise behavior are controlled by the various government establishments. In fact, in Communist China, productive enterprises in the modern economic sense do not really exist. China's productive enterprises are practically the "belongings" of the Communist bureaucracy.

In the 1980s, to improve production and management quality, Deng's reform evolved a cute slogan: "Give decision-making authority to the enterprises." Yet slogans by themselves do not change reality and this is especially true of Communist slogans. However, this kind of slogan has offered moral support to many people during China's enterprise reform.

So far, the enterprise reform results have not been nearly as impressive as the rural reform or the urban commercial reform. The enterprises are the core of the Communist economic system. They are still tightly controlled and run in the old Communist style. In short, they are not independent and have little decision-making authority.

China's current trend is to let the enterprises have more power and responsibility. How does the Beijing bureaucracy pass the decision-making authority down? It is done through the bureaucratic ladders within the Communist system. The productive enterprises are at the lowest end of the bureaucracy.

Prior to reform, the central government held the sole decision-making authority on most, if not all project investments. The province-level governments had little money or authority to make independent investments. Reform has raised the level of participation by the provincial governments who now can invest without prior approval from the central government. In turn, the various province-level governments allow the city-level and county-level governments more authority over their own investment. At the bottom, the city-level and county-level governments let the production-level enterprises have more investment authority. In this way, bureaucrats at each step down the ladder have gained considerable authority to make decisions.

However, the key factors about the relations between the government and productive enterprises have not changed. The enterprises remain a part of the government establishment and they continue to occupy the lowest rung of the bureaucratic ladder. The various higher bureaucracies still have the final say on almost anything important concerning the enterprises. In particular, the promotion and appointment process for directors and managers of the enterprises are still directly controlled by the higher bureaucracies.

There have been many other changes over the last few years. The bureaucrats at all levels have been forced to learn the art of negotiating both with their superiors and with their subordinates, especially the latter. The higher bureaucrats increasingly have to acknowledge the officially pronounced rights of the lower bureaucrats. This allows the lower bureaucrats to feel more at ease when negotiating with their superiors and enables them to better defend their own interests. This right is very important in today's China. During Mao's era the lower bureaucrats could claim hardly any interest, let alone defend it. Prior to the reform, the interests of the superiors alone would determine all decisions. Now lower-level bureaucrats contribute their ideas and opinions to the decision-making process.

A common situation faces sensitive bureaucrats at all levels, including enterprise directors and managers: now handling lower bureaucrats is equally as important as dealing with superiors — if not more important. The higher you rise in the bureaucracy, the greater the number of levels of bureaucrats beneath you. And, significantly, these lower bureaucrats have the capacity to create the actual profits and benefits desired by the superiors. It is true that the bureaucrats at all levels must contribute money, food, and other assigned quotas of products to the higher levels. Most lower bureaucrats can often force their superiors to give in on some of their demands, but it is getting more and more difficult for higher-level officials to enforce their will on lower-level officials. In particular, no grassroots workers would agree to accept lower salaries and fewer bonuses, and equally no director or manager would agree to keep less profit from the enterprise. The higher bureaucrats cannot keep all the profits they receive from the lower bureaucrats: they have to hand a considerable portion of the monies they receive over to their superiors in the same way as their subordinates pass a percentage of profits on to them. So the higher officials may find it unwise to put too much pressure on their immediate subordinates. Therefore, the lower-ranking officials are left with a larger space in which to enjoy their own interests. In particular, all the higher bureaucrats have to pay more attention to the ultimate source of all profitmaking: the productive enterprises. That is why in the last few years, the governors, mayors, magistrates, and even the central government officials have shown up in the workplace more often than in any previous time. In this manner, factory workers and their managers have taken a big step forward in the process of promoting their own interests.

In fact, negotiations between the lower and higher ranking bureaucrats have become increasingly popular throughout China in the last few years. Officials at all levels of bureaucracy now spend considerable time and energy around the negotiation table. This change in itself fosters a more positive atmosphere toward creating a market economy. After all, a market economy is one in which the buyer and the seller are equal, independent individuals at the negotiation table, where bargains are reached at "arm's length," and where no party can impose its will on the other. Prior to the reform, under the central planning system, negotiations took place only within the small circles of the higher bureaucrats. All deals were made in rooms with "iron curtained windows." China's enterprise reform so far has brought the closed bargaining process of the old central planning system out into the open and has involved far more people and many more levels of the bureaucracy in all kinds of decisions that effect economic activity — these changes constitute true positive progress in China.

Over the last ten years, the struggles between the central and the regional governments have not slowed down a bit. Indeed, these struggles have intensified. The provincial and local officials are trying to extend their activities, but the Beijing leaders try equally hard to stop this trend. In reality, it is this attitude of the central government that has restricted the scope and progress of enterprise reform. All the consequences have been shaped by these struggles.

The most dramatic change in the last ten years is that the mechanism of China's economic system has fundamentally changed.

This is particularly manifested in the rapid creation of the various new economic forces, from individuals and enterprises to the provincial and local governments. This can be seen in terms of the sources of the various economic investments. Before 1979, most investment was controlled and directed by the central government. In 1978 the investment of the central government took about 80 percent of the total fixed assets, but this has since been reduced to less than 20 percent as of 1988.[7] The different bureaucratic organizations, the enterprises, and even individuals can invest in all kinds of projects and enjoy the consequent benefits from their investments.

These changing dynamics coincide with the rapid relative attenuation of power of the central government. The ability of the central government to control the direction of investments has become weaker and weaker. Now the provincial and local governments and enterprises retain control over much more of their own money and thus have more power to invest independently. Central planning is practically nonexistent at both the national and regional levels. Yet this does not mean that the central government can no longer determine economic development in crucial ways. Indeed, the central government is still powerful enough to limit the outcome of China's reform through personal decisions. In particular, all the significant officials at each level of the bureaucracy are appointed directly by the central government. Even the directors of the large state-owned enterprises are still directly appointed by the central government.

Moreover, restrictions by the central government on the scale of investment and limits on loans have often prevented the provincial and local governments, as well as the enterprises, from taking actions they desire to take. In general, the mere existence of the various central government ministries and agencies restrict and inhibit provincial and local governments, the enterprises, and individuals, who continue to have only that much freedom as is "granted" by the central government. Naturally, these conflicts determine the nature of the processes and the outcome of China's economic reform.

On the one hand, the central government tries to keep as much control as possible in its own grip. On the other hand, one can easily imagine, all the provincial and local officials try equally hard to resist the still powerful grip of the Beijing leadership. This tension between stubborn central control and active resistance by provincial and local governments and individual enterprises is one of the fundamental factors that continues to inhibit economic development. In fact, all the policies of the central government are the results of these endless struggles, whether they increase tensions or soften the existing conflicts.

Of course, subordinate officials often must act with restraint in dealing with their superiors. After all, all decisions about promotions are made by bureaucrats on the higher rungs, and these superior bureaucrats also determine all rewards and punishments. China's economy has been struggling because it is burdened with the weight of such subtle balancing. Any economic achievement is a direct result of a positive shift in the power balance among the various power divisions. So far, China's reform has not managed to overcome this basic defect in the existing Communist system. Rather, it has expanded the problems of the existing Communist system logarithmically. Hardly anybody knows what is legal and what is right anymore. The central government has lost much of its authority over China's economic life and exposed the system's inability to cope.

In terms of investment, every bureaucrat seeks to find a way, sound or otherwise, to make a "big kill." Each bureaucrat employs optimal charm, his accent, his connections, his "fishing skills" to get desired directives from the higher offices. After all, China's economic life is completely controlled by the numerous directives from the top. The bureaucrats who can "hook big fish" are the heroes of this age in China. One of the most popular heroes is the former Tianjin major, Li Ruihuan, who is now on the six-member Politburo Standing Committee. When he was the Tianjin mayor, he hooked up a "big fish": his costly project of building a canal from the Luan River in bordering Hebai Province, many miles away from Tianjin. True, this canal is vital to the economic progress in the greater Tianjin area, the most important seaport of Northern China. Yet there are hundreds of other regional projects that are as important as this one — if not more important. Only Mr. Li's dream has come true. The other provincial leaders were amazed that Mr. Li had the magical influence necessary to win billions of yuan from the Beijing government. Even the Beijing officials were amazed that Mr. Li could find so many top leaders to back his costly project. Therefore, he was bound to become a national figure, as has happened, since June 1989.

There are various economic issues that focus attention on the conflicts and the struggles between the central government and the provincial and local governments as well as the enterprises. We will consider these economic issues one by one, including economic plans, revenues, loans, materials, and foreign currencies.[8]

The central government controls the scale of investments. This power of central planning rests exclusively in the hands of the so-called State Planning Commission, consisting of the premier and a dozen or so leading central bureaucrats. This commission controls the scale of total investment for every province and region annually. Also, it sets the limits for the amount of investment in each project. Permission from the central government is required if any project exceeds its assigned investment. To reinforce its policies, the central government keeps continual watch over local officials. However, central government policies are followed by the provincial and local officials with little deference. The central planning for each region is done in the following manner. Based on the total investment for each region given in the last year, the central government adds a certain percentage for this year. Usually, provincial and local officials can find sufficient reasons to ask the central government to change the old figures. Also, the results of these central plans can vary considerably among the different provincial and local governments. Usually, the well-organized and well-administered provincial and local governments, such as Shanghai, are able to follow the central plans much better than the less ably administered ones, such as Guangdong Province. Not a single governor or mayor has ever lost his job for his failings in the execution of the central plan.

The central government also controls the revenues of the lower levels of government. Since 1979, the local governments have gradually gained some independent revenues as an important result of reform. In general, the central government and the provincial and local governments have very different ways of sharing these revenues. Roughly, from the total funds the central and the local governments decide the share for each. However, this share of revenues is not based on taxes, for China does not yet have a clearly defined tax system. The central government has been strict about the portion of revenues it expects to receive from the lower governments. In addition, to raise its income, the central government issues bonds to the lower governments, to enterprises, and even to individuals. However, for the last few years, the central government has kept borrowing money from the lower governments with no scheduled payback. Since all lower officials are directly appointed by the central government, they are afraid that registering a complaint about these "loans" will jeopardize their future. However, local officials do have their own unique ways to resist the heavy-handed central government bureaucracy. The commonly adopted method on the part of the lower bureaucrats is to collect fewer taxes from the enterprises under their control, and thus decrease the state revenue. The lower income will mean less revenue to turn over to the central government. In particular, for locally owned enterprises, the local officials would let these enterprises be directly responsible for their own share of investment. In this way, and also partly due to inflation, the central government has collected less money year after year. For example, in 1988 the central government was very pleased to announce that its income had increased by 15 percent. But the inflation of that year was more than 20 percent.

Concerning the public policy behind loans, the central government also determines the targets of its loan programs. The central government always places priority on its own enterprises and on the purchase of agricultural products. Whenever the central government determines to modify its policies, it always picks on the lower governments, including putting an end to the locally owned enterprises. Naturally, this alienates lower officials who are concerned for their own enterprises, prompting the local officials to look for ways to hit back. For example, local officials have very strong control over the appointment of centralized bankers in their regions. They can force the central banks to guarantee the allocation of money, giving priority to their local projects. At the same time, they inhibit bank loans to the state-owned enterprises. Local officials may go so far as to spend state money, which is intended for purchasing agricultural products, on local industrial projects. When these things happen, the central ministries do have their ways of getting more money for their enterprises as well as the agricultural products. At the end, the central government always has a lot of holes to fill. This is the reason why the central government cannot stop expanding its expenditures, though it is already in serious debt.

As far as the fourth economic issue, raw materials, is concerned, the central government has sought to determine the use and the distribution of these resources. It used to exercise exclusive control over materials such as steel, coal, wood, and cement. Now, it controls only a portion of these basic materials. It now controls about 60 percent of steel, 40 percent of wood, 20 percent of coal, and less than 10 percent of the cement of the country.[9] The central government must now buy the raw materials for its own enterprises from various local governments and locally owned enterprises. For the last few years, the central government has attempted to allocate more materials to itself at the expense of the provincial and local governments. The latter are afraid to force a direct confrontation, but they ask for more power sharing from the former in return. In particular, these lower governments ask the central government to supply more money and technology, or even to relax cumbersome central government restrictions.

Regarding foreign currency, the central government has almost complete control of all foreign currencies. During the last few years, efforts have been made for greater sharing of the foreign currency with the central and the lower governments as well as with the enterprises. In return for allowing more sharing the central government hopes to encourage the lower governments and the enterprises to earn more foreign currency. However, the central government has made many regulations to govern the use of foreign currency. These regulations are so severe that the lower governments and the enterprises cannot even use their own money free of central government restrictions. What is worse, their portion of foreign money is kept in banks and can be withdrawn only by the central government. Very often when the lower governments and the enterprises ask for their foreign funds they discover that the central government has already withdrawn them.

Deng's reform, despite its imperfections, is supported by all the provincial and local governments. All of the lower officials have gained advantages in their own way. Some China-watchers outside China have argued that only the eastern coastal provinces have enjoyed much benefit from the favors and the policies of the central government in the last ten years. However, such benefits have not been restricted to the coastal provinces. The poorer, inland provinces have also reaped advantages during the period of reform.

First, the inland provinces have also gained the right to draw investments from outside China. They also draw investments from the coastal provinces. In fact, the inland provinces have benefited from investments from both these sources.

As a result of the reform, inland provincial and local governments have become less dependent on the central government. Prior to the reform, the inland provinces had very few enterprises owned under their names. Most factories, such as the steel mills in Gansu Province and Inner Mongolia, and the arms-building factories in Shaanxi Province, had been built and operated by the central government. Therefore, these provinces could not derive much profit generated by the large-scale, state-owned factories. However, over the last few years, inland provinces, such as Shaanxi, Henan, Anhui, and Inner Mongolia, have gained impressive investments and built numerous factories and other enterprises. They now have direct control over these local enterprises. These enterprises have become the new industry for these provinces. The provincial and local officials in the inland provinces have gone a long way from no locally owned industry at all to much locally owned industry. This has been a gigantic change.

In this way, the local officials in these inland provinces have gained a share of economic activities. Under the protection of the lower governments, these enterprises have developed rapidly over the last few years. Now local enterprises have provided a kind of economic backbone enabling these inland provincial officials to stand on their own feet. More importantly, they can better deal with the central government as well as the coastal provinces. Also, they are in a much better position to attract investments from overseas.

In general, interregional ties between the various governments have been strengthened. This is partly due to the difficulties and cost of dealing with the central government. Most of the raw materials needed by the industry in Shanghai, such as steel, wood, metal, and oil, for example, must be directly allocated from the central government. So the Shanghai government has to hand over a huge percentage of its profits to the central government. But the Guangdong government actually hands over only a tiny percentage of profits to the central government, for most of the raw materials needed in Guangdong come directly from other provinces, especially from the inland provinces. It is not surprising, therefore, that Guangdong has surpassed Shanghai in the 1980s in terms of retained profits.

The provinces that possess raw materials prefer not to deal with the central government directly. The lower officials from different regions meet one another and treat each other as equal and independent partners. By contrast, the bureaucrats from the central government always treat the provincial and local officials as subservient subordinates who can be neglected. High-ranking officials may even try to use their administrative powers to handle the various dealings with the latter. Indeed, the central government has the authority to take raw materials from the local governments and pay so-called fixed prices that usually are many times below fair market value. The next day the central government can then sell these raw materials to the industrial provinces at a new set of fixed prices that are many times above the fair market value. Of course, the local officials are angered by this manipulation, but they dare not speak out against such "rigging" of prices. The fate of these local officials is in the hands of the central leaders. Accordingly, local officials choose not to deal with central government officialdom whenever possible.

Because of these endless internal conflicts and clashes, and despite the fact that the state-owned enterprises have been spoiled by their privileged access to raw materials, money, and labor, they now are in decline and even dying out rapidly. Shanghai offers a good example. After all, Shanghai is the key element of the central plan. Shanghai has thousands of state-owned enterprises such as steel mills, chemical factories, machine-building factories, and electronics factories. Shanghai was known for its high efficiency and productivity throughout Mao's era. It has more than one million skilled workers, many dozens of leading research institutes, and several dozen universities. But over the last few years Shanghai's economy has stagnated, and negative growth has become a common situation. Yet Shanghai's bankruptcy-torn factories are still backed by central government subsidies. This world-class city has lost its characteristic vigor and energy. It has fallen pitifully behind many once backward provinces along the eastern coast, especially Guangdong, within the last few years.

However, the loosening of government control and the production decline of the state-owned enterprises have contributed to a dramatic growth in the economic sectors outside of the central plan. There are two vitally important sectors outside the central plan in today's China. One sector consists of individual businesses: the street vendors, the barbershops, the shoe repair shops, the private taxis, etc. The activities of this sector receives much attention from most foreign China-watchers as well as tourists. The second sector consists of the various enterprises owned by the various lower governments, which are outside the central plan. Most locally owned enterprises are in this sector. These enterprises are self-financed. They keep most of their profits, and they often have intelligent methods to secure plentiful supplies of raw materials and markets. This sector has greatly expanded, growing at a rate out of proportion to others in the last few years. These locally owned enterprises have gradually built their strength to the point that soon they might be able to challenge the central plan. The further development of this sector will be vital for China as she continues to move towards a market-oriented economy.

At the present time, virtually no one from these sectors has stood up to directly challenge the central plan. We do not know when and how China will take this step in the future. Once it happens, China will have a true property ownership revolution – the creation of modern economic institutions and uniform and universal laws governing the economic life of the country.

Reasons for China's Inflation

Inflation is the stubborn disease that plagues China's economic life during this reform era. Rapid development in the 1980s brought serious inflation, first showing up around 1984 and reaching 20 to 40 percent by 1988. Since the end of 1988, the central government has tightened its money supply in order to dampen inflation. As a side effect of this policy the economy immediately plummeted into negative growth. This tight money policy is not likely to last since it has already caused negative economic growth and has the potential for causing unemployment for tens of millions as well as the deterioration of everyone's living standards. The foreseeable thing about China's future is that when the economy starts to grow again, inflation will reappear. It will then be even more difficult to put under control.

However, the causes for China's inflation are fundamentally unlike the causes of inflation in the West's market economy. It is not just a problem with money supply. Common sense about inflation tells us that it is not really the point that prices rise and fall. It is all right that prices go up and down provided that these changes occur within a stable range. Only in this way can the economy stay healthy and grow in a stable fashion.

China's inflation is caused by a number of factors.

First, the prices on almost all items in the market are not determined by the market itself, but are set by the government. The government in China is the dominate seller as well as the major buyer. More precisely, the price-setting process is determined by officials from the various ministries and agencies, after consultations between the superior bureaucrats and their subordinates. These higher- and lower-ranking bureaucrats make bargains around the negotiating table. Overwhelming government control remains a fact today. This crucial point is the key to understanding the root causes of China's inflation.

In a market-oriented economy, as in America, prices are determined primarily by the marketplace itself with minimal interference from the government; government action is usually confined to preventing price-setting conspiracies and ensuring free and fair competition. The negotiation table is a round table. No seat is more sacred than any other one. The people involved in price negotiations are, first of all, equal to one another. Furthermore, they represent independent property owners. Both parties will strive to protect, through the negotiation process, their independent rights and interests. Each party can pound on the table to demand a better deal. The price is set only when both parties, the buyer and the seller, are mutually satisfied — only then will the negotiation process produce practical results. More often, however, prices in America are set solely by markets based on fair competition. For example, the vehicle markets in the U.S. are influenced by intense international competition. That is why the same Japanese-made cars may be less expensive in the U.S. than in Japan. After all, there is higher competition in the American car markets for one reason or another.

Under a centralized economy, as in China, all the conditions characteristic of the negotiation processes of a market economy are absent. The negotiation table is not round; it has sharp edges and the chair legs are not all the same height — some seats are more holy than others. All the people who take seats are government officials and all are accountable to the government alone. After all, the government firmly controls all the nation's wealth and has the power to intervene in all areas of the economy with laws and regulations. The government is, therefore, the sole decision maker regarding things offered for sale in the markets. The officials from the central government ministries rank higher than those from the various local governments; thus they take the best seats around the negotiation table. Vital participants to the negotiation may not even be invited to attend. The productive enterprise is the lowest-ranking government agency, and thus has the lowest seat. Here, only the higher ranking guys can pound on the table — the others must sit quietly and endure the noise. Furthermore, the negotiators do not have any urgent need to defend their personal property rights. All the parties involved are government officials, and raw materials, commodities, and products to be discussed may have nothing to do with their own units. Few people involved at the bargaining table can tell clearly who actually owns what property. In this way, the negotiation process itself and the final plans to be determined result from compromises

worked out between all the government ministries and agencies involved. Every party understands that it may, through skilled negotiation with the higher ranking officials, enjoy the use of a greater
amount of the society's wealth.[10]

China's present price-setting system was established in the
1950s when the Communist government tried to achieve a rapid industrialization in China. To that end, the central government tried
to maximize capital funds and thus established the current highly
centralized system. Within this system, decision-making authority
rests in the hands of a very small number of bureaucrats in the
capital.

During the first 30 years of Communist government, the main
feature of price-setting practice was a comparative pricing system
that linked agricultural to industrial products. To make industrialization possible, the government has had to invest more in heavy industry. This was done by squeezing agriculture and consumer-
oriented industries. Indeed, the prices of industrial products were set
very high while the prices for agricultural products were set very
low. Also, within the category of industrial products, the prices of
heavy industrial products were set very low while the prices for
consumer-oriented products were set very high. This allowed the
central government to promote heavy and military-oriented industry at the expense of agriculture, which suffered from depressed
prices, and by keeping living standards low. The government also
recouped currency by keeping prices high on consumer-oriented industrial products. To ensure the effectiveness of such policies, the
central government carried out a policy that would guarantee unified purchasing and marketing of all agricultural products, especially grain. At the same time, the government wiped out the "black"
and "free" markets in both rural and urban areas throughout China.

The centralized economy, aided by its price-setting system, succeeded in putting an overwhelming amount of the wealth of the
whole society into costly heavy industrial programs that required
massive amounts of capital. A recent study by Yan Ruizhen and
others[11] shows that this policy stifled China's agricultural growth
potential and prevented the achievement of higher living standards.
In particular, it resulted in a relatively advanced urban life, but a
quite backward rural life, a relatively advanced industrial sector
and a quite backward agricultural sector. In particular, it seriously
blocked the development of the agricultural provinces, especially in
the northwestern regions.

Despite its planned economy, the government has confronted devastating failures even in its industrial programs. Investment by the central government has been hardly rational and efficient. It has created gigantic waste that would make Karl Marx, who attacked the blindness and the wastefulness of the market system, turn in his grave. For example, the failure of the forced industrialization in the Great Leap Forward in 1958–60 resulted in a severe shortage in grain production, which caused the deaths of tens of millions. Furthermore, these failures have seriously affected China's political and social stability. The chaos of the Cultural Revolution of 1966–76 was a direct result of these economic failures. Yet it has taken the whole nation some 30 years to cry out for reform.

These painful experiences have made China's people embrace the reform since the late 1970s with unaccustomed hope and eagerness. Price reform has become all the more urgent as the economic reform developed. Yet, so far, there has been more talk than real deeds in this area. This is due to the fact that price reform cannot occur without other fundamental changes in China's present economic system.

Several steps have been taken in price reform. The first steps were taken in 1979 when the central government declared price hikes for numerous agricultural products. This new price system together with the introduction of rental farming are two mutually supporting policies in the rural areas. These policies have allowed the farmers themselves to prosper in a way not possible for several decades in China's recent past. Visible progress in the rural areas has impressed urban people and made many of them realize that they too could push for changes in the same manner. It has become a fashionable idea in China to use the inducement of raising prices to encourage production in many shortage-ridden sectors, and especially in the energy, raw material, and transportation sectors. The serious shortage of raw materials, energy, and transportation was the bottleneck in China's growing economy throughout the 1980s.

The next important reform step by the central government was to offer some power to the provincial and local governments to participate in decisions concerning the prices of a limited number of items. However, the prices for most other items are still decided by the central government alone. Throughout much of the 1980s the major economic policy activities have centered on these mixed price-setting practices.

Since 1986 the Beijing leaders, especially Deng Xiaoping, have talked about more dramatic steps that could be taken to change the existing price-setting system, but no substantial change has resulted. The reform so far has not altered the basic structure of the old price system. The government, be it the central government, the provincial and local governments, a combination of all of them, is still the final decision maker on the prices. China's markets continue to be decided by government alone, though the government has become more open about its intentions and actions. Fundamentally, there is no market economy in China yet.

Another significant cause of inflation is directly related to China's present property ownership relations. The rise and fall of the price for each product is directly tied to the interests of the particular economic units as well as those government agencies that control it. The price is also related to the revenues of the particular government, be it the county, city, or province-level government, or the central government. In this way, the price can easily rise, but it cannot easily fall, for some level or sector of the bureaucracy will have a vested interest in maintaining the higher price and will work to impede price reduction.

It happens often that when a state-owned enterprise, for instance a machine-building factory, has trouble selling its product, it can easily get permission from the central government to raise its price but not to lower it. Instead of trying to make up for poor sales by lowering prices and selling more units, the enterprise compensates by selling fewer units at higher prices. This practice would be impossible in a purely market economy, but it is common in China. There will still be the same number of buyers out there to pay the higher price. After all, most of these buyers are from state-owned enterprises. The higher price can be imposed with little effort other than some extra paperwork. Even when price-sensitive buyers attempt to find other sellers to secure better deals, they are often forbidden to do so. The central plan has already fixed them as the buyers of the output of this particular factory, and the plan is harder to change than an individual price. The plan is law. Actually, the central plan *can* be changed easily if a bureaucrat can win the favor of an influential high-ranking official in the central government. China's centralized economic life is actually governed by notes emanating from the offices of high-ranking officials who order that exceptions to the central plan be made for this case or that.

Sometimes, even when the factories want to lower the price of their products so they can better compete in the markets, they are not allowed to do so by the higher bureaucracy. For example, the Shanghai Watch Factory has had trouble selling its watches during the last few years, so it has tried to lower the price of watches in order to clear its huge warehouse inventory. But the Shanghai municipal government will not give its permission for a lower price, so the factory has had to keep the watches in storage indefinitely. The municipal government wants to keep a higher price for the watches to secure a higher tax income from their sale. But what about the watches in storage? Well, the storage waste is only a waste to the investment banks that belong to the central government, and has nothing to do with the income of the municipal government. As this example indicates, price cuts affect the interests of a variety of government agencies. For this reason, affected bureaucrats are unwilling to grant permission for lowered prices, but they are quite ready to raise prices. Naturally, this problem is something Western economists, who are so used to such terms as timing, interests, and profits, have difficulty understanding.

In addition, China's present management and workers' quality are very troublesome. In the production units, the labor cost can only increase. No workers volunteer to receive less pay for the same amount of work. Moreover, there is no free labor market in China. The factories have no easy way to find the employees they want. They have a terrible time firing employees who are not needed for production. Unemployment would cause political unrest, the last thing the government wants. Therefore, the government prefers to pay equal salaries to all employees whether needed for production or not. Managers also have to pay bonuses designed to reward quality performance to these "free-paid workers" just to make life easy for everybody. It is hard to find three workers who perform in most state-owned enterprises. Instead, it is very common that three men's work is done by five men — Karl Marx could never imagine this (or many other things that take place in Communist China). Let us take as an example a fertilizer factory in the inland province of Shaanxi, pointed out by a delegate at the State Political Consultant Conference meeting in March 1990.[12] This factory has been running for three years, but so far its production is only at about 25 percent of its potential capacity. Within these three years, 11 directors have been successively appointed by either the State Council, or the central government Chemical Ministry, or the provincial and the local governments. However, despite all these changes, the situation has not changed for the better. The factory now employs 8,000 workers, though it needs only 400 for production work.

Regarding China's centralized economy, Chen Ping observes that "The biggest problem in China's economy now is with the talentless management. The main sector of China's economy is the state-owned enterprises that are run by a degenerate as well as inexperienced group of bureaucrats. This is the biggest headache to the reformers. Also, there are highly inefficient teams of workers. Yet the factory directors are unable to fire them. Sometimes when such workers do not get bonuses, they even threaten the directors with knives."[13] Chen goes so far as to suggest that Taiwanese management skills and investments should be used to help with the mainland reform. "Let the overseas and Taiwan investments help with mainland China's reform. Many Taiwan businessmen invest in mainland China with a high salary scale for employees. Those who do not perform well are fired. This has attracted many able people to their enterprises. This also challenges the state-owned enterprises and the lazy employees there, so that many able workers in the state-owned enterprises do run away. I hope that the Taiwan businessmen help the reformers in mainland China motivate the state-owned enterprise workers to give up their 'Iron Bowl.'"

In addition, Chen feels that it would be wise to let Taiwan's concerned parties manage the economy of Hainan Island Province for some period of time so as to establish a new development direction for this region. In this way, the mainland could have very progressive economic models for stimulation. Of course, at this time, such suggestions may be received with bemusement by the Beijing leaders as well as by Taiwan's concerned parties.

Another direct cause of inflation is casually connected to the central plan. Many state-owned enterprises, as demanded by the central plan, do not produce what people buy in the market. Yet they have to keep producing these items anyway just to meet quotas set by the central plan. Otherwise, the managers and directors of these enterprises could lose their jobs. Enterprises that generate no profits can still manage to operate because of subsidies furnished by the central government. But lack of ability to meet true market needs on the part of these enterprises contributes to the problem of grave shortages in other areas. While the central government subsidizes unneeded production, it underfunds or totally ignores enterprises that produce demanded products. This is why economic sectors outside the central plan were able to develop so rapidly over the last few years. The unplanned economy is growing rapidly because it produces what the market demands and the market is vast because so many demands go largely unsatisfied in China.

It must be said that China's senior leaders are well aware of many of the root causes of China's economic troubles in general and of inflationary pressure in particular. For example, many of the problems we have listed above are discussed in the writings and speeches of the second most powerful Chinese leader, the number one central planner Chen Yun. Furthermore, the Beijing leaders understand that many of China's economic troubles can only be resolved by reforming the Communist system. But that is not what the Beijing authorities have done. Rather, the Beijing authorities try to "repair one broken wall with the bricks taken from another wall." Naturally, the Communist bureaucracy, by operating in this fashion, has created more problems than solutions.

In summary, the present monetary and price-tightening policies against inflation do not really solve the inflation problem by attacking its root causes. These policies have attenuated economic growth since 1989. This will have very severe consequences. Factories are closed and unemployment has already climbed drastically. Living standards are deteriorating. All of these problems could push China's economy into a dead end and China into political chaos.

In the future, if China continues her reform, the authorities will have to reform the present system completely. Only by total reform can China rid itself of the root causes of its stubborn inflation. To reach that end, China may have to go through some painful times in the near future. The current Polish reform is undergoing a painful transition even under an innovative government. Relatively speaking, it was easier for the Communists to install the centralized system on China than it will be for the central authorities to make necessary fundamental reforms in the system.

The Changing Roles of the
Various Social Forces in the Reform Process

It is quite untrue to think that the existing Communist system in China is supported only by a few stubborn and doctrinaire leaders, and that the rest of China's people are reformers. Rather, the Communist dictatorship has gained wide support over several decades, though its popularity has suffered substantial decline, especially since the end of the Maoist Cultural Revolution in 1976. After all, the ordinary people believe that they need a political authority to maintain order and secure their lives against famine, disaster, disease, etc.

The truth is that the Communist government has offered much more protection to ordinary "peaceful" citizens than any previous government in China's long history. No previous government had expressed so much concern about the common citizen's food, shelter, job, education, and health as the Communist government or had done as much to alleviate poverty and misery. For example, a Chinese student would be surprised to find out that his American counterpart is not automatically provided with free tuition, a free apartment with assigned roommates, an assigned set of classes for each semester, as well as an assigned job for life upon graduation. He may be shocked to discover that an American university graduate might have to write 100 applications to secure a job that may last only a year or two.

Nevertheless, hardly any living Chinese are now satisfied with the Beijing authorities. The college students enjoy the biggest benefits next to members of the Communist hierarchy, but they are probably the least satisfied group in the existing system. Throughout the past 41 years, the Communist authorities have created many man-made tragedies: famines, civil unrest, chaos, and stagnations. The other truth is that this government has deprived some people of more things than any of the previous governments in China's long history. The biggest thing the government has destroyed since 1949 is modern knowledge and the conditions for the birth of such knowledge. Any part of Chinese society that exercises any degree of freedom in thought and expression has become an enemy to the Beijing authorities.

Simple truth is shocking: almost all the enemies of the Communist government have been created by the government itself. Though this government could effectively stop free thinking and the pursuit of knowledge for a long time, it could not stop life itself. Life produces endless problems whose solutions demand knowledge and ingenuity. Therefore, the Beijing authorities have had to seek new ways to substitute human knowledge and inventiveness in order to deal with these problems. China has been deprived of the power of modern scientific knowledge for most of the last 41 years. Government policies themselves, to name one complication only, have had to suffer the consequences. Many Communist policies have created more problems than solutions. For example, like Lenin and Stalin before him, Mao Zedong introduced a system of "communist class struggle," requiring mass purges, and various penalties — including execution — as a substitute for human knowledge in governing the country.

Many different political ideas characterize Chinese society. All of them have their representatives in the Communist leadership. Camps continually evolve and change, but certain general factions can always be discerned within the leadership. The constant power struggles reflect these forces.

The Communist party does not have clear political divisions in the manner of Western political systems, with their various parties. Within the Chinese Communist party, different political groups do exist, but they do not take coherent form and define themselves by means of platforms and slogans. In fact, often the disputes within the Communist party are kept hidden from public eyes. Moreover, as usually happens, the central authorities' policies are supported by most of the cadres. Generally, it is hard to determine exactly who are Maoists, or Dengists, or Chenists. Cadres switch positions as the political situations vary. In reality, when the Maoists gained the upper hand, few people failed to declare themselves as Maoists. In this reform era in China, few people dare to publicly oppose the reform movement. The following groupings of the Communist hierarchy must be viewed in the light of political reality in China yesterday and today: factions always exist within the government, but the dividing lines between factions are usually difficult to define.

The Maoists gained power and enjoyed the public favor for some three decades. These men and women advocate class struggle and political propaganda as the means to extend the productive energy of the masses. To them, Mao's China was and remains the golden age in Chinese history. After all, in Mao's era, they sat on top of all China. Today, they have little interest in any kind of reform. They focus on the retention of their power by all possible means — power can always justify the means. In their view, those people who favor reform are class enemies. To them, the reformers are people they equate with such previous enemies as the Kuomintang, the Americans, or Soviet imperialists. They believe that the current reform movement in China demonstrates that there are many class enemies still in existence, enemies who managed to survive the various purges and campaigns in Mao's era. They believe that more class struggles are needed to exterminate these bad elements. These men and women believe Mao's slogan that 10 percent of the people in China are class enemies. Thus, to move China "forward" about 110 million people should be treated as criminals or "class enemies." In particular, Maoists believe that whenever government economic policies fail, the blame must fall on the destructive efforts of the class enemies. Therefore, the former rich farmers and landowners, the former industrialists and private businessmen, educated people and intellectuals are among the suspect social elements to be struggled against.

A second Communist opinion group consists of the central planners, led by the aging leader Chen Yun, now 85. These men and women do not believe that class struggle is the road to Communist utopia. Rather, they believe that the Communist bureaucracy must have a monopoly over China's economy in the form of central planning. After all, the Communist goal is to hold the supreme power for all generations to come. Thus, how could they afford not to control the economy tightly? Therefore, it is natural that China's economic activities must be tightly controlled in the hands of the Communist bureaucracy. In particular, all government policies must go through procedures that should be centered on the top leaders — the central planners. Private sectors may supplement and provide some services to the central plan and therefore should be allowed to coexist along with the planned state economy. But there must be limits to the private economy; when it tries to escape its bounds, it must be disciplined. Chen Yun stresses institutional and programmable methods as the proper means to deal with China's economic and political life, but he also believes that the Communist bureaucracy must be placed above all. Chen Yun's faction understands that such practices may limit China's progress, but they prefer slow progress to ending Communist power. These people believe that the end of Communist power would mean the end of China's peace and unity. To them, "without the Communist Party, there is no new China." Therefore, to protect Communist interests, even bloodshed is justified.

The third Communist opinion group consists of those cadres who want to do away with central planning and find alternate ways to govern China. They believe that the Communist government must let the various economic sectors share responsibility for improving China's economy, thereby lessening problems for the government. In this way, the Communist authorities can maintain their political power by establishing a much firmer foundation. Deng Xiaoping is the leader of this faction. He and his followers have completely lost their confidence in the omnipotence of a centralized economy. Though they see somewhat the consequences of decentralization for the Communist power monopoly, they believe that many existing problems and explosive underlying conflicts can be resolved by a well-managed decentralization. Indeed, they view decentralization as the only way to revive China's economic system. At the same time, they realize that gradual decentralization can gain them wide support from the people as well as from the tens of millions cadres. Thus, as far as political power is concerned, they have nothing to lose and much to gain.

It must be said that the Maoists, Dengists, and Chenists differ with each other regarding tactics, but not in essential beliefs. All three groups want to preserve the supremacy of the Communist authority, though they each have different ideas as to how to achieve that goal. When confronting the common people, they would immediately stick together.

There have been many changes within these three Communist opinion groups over the last ten years. The deepening reforms have opened up new dimensions and have thus brought new thinking as well as new social forces to the fore. These new forces, not the doctrinaire thinking of the politicians discussed above, will determine China's future.

In reality, neither reform camps nor antireform camps are clearly identifiable within the Chinese Communist bureaucracy. For many years Deng was labeled as China's number one reformer, but it was he who ordered the bloodshed in Beijing in June 1989. If one followed the intensive international media coverage on China, one would think that aging doctrinaires such as Chen Yun and his top aides Hu Qianmu and Deng Liqin, who were the chief executives for the various Anti-liberalization Campaigns in the 1980s, would have been responsible for violent repression. However, events have not turned out this way at all. Indeed, Chen Yun and some of his followers have tried to blame Deng Xiaoping for the enormous damage done to the Communist establishment by the June 4 slaughter. Nothing better underscores the complexity of China's present political reality.

In this reform era, the Chinese people have successfully dumped the Maoists. The Maoists have lost almost all the prestige that once enabled them to dominate Communist China. Now, they have become political beggars and "society's pets," as they are called by the man on the street. Maoists must now present themselves as supplicants before the other powerful political groups in order to obtain realistic advantages such as government offices, better apartments, and more money. Nonetheless, they still dream that someday they will regain their lost power and glory. More often, these men and women are now despised and ridiculed by the public as never before.

Deng's opinion group became the leading faction during the 1980s. The common feeling was that Deng Xiaoping was the reform banner-holder for much of this period. However, as the reform developed, the unity of this opinion group has been completely broken. In the most crucial stages of reform, especially in 1989, Deng Xiaoping betrayed his great reform and willingly stood on the opposite side of the people. To maintain his supremacy, Deng Xiaoping rallied to the side of other doctrinaire party hacks. They master-minded the June 1989 massacre. Now Deng is attempting to repair his damaged image as a reform-hero and humanitarian.

In the process of deepening reform, Deng's opinion group has produced a fresh group of reformers such as Deng's heirs apparent: Hu Yaobang and Zhao Ziyang. Hu and Zhao adapted themselves to the rhythm of the reform as it was deepening. These leaders started their high court life by following closely the instructions from Deng Xiaoping. They have lived in the shadow of Deng for some years. Deng's ideas were their ideas; Deng's dreams were their dreams; Deng's goals were their goals—Deng was their leading inspiration. But these men have their own ideas and their own dreams as well as individual aspirations concerning the reform processes. Recently, they have depended less on Deng and more and more on public opinion to shape their policies. They have desired to depart from those supermen to some degree, thought their determination has not reached a decisive level in most cases. However, both Hu and Zhao have gained enormous popularity with the people, especially since 1986 (for Hu) when Hu showed sympathy for popular political reform demands, and since 1989 (for Zhao) when Zhao refused to condone harsh means to deal with peaceful demonstrators.

The Communist ideaologues, especially the central planners, have found ample excuses—the troubles associated with reform, such as inflation and popular demonstrations—to reestablish their old power. These men do not appreciate or utilize the tremendous energy and the creative talents of the Chinese people. Reform progress scared these politicians. In order to regain their lost power, they believed that they must reverse the reform and act quickly to wipe out new economic forces. Their zeal for more power reached madness following the June 1989 crackdown and has since continued to advance in this direction, especially within the world of palace politics. As their efforts progressed, these ideologues have encountered many obstacles. Their biggest obstacle is that they do not have able and talented cadres and cannot find successors. They cannot even secure the support of the provincial and local officials, not to mention the younger generations of Chinese people. These men can turn friends into bitter foes. Their policies and attitudes have been opposed by all the people. They may resist reform, but they cannot defeat it.

Overall, a realistic assessment of Communist China suggests that all of these three Communist power groups reached their maximum influence by the end of the 1980s. None of these groups can walk ahead any farther in their chosen direction without stepping into traps of their own construction. This truth is best shown by the 1989 democratic movement and the consequent bloody crackdown. Neither the Dengists nor the Chenists could have avoided the use of violent means to protect their remaining, but declining, personal power.

At this time, more roads have opened for China's new social forces. At the bottom, the wage-earning class demands that living standards continue to improve, and that improvement must take place annually, monthly, and even weekly. Strangely, as the reform has progressed over the last few years, hardly any people have the patience to wait for a better life. They want signs of a better life *now*. China's working people have gained benefits from the reform. They want to protect what they have gained, and win more benefits through continued reform. To meet this popular demand, the economic reform must move ahead.

At the next level, various individual entrepreneurs and productive enterprises also have gained rapid independence and progress in the 1980s. Their desire for more independence and political responsibility has grown in proportion to their economic advancement. The productive enterprises have especially increased their drive to achieve these goals.

In addition, provincial and local officials will have more to say as long as China's future is considered. It is these provincial and local officials who have been the recipients of the most direct incentives and who have most benefited from China's current reform centered on sanctioned decentralization. They have increased their economic strength through the reform. They have also amassed enough political power to protect their interests. Doubtlessly, their desire for more political power will only increase. These officials now have clear goals in sight. Nobody can easily deprive them of the benefits already in their hands.

The brightness of China's economic and political future will depend upon these three new forces created by the reform. In fact, once like-minded people as these three levels recognize their shared interests and move in the same direction, a new political-economic system will have an ample chance to form on Chinese soil. This new system would provide all the social groups in China with their own incentives to pursue and to protect economic and political choices.

In fact, throughout the 1980s, the biggest lesson these people have learned is that the government cannot guarantee a good life for them and they must learn to depend upon themselves to make real progress. The truth about Chinese Communist reform is this: progress has been made wherever the Communist government retreats a step. China's people today understand more clearly than ever that they cannot depend on the Communist authorities to advance their interests. This new way of thinking characterizes not only China's new generations of educated people, but also the farmers and the street vendors. This new realization will push aside palace politics in China's future. Once palace politics is replaced, China's new system will be closer at hand.

How soon can a new system come to China? The answer to this question depends on the position of the Beijing government. The continued existence of Communist government in China depends upon the party's willingness to relax its grip on power. Communist doctrinaires cannot coexist with the reform. They do not want to reform the Communist power monopoly one bit, but the reformers will not let them get away with doing nothing.

Undoubtedly, the new social forces, such as individual entrepreneurs, productive enterprises, and provincial and local officials, will provide the strongest push for the creation of a new system in China. If the Chinese people had no vision for their future ten years ago at the start of the reform, they have a vision today. More and more people now understand that a clear and well-defined system of property ownership and a new economic order based on free markets must be the ultimate goal of the reform. Only such changes can bring fruitful results of all these new social forces. Overall, the visions of China's people have now reached new dimensions. These new visions will demand the greatest courage from China's people as they struggle for a better life. The 1989 democratic movement shows us the degree of the people's determination.

Notes for Chapter 2

1. This terminology is taken from Fernand Braudel. *Civilization and Capitalism, 15th–18th Century*, 3 vols., translated by Sian Reynolds (New York: Harper & Row, 1982).

2. On May 31, 1961, Liu acknowledged that the failure of the Great Leap Forward was mainly due to the mistakes of the government. See his official selected works.

3. See Liu Shaoqi's speeches from 1961–62. There he ordered officials to stop the farmers from splitting up the commune system. Also see Gao Shanguan and others, *Contemporary China's Economic Reform* (Beijing: China's Press for Social Science, 1984).

4. This story is also told in Gao Shangquan and others, *Contemporary China's Economic Reform* (Beijing: China's Press for Social Science, 1984).

5. See the book cited in note 4 above.

6. Comprehensive Study Group of the Development Research Institute, "Farmers, Markets, and New Systems," *Economic Research* 1 (1987).

7. Chen Shenshen, "China's Economic Mechanisms and Comments on the Policies of Zhao Ziyang and Li Peng," *China Times Weekly*, July 1, 1989.

8. This line of argument follows Chen Shenshen, *China's Economic Mechanisms and Comments on the Policies of Zhao Ziyang and Li Peng.*

9. Chen Shenshen, *China's Economic Mechanisms and Comments on the Policies of Zhao Ziyang and Li Peng.*

10. This argument follows Chen Shenshen (guest editor), "Price Reform in China," *Chinese Economic Studies: A Journal in Translations* (Spring 1989): 1–13.

11. Yan Ruizhen and others. "Current Situation, Developing Trends, and Countermeasures Toward China's Price Scissors in the Exchange of Industrial Products for Agricultural Products," *Economic Research* 2 (1990).

12. *World Journal*, March 24, 1990.

13. *World Journal*, January 2, 1990.

3

DIFFICULTIES IN THE POLITICAL REFORM

Could the killings of June 1989 have been avoided in Beijing? Could the Beijing authorities have maintained political order, or, even better, pushed reform efforts forwards, without resorting to political repression, cruelty, and bloodshed?

Choices, Mistakes, and Dead-End Streets

A positive answer to the above questions should have been possible. China would have taken a gigantic step toward a truly great modern society. Indeed, top leaders such as Zhao Ziyang and provincial and local officials wanted a very different resolution and dealings were already in existence. Party chief Zhao Ziyang openly called for a peaceful and rational resolution. The overwhelming number of local and provincial leaders in several dozen demonstration-filled cities successfully handled the reform movement and its marches and demonstrations peacefully. There was only one exception, Chengdu, the provincial capital of Sichuan, where the same sort of violent repression took place in June 1989 as that in Beijing.

It must be said that the student-led democratic movement was generally so peaceful and orderly that the movement could be praised for that reason alone. In Beijing, a city with a population of nearly 10 million, almost all the residents became involved in the unfolding events of the democracy movement and most went into the streets to support it in one way or another. Yet there were hardly any crimes, disorder, or even traffic accidents — though no police were in sight for a few days. The people created a human sea in Beijing, but everyone was polite and courteous, an attitude that had disappeared after the beginning of the Maoist Cultural Revolution.

The students did not ask for too much. The main spokesmen

for the demonstration focused on widespread official corruption, painful inflation, and the rigidity of the Communist system. All of these ills are known to and even acknowledged by the Communist authorities. Indeed, party boss Zhao Ziyang viewed the crisis as one that could be resolved through sincere dialogue and negotiation, thus opening a new road for the authorities as well as the people. He felt, like millions of the Chinese people, that violence could push China into civil war. After all, the young students and workers did not propose to overthrow the Communist government, or ask for free elections, or anything of that sort. Instead, they only wanted to communicate directly and openly with the authorities, and to improve relations between the authorities and the people. In fact, several thousand students in Beijing had staged a week-long hunger strike only to demand that the Beijing authorities acknowledge their actions to be patriotic and grant acceptance to their independent student unions. Most of the Beijing demonstrators sincerely wanted to help the Communist authorities deal with widespread official ills and to promote the Communist reform, among other things. But even these decent wishes were met with bullets and rolling tanks.

At the same time, there were also numerous student-led demonstrations in several dozen cities throughout China. Numerous provincial and local officials throughout China had already opened a dialogue with the local protesters in one way or another, with perhaps the single exception of Chengdu. In some regions the local officials and the demonstrators had even reached agreements to restore the local peace and normal life. For example, China's great cities such as Tianjin, Xian, and Wuhan reached accommodation with the demonstrators in this way.

Events did not turn in this favorable direction in Beijing, but, instead went to the other extreme. Deng and other aging leaders, together with their foot soldiers such as Premier Li Peng, rejected Zhao's methods and called in hundreds of tanks and hundreds of thousands of troops to crush the peaceful students and workers in Beijing. Automatic rifles were fired into the peaceful crowds, tanks rolled over the human chains.

It is striking that the killing did not occur any sooner. It did not occur at the height of the demonstrations first held in late April, or other demonstrations held in mid–May, or even around May 20 when large troop contingents entered the city from all directions. Rather, the repression took place on June 3–4 when the demonstrations were losing momentum and already seemed to be coming to an end. Immediately before June 3, things were returning to normal in Beijing in general, and in Tiananmen Square in particular. At this time few peaceful demonstrators still remained in the square, but their numbers were greatly reduced from just a few days earlier. The massacre really could have been avoided altogether. Most tragically, Deng and the other aging leaders hesitated for more than a month, but finally decided to revenge themselves on the young students at this moment despite changed circumstances and potential shocking consequences.

Most obviously, Deng Xaioping committed the biggest mistake in his political career. The consequences of his June 1989 bloody crackdown are devastating and they will last much longer than Deng himself, who is now in his late eighties. History will not forget this great cruelty. But the immediate crisis resulting from the bloodbath is beyond comprehension.

Only a few months prior to the bloodshed, Deng's China still set the standard for the rapidly reforming Communist world. China's attempt to become a modern economic power was universally praised by the Western democratic powers. Deng Xiaoping was regarded throughout the world as a reform hero as well as a great statesman. Who, other than Deng Xiaoping, could have reopened China's universities, closed by the Maoists for some ten years? Who had done more than Deng Xiaoping in turning China away from the Maoist hell? Who, other than Deng Xiaoping, could have opened China to the outside world, thus enabling China to start her greatest modern adventure since 1840, the year of the Opium War? In short, who could deny that Deng Xiaoping would become one of the greatest heroes in the history of mankind? Nobody except Deng Xiaoping himself! He personally ordered the June 1989 massacre in Tiananmen Square. Hundreds were killed and thousands wounded because of his orders.

Because of this grave mistake, China's great reform under Deng's leadership ended tragically in bloodshed. China's people have been pushed to the conclusion that they face a government that kills its own citizens. Many of China's best citizens have been put in prison and many others have fled abroad. Some of China's leading intellectuals and citizens have been forced to take shelter in the American embassy and other foreign embassies in Beijing. In the greater China sphere, the Chinese people in Hong Kong have lost their confidence about life under Chinese rule after the great unity date of 1997, a year that has been dreamed about by most Chinese for some 100 years. Overseas Chinese have felt terrible shame about the actions of the Beijing authorities. Separatists in Taiwan have found striking reasons for the continued independence of that rich Chinese island.

In the international community, China has suffered its worst setback since her brilliantly fresh and cheerfully engaging global debut in 1979. But now China is semi-isolated again. Things have deteriorated to such an extent that hardly anybody feels it an honor to be friends with Deng and the other aging leaders, as former President Richard Nixon, one of China's best Western friends, remarked in his Beijing trip in the fall of 1989.[1] Sadly, the international community has again turned against China.

However, the other Communist states have learned their lessons from Deng's mistakes. Positive changes have taken place in the Soviet Union, Poland, Hungary, and many other Communist states throughout the world. Deng is no longer their reform hero; the Soviet strongman Gorbachev has stolen his thunder. The Eastern European states are now receiving most of the international investments and technical help that might have been directed at China.

It is not Deng but the Soviet Gorbachev who has become the man of the 1980s, at least according to *Time* magazine, despite the fact that China's wealth doubled under Deng's reform, while Gorbachev's reform has not added even a penny to the Soviet economy, let alone filled the empty stores in Moscow. Since at least 1989 many people suggested Gorbachev for the Nobel Peace Prize, which he won in 1990, while many other people have demanded that people's courts try the criminals of the June 1989 massacre in Beijing.

At the next level, such mistakes on the part of the Beijing leadership have pushed the unity and peace of Chinese society into a dangerous state. This danger is reflected in the increased power struggles taking place within the top leadership housed in the ancient Beijing palace. Zhao Ziyang and his followers have been purged for refusing to use harsh means to deal with the peaceful demonstrators. The real criminals, Li Peng and his followers, have pushed to try Zhao for his "crimes," and to further punish the poor students who starved for a week in hopes of producing greater things for China. China has been driven to the edge of chaos and civil war.

Now, even if Zhao Ziyang and many of his followers have been ousted from the Communist leadership, the split in the Beijing palace cannot be hidden. For example, the two new members of the most powerful six member Politburo Standing Committee, Jiang Zemin from Shanghai and Li Ruihuan from Tianjin, have no blood on their hands from June 1989. It will be difficult for them to take the same stand as such members as Premier Li Peng, who was one of the people most responsible for the June 1989 bloodshed.

The relations between the central authorities and the various regional and local governments are bound to grow worse. What about the provincial and local officials who did not employ violent means to handle the demonstrations? Would these powerful officials agree with the bloody event's planners in any way? Should the Beijing authorities find themselves in trouble in the near future, who would stand on their side if not the local powers?

One almost unbearable fact is this: on June 9, 1989, Deng indicated that the bloody crackdown was necessary, but he also said that the reform must continue.[2] In a sense, he has realized his grave mistake, though he has not admitted his error or apologized for it. What kind of reform is he really talking about? Another series of economic changes, then another bloody crackdown?

The Communist authorities have made many grave mistakes in the last four decades and they have had to correct these mistakes to their discomfort. Again and again, these mistakes have caused the Communist government to wind up in a dead end. Thereupon, it has had to stop, turn around, and reverse direction to get back from that dead end. The Communist leadership has lived this way since 1949 or before. The more than forty-year record of Communist rule is a record of one evil mistake after another.

In the early years of the Communist takeover, from 1950 through 1952 alone, as acknowledged by Mao Zedong in 1957, more than 700,000 people were killed by the Communist government. In the old Kuomintong capital Naijing and many other cities such as Wuhan, Tianjin, and Xian, within a few days of the takeover, the Communist police arrested thousands of leading citizens, the schoolteachers, bankers, managers, professors, and publishers. Immediately, Naijing reached an explosive point and the people were terrified to the point of seeking any means for survival. Then the Communist authorities had to order the police to release a few prisoners in order to calm down the panicked people of Naijing. Similar things happened throughout China in the early 1950s.

On February 27, 1957, Mao tried to summarize the experiences of this period at the Supreme State Conference in Beijing. In particular, he had to offer an explanation for why more than 700,000 people had been put to death by the Communist authorities in 1950–52. He said:

> The Soviet Union was too leftist, Hungary was too rightist. We have drawn a lesson from this; it is not that we're especially clever.... There were two sides to him [Stalin]. One side was the elimination of true counterrevolutionaries; that was the correct side. The other side was the incorrect killing of numerous people, important people. For example, a high percentage of delegates to the Communist Party [National] Congress were killed. How many in the Central Committee did he kill? He seized and killed XX percent of the Seventeenth Party Congress delegates, and he seized and killed XX percent of the Central Committee members elected at the Seventeenth Congress. We didn't do this sort of thing, having seen his example. Have there been any people unjustly killed? Yes, at the great [campaign] to eliminate counterrevolutionaries [sufan], 1950, 1951, 1952, in those three years of the great sufan, there were. [When] killing local bullies and evil gentry in [the campaign against] five types of counterrevolutionaries, there were. But basically there were no errors; that group of people should have been killed. In all, how many were killed? Seven hundred thousand were killed, [and] after that time probably over 70,000 more have been killed. But less than 80,000. Since last year, basically we have not killed people, only a small number of individuals have been killed. So people say, "You people are so capricious; if you had known it would come to this, why did you start as you did? And now again you want no more killing." In the past four or five years we've only killed several tens of thousands of people. From last year we more or less haven't killed, only killing a small number, a few individuals. In 1950, 1951, 1952, we killed 700,000.

Mao continued,

> The Hong Kong newspapers expanded that estimate (at that time we did not need to reckon accounts with them); they said we killed 20,000,000. If we subtract 700,000 from 20,000,000, that really leaves a remainder of 19,300,000. They were 19,300,000 over. "The tyrant Zhou cannot really have been as wicked as all this." How could we possibly kill 20,000,000 people? It is true that 700,000 were killed; [but] if they had not been killed, the people would not have been able to raise their heads. The people demanded the killing in order to liberate the productive forces. "Evil despots" — the Eastern despot, the Southern despot, the Western despot, the Northern despot, the Central despot, the backbone elements of the five types of counterrevolutionaries.

However, in the same year, 1957, the Communist authorities under Mao and with Deng as one chief party executive committed another great crime: more than 2 million intellectuals, technical specialists, and students, among other people, became purge targets and many were put in prison and labor camps. But the Beijing authorities realized that they could not run China in the same manner in the next two decades. So almost all the so-called Rightists were freed in the late 1970s. Many leading citizens of the 1980s, such as the influential reporter Liu Binyan (1925–   ) and popular writer Wang Meng (1934–   ),[3] have been through these cycles of persecution, imprisonment, internal exile, and rehabilitation in the last four decades.

The biggest crime of the Beijing leadership under Mao Zedong was yet to come. The Cultural Revolution of 1966–76 actually pushed China into a total civil war that partly wiped out the Communist bureaucratic establishment. Millions of cadres, from leaders such as Liu Shaoqi and Deng Xiaoping on down to the lowest-level cadres, were disgraced and humiliated, not to mention countless ordinary Chinese. Most of these cadres spent the next ten years in labor camps and internal exile. Many of them died in the prison. It would take the Communist leadership many years in the late 1970s and 1980s to correct this great mistake. To his credit, Deng Xiaoping acknowledged, on January 16, 1980, that within three years in 1977–80, more than 2,900,000 victims of the previous Communist wrongdoings were rehabilitated by the Beijing authorities under his personal supervision and more would be freed.

Again and again, the Communist authorities have pushed China into the same dead-end policy of blaming failure on imaginary enemies. With the June 1989 massacre, much of China's progress for the last ten years has been buried. Now, China's unity and peace are gravely threatened.

Total Control: Ultimate Chaos

One striking difference between China's old rulers and the Communist authorities is that the latter have penetrated to the lowest levels of the society. The Communists loaded themselves so heavily with control and responsibility that it would make the old rulers turn in their graves.

An example of this is an event that occurred in the autumn

following the Tiananmen Square tragedy of June 1989. After the Square was cleared by the troops, the mayor of Beijing and his municipal government officials were in hot pursuit of certain democratic activists. At the same time, they also were engaged wholeheartedly in selling cabbage that had piled up like mountains in the Beijing streets. To conduct the cabbage sales, these municipal officials were running a massive campaign in Beijing. The mayor of Beijing employed media advertising including newspapers, television, radio broadcasting, and wall posters. Numerous conferences involved hundreds and hundreds of cadres and officials assigned to deal with the cabbage issue. The mayor of Beijing used his political and administrative power to demand that the leaders of various schools, businesses, and government institutions purchase more cabbage regardless of need for it. Thereafter, to finish their assigned tasks, the unit cadres would demand that their employees take home more cabbage. Considering the intensity of the cabbage campaign, one had the impression that some unit officials and cadres would get promoted or demoted depending upon their performance in selling the "patriotic cabbage," the name given the vegetable by the Beijing municipal government.

Behind this curious scene lies the fact that China's vegetable supplies are still controlled by the government. Though it is troublesome to the officials to handle such trifles, they refuse to let the private sector and other responsible institutions manage alone.

This cabbage campaign, although real, also offers a kind of allegory about the way the Communist leaders run China. The Communist authorities constantly attempt to mobilize the entire Chinese population to carry out every new government program, big or small. The success or failure of the Communist authorities depends solely on how effectively they can mobilize the masses. This was true even before the Communist takeover in 1949. The successful mobilization of China's entire population into the Communist power struggle was the very secret of the Communist success. These practices have stayed with the Communist authorities ever since.

Several dozen national campaigns have taken place in the last four decades that have involved practically the entire Chinese population. One particular campaign was the Great Leap Forward of 1958–60. To make enough steel and iron for a rapid industrialization as planned by the Beijing authorities, the campaign involved not only the productive enterprises, but also the schools, villages, temples, and every street and every household. In short, the entire population became a single body working under the Communist authorities in hot pursuit of a Communist miracle. Even the widow of Sun Yatsen, Madame Song Chingling, then a vice-chairman of the People's Congress, could not avoid getting involved in the Great Leap Forward. With the help of her personal staff, she made a small stove at her courtyard to make some "steel." Her action was then widely publicized to promote the cause of industrialization.[4]

Another event was the Maoist Cultural Revolution of 1966–76. In truth, this was nothing more than a tremendous power struggle between the Communist "puritans" led by Mao Zedong and the "revisionists" led by Liu Shaoqi and Deng Xiaoping. During the ten-year struggle and resultant civil chaos, every citizen, from age 5 to 95, was effectively mobilized and sent into the "battleground" under Mao's personal guidance: the debate, the persecution rally, the book burning, the destruction of public properties, the storming and seizure of private homes, the ritual performances in devotion to Mao's cult of personality, the bloody factional fighting with fists, stones, rifles, tanks and artillery guns. Mao Zedong even threw his whole family—his wife, daughter, and nephew—into the power struggles to rid himself of his rivals.[5] All these things may be called the "people's war" in Mao's own terms. After all, Mao Zedong had a brilliant talent for utilizing the passions of the masses for his private ambitions.

Nonetheless, during this reform era, Deng and his reform-minded administration have regarded such mass mobilizations as unproductive and disruptive. After all, Deng Xiaoping and millions of cadres were victimized in the chaotic Maoist Cultural Revolution. It is natural that today the Beijing authorities try very hard to make it something of the past. In the mind of the Beijing leadership, the ordinary people should do their job as assigned and leave national politics to the experts. The job of students is to study diligently so they will be able to participate in the Communist modernization programs. The leaders believe that students have no rights whatsoever to talk about such big issues as democracy. After all, if China's 70- and 80-year-olds do not know how to handle the big issues, how can the 20-year-olds know what to do?

Deng Xiaoping has gone so far as to advocate complete separation between the Communist party and the government, as well as separation between the government and the enterprises and entrepreneurs. In Deng's mind, only with such separation of power can a system of clear responsibility and accountability at every level be installed. Indeed, Deng understands perfectly that without a sound system of accountability for the various institutions as well as individuals, Communist China may not be able to avoid Maoist-style civil chaos and political struggles, much less achieve an economic miracle. However, Deng's reform ideas of this nature have not produced sound results and visible deeds. Throughout Deng's era, total mobilizations have remained commonplace. The most recent example involves the vast manhunts directed at democratic activists following June 4, 1989. Beijing authorities tried to mobilize the entire citizen body, from each street and working unit, to hunt down the young democratic activists. China's recently established legal and judicial systems were totally ignored during this crackdown.

Why won't the leaders dump mass mobilization if they view it as disruptive and unproductive? If one looks at how hard Deng Xiaoping has tried to break with this method from the past, it becomes even more shocking to recognize that policy has actually gone the other way. In reality, even Deng's gigantic effort is really not sufficient to achieve the policy change he wanted so badly. Such self-destructive behavior could have been avoided by the Communist authorities. The answer to this conundrum lies in the very structure of Communist society. After all, Deng's stated goal is merely to perfect the Communist system.

What is the Chinese Communist society? In this society, the Communist bureaucracy is the only thing worthy of existence. Everything else, from the society's wealth to the livelihood of the citizen body, is in the hands of the Communist bureaucracy. This Communist iron grip of power has penetrated society to a fanatic degree. Even such things as what a monk does in his temple, how a ten-year-old girl makes her hairstyle at home, what picture book a three-year-old baby reads in his mother's arms are directly controlled by the Communist bureaucracy. Needless to say, teachers, managers, bankers, city sheriffs, grocery store clerks, shoe-repairmen, and bus drivers are all tightly controlled by the vast Communist bureaucratic structure.

Power corrupts, and absolute power corrupts absolutely, as a wise Englishman noted. The vast power of the Chinese Communist party has corrupted it. All social, economic, and political affairs in Chinese society have to be handled by the Communist authorities. The Communist bureaucracy is the only social organizer, planner, executive, provider, caretaker, trouble-shooter, birth-death announcer. In short, the Communist government plays the roles of god, emperor, boss, confident, friend, policeman, priest, fortune-teller, and devil. Each citizen has to find his place in this vast bureaucratic society. After all, each citizen is fed, sheltered, educated, and employed by the government. Everyone has to swim in the vast ocean of the Communist bureaucracy. You can't escape Communist control at any time between birth and death. Even death provides no true escape, for the Communist bureaucracy owns all the burial grounds and dictates the manner of handling burials throughout China. Also, the cadres in the deceased person's work unit are often invited to offer a speech on the merits of the dead person at his funeral.

The Communist party does not mind doing all these things. The Beijing authorities are proud to say that "without the Communist party, there is no new China" and "only socialism can save China." In truth, the Beijing authorities believe that only their iron control can ensure continuation of the absolute power of the Communist party. To that end, the Communist authorities see no other choice. Even Deng's great reform has left this vast bureaucracy intact. To Deng Xiaoping, Chen Yun, and the other top leadership, all bad things should be dumped, except this vast bureaucratic organization. However, unless this bureaucratic body is reformed, Deng's other reforms will only create more mess for China.

Like China's old rulers, the Communists have gained supreme power by organized violence. In the Chinese tradition, the Communist authority was immediately acknowledged by the population after its military success in 1949. It would be very difficult for China's people to understand that the British people did not make Winston Churchill prime minister for life immediately after victory in World War II, though Churchill was the British leader who defeated Nazi Germany. As victors, the Communists easily claimed universal power over China's population. To ensure the Communists power for "all the generations to come," the Beijing authorities understand the need for total control. Indeed, the Communist power holders have been remarkably successful in establishing their total control of China.

This is very different from China's old dynastic governments. Each dynastic government in China's long history could claim supremacy, but it could not extend its power into every village, every street, and every household. Each old dynastic government had a very limited number of officials at any given time in history. John Fairbank, among others, observed that only 100 years ago there were no more than 40 thousand officials administering a population of 400 million.[6] In fact, each old government could only extend its power to the level of the county. Outside the government, affairs were managed by the land-owning gentry class and by the educated gentry class.

China's educated gentry class consisted of scholars who usually had strong links to the landowners. Gentry scholars gained their influence through talent and intellectual labor as demonstrated by passing the civic examinations. Only 100 years ago, there were more than one million such scholars. These scholars were the major source from which to make up the deficiencies of bureaucracy beginning some 2,000 years ago and taking roots in the form of civic examination since seventh century A.D. Though a small number of these scholars held government offices, most scholars remained outside government and served as a bridge between the ruling power and the ruled. Thus both the landowners and the educated gentry linked the old dynastic government and the rural population. These people also performed the role of government in the organized effort for building roads and bridges, in organizing famine relief, in the supervision of local affairs of all kinds, and even in the maintenance of peace at the local level, especially in cases of national chaos. China's old rulers could have dreamed of extending their power, but they found it neither possible, nor needed.

Even before 1949, the status and influence of the gentry class had suffered a great deal due to the chaos brought by civil war and the anti–Japanese war. In fact, by 1905, the civil examination system was abolished. This decline of the gentry's role worsened the chaos in Chinese society in general and in the rural areas in particular. Lian Shumin, a philosopher as well as a leading advocate for the rural life, tried to redirect China's social order especially through the remaking of the gentry class in the 1930s and 1940s. However, the anti–Japanese war and the civil war made progress difficult.[7]

Since 1949, the landowning gentry class has been completely eliminated by the Communist party. The Communist government has taken all the wealth of China society into its own hands. It now can support a vast bureaucracy. The Communist government now employs some 48 million party cadres and about 30 million officials.[8] The Communist party has a very good reason not to adopt a market-oriented economy. Under such an economic system the party would lose the financial resources to maintain this gigantic body of cadres and bureaucrats.

With the aid of the gigantic Communist bureaucracy, all aspects of life of China's citizens, now 1.1 billion total, are easily controlled by the government. The Beijing authorities by themselves determine all affairs of the society. The authorities are assured of complete Communist domination and they can easily mobilize the population. After all, the Communist bureaucracy controls every street, village, workshop, working team, classroom, and even each temple. Once the Beijing leaders issue orders, the 48 million cadres and 30 million officials will rush to mobilize the whole of society. China's numerous political campaigns in the last 41 years have been carried out in this manner.

Naturally, the charms of Chinese life in old age are completely eliminated by the Communist government. The old China described by Lin Yutang in his *My Country and My People* does not exist anymore. In old China, the inability of the Son of Heaven to fully utilize his power had created a serene scene. The ordinary people did not need to care too much about the existence of the high power in their simple, daily life.

> We go to work at sunrise.
> And come back to rest at sunset.
> We know nothing and learn nothing.
> What has the emperor's virtue to do with us?

In Communist China today, the Beijing authorities can utilize their power completely and exclusively. In particular, Mao's virtue has everything to do with every citizen, even how much sleep a farmer should have. One of Mao's instructions given on August 21, 1958, runs this way: "At present, the intensity of labor is very high; the peasants must be allowed to have proper rest, two days a month, one day a fortnight. During the busy season, rest a little less; at other times, rest a little more. [Those] living relatively far away from the work site can eat and sleep [there], so as to save on commuting time and have more rest. This point should be written in the documents but not be talked about too much."

In the old China, as cited by Lin Yutang, the individual person could find much time for leisure and he was as happy as a bird if he

> Has met a monk in a bamboo-covered yard
> And enjoyed another of life's leisurely half-days.

Yet in Communist China today, such desire is indeed too much for the Communist bureaucracy. Every citizen from elementary school–age on is forced to read Mao's Little Red Book endlessly, to spend a huge fraction of his or her lifetime at propaganda meetings, and to criticize oneself and one's colleagues in the workplaces. In Deng's era, the old propaganda has been "reformed." For example, the government television newsmen can stop the people on the streets and demand their views about the June 4, 1989, killing. Of course, nobody dares to express opinions different from the official view. The people remember that one man was sentenced to ten years in prison for talking about the bloodshed with an American television team on Beijing streets in June 1989.[9]

In the old China, the poets had their ways to enjoy themselves. They could even do things like the following.

> With a jar of wine, Li makes a hundred poems,
> He sleeps in an inn of Ch'angan city.
> The Emperor sent for him and he'd not move,
> Saying, "I'm the God of Wine, Your Majesty!"

In Communist China today, the poets cannot survive unless they work to promote the cult of the Communist authorities and the greatness of the Communist leaders from Mao Zedong, Zhou Enlai, Lin Biao, and the Gang of Four, to Hua Guofeng to Deng Xiaoping and Chen Yun. After four decades of such life, beauty, harmony, and serenity have become foreign subjects to China's poets.

Nevertheless, the Communist authorities have gathered all the troubles of the society by its power grip. American politicians such as Washington, Jefferson, and Lincoln feared absolute power and understood that the best, or, more precisely, the most trouble-free, government is the one that governs the least. China has one philosophical school, the Taoists, in existence for 2,500 years, that talks about the advantages of minimal action by the government. Such a philosophy would hardly be understandable to the Communists. The Communists feed on power. Many Chinese Communist officials sent to Hong Kong during the 1980s were shocked that the British have not tried to interfere in depth in the affairs of Hong Kong. The British colonial government maintains a minimal level of governance which is responsible for public safety and protection, taxation, the judicial system, defense, and foreign relations for Hong Kong, but little more. British rule is based on a well-defined property ownership law and the Chinese in Hong Kong are left alone to pursue their economic and social interests. Moreover, the Hong Kong Chinese can even openly criticize their government officials!

But so far, China has turned in a very different direction as she failed to create modern political and economic institutions. The halfway reform adopted by the Manchu government was only short to make China a modern progressive nation. Yet the end of the Manchu government only led to national chaos coupled by the Japanese invasion. All these prompted the Communist revolution. Though this revolution has involved the entire Chinese people and sacrificed tens of millions of people, it has not moved in the bright direction of erecting modern institutions for China. Instead, it has created a very twisted society. The few ambitious politicians have found their way to become new rulers over the very many. China has been forced to return to the pattern of her dynastic changes as before.

Before Mao, Deng and the other Communists learned a trade, they become professional revolutionaries when only in their teens and twenties. Only a very small percentage of the Communist leaders enjoyed a formal education beyond elementary school. Nevertheless, the Communist Revolution opened up a brave new world for them.

Suddenly, there was no need for the Communists to learn a trade to earn a living. Class struggle became their profession. Once they gained power, they gave themselves positions as chairmen, presidents, ministers, governors, mayors, managers, bankers, and directors.

The difficulties and privations the Communists suffered during the years of warfare as they fought to win power ensured their limitless thirst for power. Once in possession of power, they wanted to claim all the privileges Chinese society could provide. And naturally, they want things to stay that way forever. Naturally, China's previous autocratic governments have shown the Communist leadership how to establish a powerful central government with absolute rights over the people.

Immediately after the takeover of mainland China, these guerrilla warriors went straight into the cities and put their hands on everything. They immediately set out to destroy all the opposition, even the traditional social organizations led by the gentry class. In this way, they made themselves the masters, the kings, the policemen, the priests of Chinese society, and the judges and the juries of how well they were performing their self-assigned tasks.

Ten times worse, millions of Maoist purge specialists joined the Communist bureaucracy during the numerous purge campaigns in the 30-year Maoist era. The Gang of Four gained their power in precisely this way. The Gang of Four and their like thrived by exploiting not only the Chinese people, but even their fellow Communists. Indeed, these gangs have been disastrous to the Communist establishment, that even the Communist strongmen Deng Xiaoping and Chen Yun would like to completely eliminate them.

In a country crowded with almost a quarter of the world's population, Mao Zedong and his colleagues sometimes appeared to be the only living beings in China. Mao was renowned for many skills: he was a statesman, a military genius, an economics wizard, an agricultural expert, a public relations expert, an industrial planner, a financial king, a diplomat of the first rank, a bridge inspector, a movie critic, an omnipotent judge of good and evil, a public health specialist, a women's rights campaigner, a market analyst, a mighty educator, a philosopher of heaven and hell, a poet of life and death, and, above all, a marathon swimmer. When he swam, the world was most delighted to discover that a human body can indeed float on water, despite age and weakness. In the post–Mao era, all the godly abilities that once belonged to Mao were bestowed first upon Hua Guafeng and now upon Deng Xiaoping.

Even if these Communist leaders did possess such heavenly abilities, the world has not witnessed any heavenly performances in the last forty-plus years. Once all their enemies – the traditional gentry class, the traditional organizations, the intellectuals, the industrialists, the merchants, the managerial people – were destroyed, the real troubles started for the Communist authorities. Nobody remained to be blamed for Communist shortcomings. The government was supposed to take care of each citizen, his birth and death, his eating and clothing, his shelter and job, his excitement and boredom. The atheist Communist leaders decided on how many monks should be added to each temple, how much cooking-oil each citizen should have each month, who should join the few non–Communist parties, what clothes the children should wear, who should associate with whom. Alas!

The Communist grip on power offers more deadly troubles for the whole of society. Since the Communist bureaucracy controls all the affairs of society, all conflicts within society eventually surface within the Communist party for resolution of some sort. All social conflicts eventually become conflicts within the party. Any change within society, economic, political, or social, inevitably causes power struggles within the Communist bureaucratic establishment. This is why there have been so many power struggles within the Communist leadership. Furthermore, such power struggles threaten Communist unity and even the existence of the Communist party itself.

Once the Communist system was established, there were no easy ways for its leaders to resolve conflicts except through power struggles. The huge Communist bureaucratic body guarantees unrest and deadly strife. The various leaders represent different interests, different sectors; each powerful leader, each faction wants more power, which can only be secured by struggle.

One of the first striking instances was the struggle between Mao and Defense Minister Peng Dehuai in 1959. Peng, observing the suffering of the people amid the fanatic attempts of Mao's forced industrial programs, opposed Mao's Great Leap Forward. He wrote a long letter to criticize Mao's policies. As result of his criticism, Peng and his followers were purged by Mao Zedong, while other powerful leaders such as Zhou Enlai and Liu Shaoqi stood by and watched. The conflicts between Mao and Liu Shaoqi resulted in the near-collapse of the Communist bureaucracy and also caused ten years of chaos from 1966 to 1976. In the 1980s both Hu Yanbang and Zhao Zhiyang became the victims of the power struggles between Deng Xiaoping and Chen Yun. In short, as long as the Communist bureaucracy is unchanged, power struggles and civil chaos will persist.

In passing, we point out that the very reason the government could not manage the centralized economy is that the central plan always boils down to a power struggle within the system. More power means a greater share in the plan. Hu Pin,[10] a critic of the Communist authorities, would go as far as to say that even if one would try intentionally to harm China, one could not do worse than the Communist authorities in its bungled effort to build a new China.

The Communist bureaucracy above all else must be the target of true reform. To replace the Communist bureaucracy with modern economic and political institutions should be the primary goal for China's modernization. Without achieving this reform, any talk of a better China would be daydreaming.

China's reform had not reached this point until 1989, when tens of millions of peaceful demonstrators demanded a change in the Communist system. Yet that peaceful movement ended in bloodshed. If China has anything to reform in the future, it is this Communist bureaucracy.

Weighted down by the gigantic bureaucracy, China can hardly stand on her own feet. In reality, Communist China does not produce even half a much wealth as China's great dynasties in the past. The Communist authorities have not managed to do half as well as the Manchu government in maintaining political stability and peace and expanding national wealth. The Communist government with some 30 million bureaucrats cannot do half as well as the Manchu government with no more than 40,000 officials.

It should be clearly understood that when any government tries to secure excessive power, it will end up with intense power struggles. Indeed, if the American government tried to handle all the affairs of American society, very soon American society would be characterized by endless unrest and power struggles. Washington would give birth to numerous Mao Zedongs, Deng Xiaopings, Zhou Enlais, Gangs of Four, Lin Biaos, and Chen Yuns. Power struggles such as those in Chinese Communist government are not a matter of ethnicity; they represent a basic flaw in any government that has too much power.

Strongman Versus Institutions

China's grave internal instability over the last 41 years has been caused by the uncontrollable power struggles within the Communist authority. To curb these power struggles is one of the most urgent issues facing the Communist authority in particular and China in general. In this reform era, the Communist leadership has tried desperately to replace personal leadership based on a personality cult by a collective leadership and collective institutions. Building institutions was one of the most difficult tasks faced by the Beijing leadership in the 1980s.

Deng Xaioping, Chen Yun, and most other senior leaders of the reform era all suffered when the Communist superman Mao Zedong played his one-man show for several decades. Deng himself was victimized twice under Mao's tyranny, but he still should believe himself lucky. For the state head Liu Shaoqi, along with thousands and thousands of comrades, perished during the years of Mao's rule.

These traumatic experiences are still fresh for many living politicians. "For more than ten years, Lin Biao and the Gang of Four have done great harm," Chen Yun, the second most powerful Communist in the reform era, remarked to his colleagues on January 4, 1979. "In the meetings [in those days], all we did was to read [Mao Zedong's] quotations, shouting three times 'Long live [Chairman Mao]'; what was more, we had to perform rituals [in devotion to Mao's personality cult] in the mornings and evenings, and recited quotations before talking on the telephone. This sort of thing was stopped only by Comrade Zhou Enlai. Without Comrade Zhou Enlai, the results of the 'Cultural Revolution' would have been more deadly. He has protected many comrades and we are among them! Due to the destructive efforts of Lin Piao and the Gang of Four, our Party has experienced many abnormal things.... In the winter of 1975, there came Chairman Mao's communications officer, a kid [Mao's nephew, Mao Yenhsin]. This kid passed Chairman Mao's directives to the Politburo and took the Politburo's resolutions back to Chairman Mao. Comrade Ye Jianying told me that as a Vice Chairman, he was not allowed to see Chairman Mao. On last December 10, I asked Comrade Hua Guofeng if he could see Chairman Mao at that time. He replied that he could not except that he chatted briefly with Chairman Mao when they received foreign guests together. Even such a Central Committee Vice Chairman had trouble arranging to see Chairman Mao; this was very abnormal indeed."

It was no wonder that a little note from Mao Zedong could make Hua Guofeng, a talentless bureaucrat, China's new ruler for several years. This particular story is worth telling. It was officially reported that the dying Mao Zedong handed a piece of paper to Hua in April 1976 with eight words written on it, but without either an addressee, a signature, or a date. (That was exactly the time when popular demonstrations against Maoists broke out in Beijing.) The eight words in the note were, "With you in charge, I feel at ease."[11] In this way, Hua was given the highest seats in the party, in the government, and in the army following Mao's death in September 1976. Thereafter, numerous cadres, Maoist writers, poets, and newspapermen showered Hua with many heavenly praises that once were reserved only for Mao: "wise leader," "people's great guardian," "people feel at ease when Hua is the leader since Chairman Mao did."[12] Fortunately for China's people, Mao did not hand that piece of paper with its powerful message to Hua's granddaughter still wearing diapers. Otherwise, Hua's granddaughter could have claimed the rulership of Communist China. In a way, that would not have shocked China's people. After all, less than 100 years ago, the last emperor of the Manchu government, Pu Yi (1906–67), claimed the throne when he was only three years old and still wearing diapers.[13]

It would take several years for Deng Xiaoping and the other once-victimized veteran leaders to rise to the top again and gather enough strength to remove Hua and his followers from the top leadership. Only then could Deng start his reform and push for gigantic changes within the Communist hierarchy and beyond.

The life-long bitter experiences of these aging leaders have made them feel the desperate need to reshape the Communist power structure, and especially to limit the power held by a few top leaders. These men believe that most Communist disasters can be avoided by the denial of excessive power to any individual. In their minds, Mao successfully put his own interests above the party and the nation. Both Deng Xaioping and Chen Yun want to establish Communist institutions to prevent any future disasters caused by personal rule.

"Some establishments we have had are actually influenced by [China's history of] feudalism, including the cult of personality, the family master ruling style or attitude, and even life-tenure for office holders." On August 21 and 23, 1980, Deng Xiaoping made this statement to an Italian reporter about the "root causes" of the disastrous Maoist Cultural Revolution: "We are now studying how to avoid repeating these things, and we are ready to start to reform the system. Our country has had a feudal history for several thousand years and lacks socialist democracy and a socialist legal system. Now we want seriously to build a true socialist democracy and a socialist legal system. Only in this way, can the problems be solved."

Throughout the 1980s, many attempts were made by Deng Xiaoping's government to promote institutional changes. Most significantly, many new and younger cadres have been brought into the system at every level of the Communist bureaucracy. Many of the aging cadres, including Deng and Chen Yun themselves, retreated to the sidelines one way or another. However, all such attempts have not lasted long. Again and again, the younger and abler leaders such as Hu Yaobang and Zhao Ziyang have been pushed aside and even purged. Most strikingly, Deng Xiaoping and Chen Yun, among other veteran leaders, were responsible for these demotions and purges.

Yet, this is not something new to the Communist party. Throughout its history, the Communist party has continually dumped some of its most able and respectable cadres. As Su Wei observed, many able and more liberal cadres suffered a bad end, such as Liu Shaoqi, Zhou Enlai, as well as Deng Xiaoping in Mao's era.[14] A bad fate also overtook reform-minded leaders such as Hu Yaobang and Zhao Ziyang in Deng's era.

In fact, the more Deng talks about his official retirement, the less he seems willing to retire. Deng has kicked out his two hand-picked heirs in the last few years. In fact, the Communist central leadership went so far in 1987 as to pass a resolution that ensured that the semiretired Deng would have the final say on anything important in China. Even after his formal retirement announcement in the fall of 1989, Deng could not stop appearing on the political stage to show the world that China is still under his personal charge. The Tiananmen tragedy might have been avoided if a collective leadership had been at work. What has gone wrong? Why have Deng and Chen Yun fondly talked about collective leadership for so long, but ended up preventing its establishment?

The issues at hand seem much more complicated than what Deng Xiaoping and Chen Yun could have expected. The key fact is this: since the Communist bureaucracy was established, even its most powerful leaders have been powerless to correct the ills of the system. Morever, no mechanism exists outside the party structure to correct Communist mistakes.

The Communist bureaucracy is modeled on China's traditional centralized bureaucratic system. Traditionally, the Chinese government, as well as the entire Chinese nation, has revolved around a paramount leader. Only under such a superman can China's unity be secured. In fact, the Chinese people have been accustomed to live under the strong, centralized rule of a single leader for nearly 4,000 years. The need for a single paramount leader, who sits high in the palace and decides on all affairs, big or small, is felt as urgently today as yesterday. All the officials are his employees and any of them can be dismissed at any time at his pleasure. In a way, without this superman to give orders, no officials would know how to get through a day. This is the nature of China's centralized political system. Throughout China's long history, a weak emperor was constantly associated with chaos and even civil war. As a popular Chinese saying declares, "A family cannot be without master for a day; a nation cannot be leaderless for a day."

In this way China's powerful autocratic government maintained its rule in the past. Ray Huang offers insightful observations about China's old imperial system: "It was neither divine nor secular, but both. It was neither irrational nor rational, but both. It was neither Confucian-humanistic nor Legalist-methodical, but both. At the dawn of the imperial era [around 2,100 years ago], the occupant of the Chinese throne was already called on to administrate a population of sixty million with the aid of some 130,000 bureaucrats. His tools were few, but his approach to problems, forced to cut through many levels of inconsistency and uncertainty, had to remain decisive."[15]

The Communist authorities could hardly change this tradition. Yet, they have added new twists to this messy old tradition. The Communist cadres must not only follow the Chinese traditions of servitude and obedience, but they must also follow all the Communist rules. The usual picture is this: when a lower-ranking cadre refuses to submit to the will of a higher-ranking cadre, this situation will change completely if the latter shouts, "Aren't you a Communist?" This question has the same effect as when a master shouts at his servant: "Aren't you my servant?" To understand this point, we cannot do better than to cite the teachings of the second most powerful Communist, Liu Shaoqi. His popular booklet, *How to Be a Good Communist*, which was written in 1939 during the Yenan guerrilla period, is particularly revealing.

What is a good communist? Liu asserts that "The test of a party member's loyalty to the party, the Revolution, and the Communist cause is whether or not he can subordinate his personal interests absolutely and unconditionally to the interests of the party, whatever the circumstances." To make sure this point is fully understood, Liu goes on to say: "At all times and to all questions, a party member should give first consideration to the interests of the party as a whole, and put them in the forefront and place their personal matters and interests second. The supremacy of the party's interests is the highest principle that must govern the thinking and actions of the members of our party. In accordance with this principle, every party member must completely identify his personal interests with those of the party both in his thinking and in his actions. He must be able to yield to the interests of the party without any hesitation or reluctance and sacrifice his personal interests whenever the two are at variance. Unhesitating readiness to sacrifice personal interests, and even one's life, for the party and the proletariat and for the emancipation of the nation and of all mankind — that is one expression of what we usually describe as 'party spirit,' 'party sense,' or 'sense of organization.' It is the highest expression of communist morality, of the principled nature of the party of the proletariat, and of the purest proletarian class consciousness."

The Communist party went through a period for several decades as a secret society during its power struggle with the powerful Kuomintang. For the safety of the members, the party was operated under a tight secretive system. Party members were restricted by severe discipline and regulations. Cadres were required to renounce not only their own interests, but also their parents, brothers and sisters, and friends for the interests of the party. After 1949, the party's activities became open, but the secretive practices that characterized the party's early history have persisted into the present.

In fact, almost every cadre has some bitter personal stories to tell. The bigger a cadre is, often the more bitter his experiences. In one instance, party boss Zhao Ziyang of the reform era allowed his father, a rich peasant, to die in the purgelike Communist land redistribution movement of the early 1950s. For that, Zhao received honorable mention from the higher cadres, through he has been hated by his home-village people ever since.[16] Though state head Liu Shaoqi diligently promoted the cult of personality for Mao Zedong for several decades, he himself became a victim of Mao's tyranny. He died in prison in 1969, though he still held the state head post.

The Communist power structure is set up in the traditional manner. Since Mao Zedong successfully led the party to power after some three decades of bloody struggle, it was natural that Mao would become the undisputed leader of Communist China. To maintain Communist supremacy, it was necessary for the party to further strengthen its unity around the deified superman Mao. Even the Communist bureaucracy built its legitimacy around the personality cult of this leader.

In fact, during Mao's era, Mao was the only person who could speak freely — not even Zhou Enlai, or Liu Shaoqi, or Deng Xiaoping could contradict or criticize Mao. The ties of the Communist authority with the people were built on Mao's cult of personality. Thereafter, everything had to revolve around him. Naturally, the power structure of Communist China was centered on Mao for several decades. Though there were a series of Communist political institutions such as the Central Committee, the Politburo, and the Party Congress, Mao was actually supreme and could walk on all of these freely and without hesitation.

In reality, this is really the way the Communist centralized bureaucracy works. During the chaotic Maoist Cultural Revolution, Zhou Enlai had to protect Mao's cult of personality with his one hand, while at the same time he tried to save as many disgraced senior comrades as possible with the other. Zhou's authority over the millions of lower bureaucrats remained legitimate only when he protected Mao's authority. The same thing works for all bureaucrats in Communist China. That is, to protect one's power over the lower bureaucrats in particular and the people in general, each cadre must first try to protect the authority of the higher-ranking cadres. In return, the higher-ranking cadres must show support at all times for the lower cadres who deal more directly with the people. This is the only way to maintain the authority of China's centralized bureaucratic system.

The nature of the Communist bureaucracy also demands that a new bureaucratic administration protect the reputation of the immediate past administration. That is why in the reform era Deng Xiaoping, Chen Yun, and the other aging leaders have had to try hard to protect Mao's cult of personality in the same way as Zhou Enlai did, even though these men suffered terribly under Mao's tyranny. In reality, they really have no choice. Mao's image is equivalent to that of the Communist party. If they lose the power they derive from Mao's reputation, Deng and Chen Yun would lose much of the authority they have over tens of millions of cadres, and they would eventually lose the authority that enables them to rule and control a billion people.

The means for running China is almost as limited as it was some 2,000 years ago, but considerably more complex than ever before. But the people would wish their rulers to lead them to prosperity overnight. That is why China's people surrendered completely all their rights to the Communist authorities in the first place. Mao was offered all the decision-making authority for several decades to make such popular dreams come true in whatsoever ways Mao would see fit. That is also why the people did not revolt when they were pushed around and overworked by the cadres. Despite the tens of millions of lives lost by the failure of the Great Leap Forward, Mao still maintained his supreme position in China and even had the power to mobilize the entire Chinese population for the Cultural Revolution before he died in 1976. His photo still hangs on the Tiananmen Tower and his ghostly shadow still shapes the lives of hundreds of millions of people in China today.

Once the cult of personality had become effective, all other Communist institutions became "paper tigers," to use Mao's own slogan. Small wonder that for several decades Mao was the only person who had freedom of speech in a country with almost a quarter of the world's population. In March 1981, Chen Yun told his colleagues, "The high esteem of Comrade Mao in the party was established only through the long revolutionary war and experiences. That is why even when he made mistakes and when so many veteran leaders received such ill-treatment, these men could still trust him and remember his achievements. The veteran leaders' support of Comrade Mao Zedong is fully sincere and honest." This may not be a dishonest speech. But the deeper truth is that the Communist authority has not established institutions that can effectively stop the evil doings of its leaders. Therefore, even when they themselves became the victims of the system, they had no way to escape. The common people have even less chance.

Actually, the courage of the Communist officials can hardly match that of the Confucian officials in China's dynastic past. Throughout China's dynastic history, there were many tyrants, but there were even more fearless officials. Those officials would put the interest of the empire much above their life. In fact, for hundreds and thousands of Confucian officials, to meet death in the process of preventing the emperor's errors was regarded as the noblest action. During the Ming Dynasty (1368–1644) alone, thousands of officials chose such a noble death. It is most shocking that the Communist party has produced more cowardly officials in the last forty-odd years than all of China's previous dynasties put together. No wonder that the Communist party has committed so many mistakes so far.

Benefiting from his cult of personality and enjoying unchallenged power, Mao believed that he owned China just like the old rulers. He could do whatever he pleased. After all, in his mind, whatever he did was for the interests of the people. Any cadres who might have higher talents than he must be gotten rid of in the "interest of the people." When Mao did not produce miracles with his "class struggle" and "politics-in-command" ideas, he would not tolerate any other ideas from his colleagues. Finally, when leaders like

Peng Dehuai, Liu Shaoqi, and Deng Xiaoping, at different times, tried to remake the economic system by "economy in command" and "profits first," Mao punished these men regardless of the terrible consequences for China's well-being.

The very legitimacy of the socialist system was tied to Mao's cult of personality in Mao's era. Just before he died, Mao seemed sad that nobody would protect the things he had spent his lifetime to build up, especially his theory of class struggle and his socialist system. Mao's worries were justified. Less than one month after his death, his wife and nephew were sent to prison by Hua Guofeng, Mao's number four handpicked successor. More significant, Deng Xiaoping could easily dump Mao's brand of socialism and pursue his own "socialist" programs.

Now Deng seems to be in the same kind of mess. For instance, he cannot be sure that his only son, who is widely rumored to be tainted with corruption, will not be sent to prison. Of course, he has more important things to worry about, especially the fate of the Communist empire.

More abnormal things did happen. During the height of the power struggle between Mao and Lin Biao, as pointed out by Hu Ping, Lin had many chances to strike ahead.[17] Yet Lin was acutely aware that he might not be able to unite Communist China without using Mao's flag. In this way, he had to design a series of rather careful schemes to get rid of Mao. Then he could take the supreme seat in the name of Mao's personality cult. That was perhaps the main reason that Mao had the chance to strike at Lin first. Therefore, it was Lin Biao, not Mao, who met an untimely end.

In this reform age, the power structure of the Communist party is built around the second-generation strongman Deng Xiaoping. Everything revolves around Deng at this time. Socialism is now labeled by Deng, the party is now commanded by Deng, the people are now under the personal protection of Deng. Every cadre has to protect Deng's personality cult in order to advance his own interests.

In Deng's era, all official orders must come from Deng. Without him, the army generals would fight with each other; the cadres would forget which province they serve; the officials would have trouble spending even a day without receiving directives from him; many overseas Chinese would weep over the approaching disasters.

Since June 1989, Deng has had to get out and stand in front of the television cameras. Otherwise, Communist unity would be in question; the Hong Kong stock market would plunge; the doctrinaire hard-liners would feel more isolated. When the June 4, 1989, massacre was over, all the provincial and local officials watched carefully to see if Deng would leave his bedroom. When Deng appeared in public on June 9, 1989, and made a speech to the officers of the martial law troops, supporting telegrams from all corners of China immediately flooded Beijing.

In a sense, Deng had to kick out both Hu Yaobang and Zhao Ziyang, his two most useful aides during the 1980s. These two men lacked the will to reach for absolute supremacy. Both Hu and Zhao were most reluctant to apply harsh means to deal with China's young generations of students, workers, and intellectuals. How could such weak characters unite a vast party with 48 million ambitious cadres, a bureaucratic body with 30 million officials waiting for orders, and a nation of 1.1 billion poor souls in need of a benevolent emperor as well as bread?

Now, although Deng has chosen a new successor, the provincial Shanghai bureaucrat Jiang Zemin, and has announced his formal retirement in November 1989, he has not retreated to a vacation home to spend quality time with his grandchildren, a practice usually loved by 80-year-olds in China. He continues to show up from time to time to tell the world that Communist China is safe, and that his brand of socialism is operating and in order. The more troubles other Communist states are in, the more often he has to appear on television or in public to shake hands with foreign guests.

However, the loss of his aides Hu and Zhao has significantly reduced the personal role of Deng Xiaoping on China's political stage. Now he has tremendous problems dealing with power contenders, especially from Chen Yun's faction. Deng maintains his supreme position partly because the big central planners realize that they cannot retire Deng without causing great troubles to themselves. Moreover, whenever anything goes wrong, the central planners can blame Deng.

There is a problem for the Communist party, for the nation, for the people, and for Deng himself. Deng cannot pass his power to anybody else without perhaps causing chaos and even violence. Mao Zedong had tremendous troubles passing over his power. Mao had to start a civil war, the Maoist Cultural Revolution, to get out of the mess he had created, but only ended up stepping into a more deadly trap. What can Deng Xiaoping do now?

"Monks Are Burning Down the Temple!"

Power struggles and palace intrigues occur in every country. What is really unusual about the Chinese Communist power struggles is that these things take place so constantly and are so devastating that they would even shock China's old rulers.

The old China's palace struggles were always kept secretive and mysterious. Though the Communist power holders do their things in secrecy, they have failed to keep their power struggles within the walled palaces and out of the sight of the people. Indeed, the Communist authorities have often purposely promoted their power struggles before the public. The Communist authorities have gone so far as to mobilize the entire population and send the people into the actual battleground of the Communist power struggles. Moreover, as an unfailing law, the winners of the power struggle always condemn the losers publicly in ways that would do more damage to their prestige than what its enemies, such as Jiang Kaishek in Taiwan, could dream of. So obvious is the damage, for example, that one day Liu Shaoqi, the second most powerful cadre in the government, was suddenly denounced as the worst criminal of the party, the nation, and the people: "renegade, hidden traitor, and scab." To an honorable cadre, these power struggles would be unspeakably ugly even viewed in retrospect. So, why do the Communist power holders want to jeopardize their own prestige in the first place?

Most Communist party power struggles are centered on the power succession. Each power struggle has resulted in a partial or even complete destruction of certain divisions in the Communist authority. Many Communists did not die at the hands of their enemies during the civil war with the Kuomintang or the anti–Japanese war. Many met violent deaths in the hands of their colleagues. It is a painful truth to the tens of millions of aging cadres that hardly a single cadre has not been humiliated and disgraced by his own colleagues at some time during the last four decades. The biggest power struggle, the Maoist Cultural Revolution, actually almost managed to destroy the entire Communist bureaucratic establishment. That civil war caused the deaths of thousands and thousands of cadres, starting with the state head, Liu Shaoqi, and also caused the deaths of countless common people.

Such power struggles have not slowed down but have intensified in this reform era in China. Many people dreamed that the reform of the 1980s would do away with these ugly power struggles. Many people hoped that the Communist winners and losers would kindly shake hands with each other in front of the T.V. cameras like the American Republican and Democratic office candidates so often do. All human beings can shake hands to end their conflict. Even the Jews and the Germans, the Americans and the Soviets can achieve a reconciliation, so why cannot the Chinese Communists reconcile after their power struggles? Reconciliation has never happened thus far. Reform has not resulted in a unified leadership, or even in a display of more common sense and mutual understanding.

Fundamentally, Deng's reform has not created any working institutions, within the Communist system or without, that can put an end to these deadly power struggles. In fact, no Communist, not even powerful party chiefs such as Hu Yaobang and Zhao Ziyang, can be sure what the next days hold in store for them. Why cannot the Communists learn some lessons from their own sufferings? Why do these "monks" keep burning down their own temple?

Again, this issue is very complex. The Communist system is constituted in a manner that cannot avoid, indeed even invites, such deadly power struggles. Like China's old dynasties, the Communist party retains its supreme power by means of violence. Yet, the power succession in the Communist government is very different from the power succession in China's old dynasties. Under the dynastic system, the leader of a successful revolution would become the absolute ruler in the new political establishment. The succession of the rulership was completed within the royal family. This has been universally accepted in the Chinese culture. It continues to influence succession practices to some extent in some of the Chinese culture–dominated societies. For example, the Kuomintang superman Jiang Kaishek could let his son, Jiang Jingkuo (1910–1988), succeed him in Taiwan. Also in North Korea today, the supreme ruler Kim Il Sung is trying to pass his power on to his son.

The Chinese Communist authority can hardly follow this old dynastic practice. After all, the Communists claim that they have ended dynastic rule and founded a socialist republic. Mao could not name a relative as his successor, and neither can Deng.

In reality, the Communist power succession is very difficult to carry out even within the system. This is due essentially to the fact that the Communist government is not electoral. The common people have no direct influence on the choice of the leadership. There are hardly any democratic measures within the party, so that even the cadres cannot choose their leaders. In this reform era, the Beijing leadership has tried desperately to resolve this problem. Yet all their efforts have ended in grand failures so far. Leaders such as Li Peng are publicly despised, while party chief Zhao Ziyang is applauded worldwide for his reform effort. However, Li Peng still holds power, but Zhao has been ousted, publicly condemned, and remains haunted by the threat of standing "criminal trial" for "splitting the Communist Party" and for showing sympathy for the 1989 "counter-revolutionary uprising."

In the 1980s the Communist authority has supported the theory of involving more people in the decision-making processes. The Beijing leadership has gone so far as to allow the lowest-level offices, such as county-level offices and local people's congress members, to be directly chosen by electoral vote. Yet they soon found that granting even this small right to the people would damage Communist domination of Chinese society. As events turned out, democratic activists tried hard to win elections and usually gained the majority of such elections. Due to the unexpected success of activists and reformers, conservative cadres overreacted, thereby promoting unrest in the various regions since 1979. This unrest can be traced to election abuses committed by local officials in such elections. The most serious incident of this kind occurred in December 1986. Opposing the cadres' wrongdoings during the selection of representatives for the local people's congress, the students at the Chinese University of Science and Technology in Anhui Province took their cause to the streets. The demonstration movement immediately spread to other major cities in China, including Beijing, Shanghai, and Naijing. The Beijing authorities panicked, almost to the point of declaring martial law.[18]

Over the last few years, the Beijing leadership has even tried to introduce some democratic measures at the very top. In the 13th Party Congress in 1987, the leadership made a historical breakthrough by allowing the list of candidates for the Central Committee to be a few persons larger than the actual number required. As a result, the Maoist ideologue Deng Liqin, who is said to want the party chief seat, lost his seat in the 285-person Central Committee. Deng Liqin's misfortune struck other powerful Communist leaders like a lightning bolt and made them realize the risks they faced with any form of free elections.[19]

It is a small wonder that the last thing the Communists would want is a government by election. For decades, the people have been the favorite cards for the Communist leaders to play with, but now the people may become an unspeakable nightmare for them.

The problems surrounding the Communist power succession need to be resolved within the Communist party itself. However, it is not an easy job, for there is very little popular consent for the leadership, even by the cadres. All the governors and mayors are directly appointed by the central authority. Moreover, there are hardly any regulations or laws concerning the selection of new leadership. One popular way seems to be based on the merits of the particular cadres. This method is very troublesome. Every ranking cadre believes in his or her worth. Everybody wants to stand above everyone else. After all, the winner takes all. Many Communist factions have gradually developed since the Communist guerrilla era. Each top leader heads one or more of these factions. The final selection, therefore, usually boils down to the political balance of the various political divisions. Everybody wants to prove that he is the supreme boss, and endless struggles are the result.

It is natural that the Communist power struggles will continue after Deng's era. Indeed, the millions of cadres will only increase their struggles upon the disappearance of Deng. Such power struggles are already under way. In short, the political problems facing the Communist government now will only mean more and more power struggles. The Communist system itself is the very source of the Communist power struggles.

So far, the Communist power struggles have been very destructive. They are often fought not just for power, but for life and death. This is not surprising. The dominating majority of the Communists come from extremely poor peasant backgrounds. They never learned the art of negotiation or the value of compromise for the sake of coexistence.

Communist power was established after a long and bloody revolution. Throughout China's long history, such highly destructive power struggles have been characteristic of peasant uprisings. The Taiping Rebellion (1851–1864) had many similarities with today's scenes as far as bitter power struggles are concerned. The Taiping rebels were so successful that they controlled the better half of China within three years or so. Yet they failed to maintain a reasonable unity within the system. Destruction soon set in from the inside; endless power struggles led to the deaths of tens of thousands of the rebels at the hands of their comrades. But the Communists have outdone the Taiping rebels in their self-destruction. Starting in the 1920s, the power struggles have been bitter and bloody. The winners have gained everything and the losers have lost everything. The losers suffer house arrest, forced labor, lifelong imprisonment, and even death at the hands of the winners. Both Liu Shaoqi and Lin Biao were second-in-command to Mao at their peaks of achievement, but both men met violent deaths during power struggles. Mao Zedong purged many colleagues, but he could not prevent his survivors from imprisoning his wife, nephew, and other followers just a few weeks after his death.

The other side of the story of the Communist power struggles is also chilling. Though the choice of leadership is not determined by the populace, the Communist authority must sell its new leader to the people. In particular, it must convince the people that such a choice is made in the best interests of the nation and the people. So the new leader must try to gain popular consent one way or another. However, the Chinese people are accustomed to acknowledging power succession only within the royal family. The Communist power succession is something new to the people. It demands extra effort on the part of the Communist leadership to make its power succession acceptable. Only in this way can the new leader be elevated to the superman position.

However, the Communist authority has not done a good job of proving that whoever wins the power struggle is the best man to rule China. China's people want to believe in their government. Once a new leader is chosen, the people want to show immediate affection and loyalty. Yet, this kind of popular obedience has caused grave troubles for the Communist party since the Communist authority chooses new leaders almost as often as the seasons change. Since 1949, seven party chiefs have been chosen, and all but the latest have met with a bad end. Two, Liu Shaoqi and Lin Biao, met violent death; three men, Hua Guofeng, Hu Yaobang, and Zhao Ziyang, were disgraced publicly; the sixth was Wang Hongwen, who was given a 20-year prison sentence and is still in prison somewhere in China. The seventh is Jiang Zemin, who replaced Zhao following the June 1989 bloodshed. Chinese newspapers worldwide already contain intense discussions about the probable fate of this new party chief.

The Communists have not been kind to their own chiefs. One day, the people are told that the new boss is the greatest man alive next to Mao or Deng. But the next day the people are told that the new leader is a "renegade, hidden traitor, and scab"—as happened in the case of Liu Shaoqi. Indeed, Lin Biao, who pronounced these famous words during a speech at the Ninth Party Congress in 1969 after Mao's decisive victory over Liu's camp:

> Our present congress is convened at a time when a great victory has been won in the Great Proletarian Cultural Revolution personally initiated and led by Chairman Mao. This great revolution has shattered the bourgeois headquarters headed by the renegade, hidden traitor, and scab Liu Shaoqi, exposed the handful of renegades, enemy agents, and absolutely unrepentant persons in power taking the capitalist road within the party, with Liu Shaoqi as their archrepresentative, and smashed their plot to restore capitalism; it has tremendously strengthened our party and thus prepared ample conditions for this congress politically, ideologically, and organizationally.

Lin Biao himself was Mao's next choice. The Communist authority pronounced him to be the "second wisest man alive" one day. But the next day, he had fallen from the pinnacle of power and was publicly denounced and charged with nasty crimes: "traitor, spy, national enemy." Note this statement by Premier Zhou Enlai in 1973 on Lin Biao:

> The smashing of the Lin Biao–Anti-Party Gang is the biggest victory of our party since the Ninth Party Congress, which is a heavy blow to all domestic and overseas enemies.... Lin Biao, the bourgeoisie careerist-conspirator–double dealer, has engaged in machinations within our party not just for one decade but for several decades.... At all the important turning points of the Revolution he invariably committed the rightist opportunist errors and invariably played double-faced tricks, putting up a false front to deceive the party and the people.... Lin Biao and his followers, who have been capitalist roaders in the leadership and only working for the interests of the few and whose dark ambitions grew with their rising positions, overestimated their strength....

After Lin Biao, four other leading politicians chosen as heirs fell in quick succession; all were reduced from glory to either imprisonment or public disgrace. However, these sudden changes have finally proven to be too much for the people, even the most patient and loyal ones. The following statement was given by Chairman

Hua Guofeng in August 1977 from his "Political Report to the Eleventh National Congress of the Chinese Communist Party":

> The struggle between our party and the Wang-Zhang-Jiang-Yao Anti-Party Gang of Four is the eleventh major struggle between the two lines in our party's history. It is a life and death struggle between the proletariat and the bourgeoisie, and on its outcome hinges the future as well as the destiny of our party and nation. The tremendous victory won in this two-line struggle should be ascribed to our great leader Chairman Mao, to the greatness of Mao Zedong thought, to Chairman Mao's revolutionary line, and to our great party, army, and people..... Our wise and great Chairman Mao became aware of the anti-party activities of the Gang of Four a long time ago. He sternly criticized and admonished them on many occasions and took it upon himself to lead the party in repeated struggles against them.... However, the Gang of Four were not in the least repentant.... They stepped up their factional activities in order to usurp party power and plotted to set up their own cabinet and seize state power.... Prior to the death of our esteemed and beloved Premier Zhou and in the days following it, the Gang of Four ran amok again. They made unbridled attacks on Premier Zhou and suppressed and persecuted vast numbers of cadres and people in mourning for him. Defying Chairman Mao's instructions and going their own way, they attacked Comrade Deng Xiaoping and brought false charges against him.... Thwarted at every turn, they hit back ten times more vehemently and a hundred times more vengefully and stepped up their machinations to usurp party and state power....

In these and other ways, the Communist party itself has destroyed the myth of its infallibility. No institution other than the Communist party itself has the ability to show the dirty, the unspeakable, the naked, and the evil things it has been doing behind the backs of the people. And yet the party itself through its contradictory actions arising from internal power struggles reveals its own inconsistencies, errors, and even criminal activities.

The effects on China's people are explosive. The repeated power struggles have resulted in severe damage to the people's emotional bond with the Communist government. It is shocking to the millions of Communist worshippers that this great People's Government has turned itself into banditry. Qian Jaiju, a member of the People's Political Consultative Conference, is among these outraged people: "Since the victory of the Communist Party in mainland China, I had believed that there would be no more student movements against the political authority forever." But in the fall of 1989 he reflected:

The Communist authority had well represented the authority of the people and the interests of the overwhelming majority of the people. How would the students organize themselves against the people! Not only the Communists believed this; we, as the democratic representatives [of the government], as well as the overwhelming intellectuals believed so. In the 1950s, we worshipped the Communist party and the "great leader" Mao Zedong, and that made us really happy. Our faith in Marxist-Leninism and Mao Zedong–thought reached a fanatic point. I believe that I was not the only person — my friends including Ba Jin and Bin Hsin [renowned writers] acted in the same way. However, having been through numerous political campaigns, especially the Anti-Rightist campaign which sent more than a half-million of the best Chinese intellectuals to the labor camp as Rightists, my doubts have started to surface. What was more to my eye, the revolutionary heroes such as General Peng Dehuai, who helped the Communist party gain over China, were condemned down to the 18th Hell by Mao Zedong for just expressing a few honest words on behalf of the common people. What kind of "Marxism" was this? Up to the Cultural Revolution, a few black-ambitious politicians, fighting for the "successor position," turned China into chaos and darkness. I gradually, but finally, awakened. In my "Seventy Years' Experiences," I wrote . . . only the "Great Proletariat Cultural Revolution" affected my conscience so that I began to see the true face of the Socialist China.[20]

That is why Western journalists found that many Chinese have become cynical about the palace struggles. The Chinese are accustomed to speaking very highly of other people, especially their political leaders. But this old tradition was destroyed at the hands of the Communist authority. Indeed, many people no longer have great interest in the politicians, let alone palace politics. Even Western journalists hear that some people on Beijing streets go so far as to view the power struggles today as "dogs bark on dogs."

More consequences are bound to come. The ugliness in the walled palaces has made millions of cadres feel that they have been betrayed. The top leaders do not bother about the interests of the party but madly satisfy their own power hunger. How should the cadres feel? Once cadres gain power, they also abuse it in any way they see fit. This is exactly what has happened over the last ten years. Almost every official, big or small, has been engaged in pursuing his own interests, sound or otherwise. Of course, the official corruptions have grown wilder and more madly than the boldest critic could have imagined only ten years ago.

Notes for Chapter 3

1. For Richard Nixon's trip to China, see the *New York Times; World Journal*, October 28–November 2, 1989; *China Times Weekly*, November 18–24, 1989.

2. Deng Xiaoping's speech on June 9, 1989, was published by the *People's Daily*, on June 29, 1989. His first words were: "You Comrades are working hard!" Also see the new party boss Jiang Zemin's speech on September 30, 1989, published in the *People's Daily*.

3. Biographical information about Liu and Wang Meng can be found in Liu Binyan, *A Higher Kind of Loyalty: A Memoir of China's Foremost Journalist*, translated into English by Zhu Hong (New York: Pantheon Books, 1990) and in Wang Meng, *Selected Works of Wang Meng*, vol. 1: *The Straw of Meeting*, translated by Denis Mair; vol. 2: *Snowball*, translated by Cathy Silber and Deirdre (Beijing: Foreign Language Press, 1989).

4. Su Xiaokang, Luo Shishu, and Chen Zhen, *A Feast of "Utopia" — The Summer of 1959 in Lushan* (Beijing: China News Press, 1988).

5. Mao Yuanhsin is Mao Zedong's nephew, born in 1940. By his mid–20s, Mao Yuanhsin had already become one of the most powerful provincial politicians in Northeastern China. Later he became Mao Zedong's personal liaison official, almost the chief of staff of Mao, in Mao's final days. At age 26, Mao's elder daughter (mothered by Jiang Qing), Li Na, became the editor-in-chief for the powerful *Liberation Army Daily*. A few weeks after Mao's death in September 1976, Mao's nephew and Li Na, together with the Gang of Four, were put in prison. For more information about Mao Yuanhsin and Li Na, see Ting Wang, *Biographies of Yao Wan Yung and Mao Yuan Hsin* (Hong Kong: Ming Pao Monthly Press, 1979).

6. John King Fairbank, *The United States and China*, 4th ed. (Harvard University Press, 1983).

7. Liang Shumin, *Best Scholarly Writings of Liang Shumin* (Beijing: Beijing Normal University Press, 1988).

8. See the *People's Daily*, September 16, 1989. It reports that in the early 1950s, the bureaucracy had only 1.7 million officials. This number climbed to 6.63 million by 1954. By 1989, this number had reached 30 million. Note that most officials are Communist members and a big percentage of the cadres are also officials.

9. Jin Zhao, "History Will Remember Them — The Traces of a Few Individuals Involved in the June 4 Event," *China Spring* 6 (1990).

10. The Nineties Monthly Journal Editors, "The Intellectual Circle Views of the 40 Years," *Nineties Monthly Journal*, October 1989.

11. See the official and semiofficial books on the promotion of Hua Guofeng: *Chairman Hua Is Our Great Leader: Hunan People Recall the Glorious Revolutionary Experiences of Chairman Hua* (People's Press and Hunan People's Press, 1977) and *Chairman Hua Is Closely Linked to the Hearts of Hundreds of Millions of People* (Beijing: People's Press, 1976). Also see works by Huang Shenxou and others, *Chairman Hua's Footsteps* (Huan People's Press, 1977).

12. See all the books cited in note 11 above.

13. See Pu Yi's autobiography, *From Emperor to Citizen* (Beijing: Foreign Language Press, 1964 and 1965).

14. Li Yi, "Return to Face Some Fundamental Questions: A Visit with Chinese Intellectual Sui Wei," *Nineties Monthly Journal,* November 1989.

15. Ray Huang, *China: A Macro History* (New York and London: M. E. Sharpe, 1988).

16. Yi Hua, "The Rise and Fall of Zhao Ziyang," *Nan Bai Ji Journal,* June 1989.

17. Hu Ping, "On the Future Perspective of the Chinese Communist Leadership Power Struggles" *China Spring* 77 (1989).

18. Willy Wo-Lap Lam, *The Era of Zhao Ziyang: Power Struggle in China, 1986-88* (In English) (Hong Kong: A. B. Books & Stationery, 1989).

19. Willy Wo-Lap Lam, *The Era of Zhao Ziyang.*

20. Qian Jiaju, *China Times Weekly,* September 1989.

4

TROUBLED COMMUNICATIONS

The June 1989 massacre in China indicates that the most serious problem for the Communist government is that it is unable to communicate with the people. The Beijing authority does not know how to deal with the Chinese people.

The means of communication between a government and its people are determined by the political structure. Once a political-economic system is established, a government will have a fixed structure for communications within society. In American culture, the government is a service body to the society and political authority rests upon popular consent and direct election. Therefore, to gain popular support, the American president has to pay attention to what the voters think and desire. After all, the American president is elected by the population. If he does not pay attention to the people he will not become president in the first place. If he stops listening to the people after his election, he will not win reelection.

But China has a centralized political system. A Chinese government is a government that stands above the society rather than as part of the society. Fundamentally, the centralized political system in China demands that the entire population revolve around the central authority and the whole bureaucratic body around the head of government. Thus the maintenance of the absolute power of the leadership is the number-one priority for maintaining national unity.

Two most important traditions that contribute to China's centralized system are the Confucian and the Legalist systems. The Confucian government is a government ruled by means of virtuous example, kindness, benevolence, religious rituals, gentlemanly conduct, direct personal supervision, and careful trustworthiness. Violence and ruthlessness to Confucians are what wolves and tigers are to people. Under a Confucian government, only 58 people were executed by the government state during one year of the Tang

Dynasty (618–907) even though China at that time already had a population of about 60 million.

Indeed, the Confucian mentality is still strong in China today. Chinese understanding of democracy is quite influenced by Confucian ideas. At the core of the 1989 democratic movement was a Confucian belief that the leaders must try to understand the sufferings of the people and that the people have the rights to freely express their feelings and thoughts.

Legalist government is a government ruled by a set of uniform laws and regulations. These laws and regulations include systematic rewards and punishments for the people ruled. In particular, the Legalists emphasize the absolute need for terror and intimidation. Legalists believe that man's nature is basically evil. Therefore, the relations between the authority and the ruled should be like those between the trainer and his tiger. The first imperial dynasty, the Qin Dynasty, was ruled exclusively according to a Legalist philosophy, and led to the creation of nothing less than a police state. Neighbors were organized to watch over each other, and the entire neighborhood was held responsible for any individual's bad behavior. Nine neighbors were punished for any crime committed by the tenth neighbor, for example.

This Legalist tradition still exists in today's China. In Communist China today the neighborhood responsibility system has been replaced by the street committee. The street committee is an extension of the police forces. Following the June 4, 1989, bloodshed, numerous democratic activists were arrested by the police through the work of the numerous street committees in China.

One thing must be said: no government in China's history approved when the people took their demands to the streets. Popular street demonstrations in Communist China today stem directly from the fact that all the usual communication channels are destroyed for both the government and the people. And the Beijing bloodshed will only make China's communication troubles worse.

Propaganda and Agitation

The Communist authority may be unable to handle China's economic life as well as the Kuomintang in Taiwan and the British in Hong Kong, but it can certainly handle propaganda. The intensity of Communist propaganda has no equal in China's history. Yet, the goal of Communist propaganda is not any different from the goal of propaganda created by the old dynasties in China.

Throughout history, China's political foundation has remained virtually unchanged, though the superstructure in various periods has differed. The legitimacy of the political authority rests upon the Chinese concept called the "Mandate of Heaven" — the right to rule. The government must convince its people that the people, for their own good, should obey its rule. In China's long history, each government, whether it has succeeded in holding rule for a long or a short time, has had to do the same things.

Within the Communist system, the Beijing authority has one great defect: it has trouble opening dialogues with the people, especially when the alternatives threaten Communist rule. The June 1989 Beijing massacre is a striking instance of this problem. That bloodshed would have been avoided altogether if the Communist authority could have opened some sort of dialogue with the peaceful and mostly youthful demonstrators. One cannot but wonder, why has the Communist leadership failed to maintain dialogue with the people they rule? Why does the leadership fear such dialogues? The answers to these questions lie in the nature of Chinese methods for communications between the authority and the people.

In passing, one striking thing about Chinese government should be mentioned: it can survive many deadly mistakes that would have toppled numerous governments in Europe and America. China's political authority can remain in power despite its repeated mistakes. This striking difference must be understood in the context of China's political-social traditions, though it is much beyond the scope of our book to offer discussion of these traditions. Perhaps our understanding of Communist propaganda may shed some light on this extremely complex phenomenon.

Almost as an unwritten law, each new Chinese government has to condemn its predecessor. It must convince the people that the previous government did little good, but much harm; the new government must continually point out how rigid, corrupt, selfish, and stupid the old government was, and how much it deserved to be destroyed.

Following this traditional practice, the Communist authority has condemned the Kuomintang for decades. Each succeeding Chinese political authority must rewrite history, and the Communist authority is no exception: it has employed several generations of writers, poets, journalists, philosophers, and historians, among others, to devote their skills to portraying the Kuomintang as corrupt, violent, stupid, and dictatorial, and the Communist government as "majestic, glorious, and always correct." Indeed, it would be hard to exaggerate the effect of this propaganda in the Communists' success in 1949. The birth, growth, and ultimate success of the Communist power was tied to its use of extensive propaganda. Naturally, the Communist party did not invent this type of propaganda, but it employs it with greater intensity than any previous government.

The American reporter Edgar Snow, among others, went to war-torn China in the 1930s and 1940s. He vividly reported Chinese life at the national political level in his *Red Star Over China* and *The Battle for Asia*. There he talks about how fat the wallet was that each high Kuomintang official carried, how many servants they had in their luxurious homes, and how little they cared about the suffering of the people. In contrast, in the jungles of northern China, there was a red star shining: Mao Zedong and his Communist guerrillas.

In the Communist guerrilla base of Yenan in northern Shaanxi, Snow suddenly discovered China's future: Mao and his comrades had just marched on foot several thousand miles from southern China to this remote and shabby Yenan "in order to start the long journey to save China from the ruinous Japanese invaders." Mao and his colleagues wore the same cotton-padded clothes as the common soldiers; Mao lived in tiny rooms and ate simple food, just like his soldiers. Snow even took the trouble to write down the numerous mottoes of Mao and his colleagues on his notebook; the Communists talked about people's rights, people's happiness, people's freedom, people's democracy, people's republic, people's China. Snow's reports on Mao and the Communists and their beliefs played a significant role in the Communist success. In his wartime book, *The Battle for Asia*, published in 1942, Snow reported vividly on the Communist activities in this period.

Japan's war machine conquered and occupied the better half of China. Japanese success roused the Chinese population for a great national movement for survival. At this period of history, faced with Japan's threat, China's people put aside politics. The Chinese people worked together in a united front to repel the Japanese invaders. What was going on in the minds of Mao and his colleagues in Yenan at this time? Snow reported his historical conversations with these guerrilla warriors. "While admitting that political progress made since the war began was quite slow, Mao believed that there was 'democratic movement growingly widespread among not only workers and peasants but also among students and youth, intellectuals, scientists, statesmen, military men, writers, teachers, and so on. The obstacle that confronts this movement is an archaic political system. The problem is how to change that political system (without endangering resistance), *for unless it is changed, and unless democracy is realized, there can be no victory.* Resistance and democracy are the two edges of a single sword. Some people pretend to support resistance but to reject the principle of democracy. In reality they do not want to use either edge of the sword.'"

Snow asked what everyone wanted to know: "How sincere are the demands of the Communists for a democratic republic? The Reds say, in answer, that they fought ten years of civil war to establish that sincerity; that theirs was a struggle against a 'counter-revolutionary' Kuomintang which has rejected completely democracy for dictatorship. In any case, just as their demand for a 'unified front' was honest simply because it coincided with all the dynamic needs of the Communist position — and hence has been loyally upheld by them — so the agitation for democracy may be taken as sincere just because it also corresponds with the objective realities of the living situation."

Tens of millions of Chinese felt the same way as Snow. "The Communists have always maintained that only a democratic republic can accomplish the 'bourgeois-democratic' tasks of the revolution — attainment of national independence and the liquidation of remaining feudalism. Only a democratic republic could guarantee to the peasantry and the working class the right to organise and win their internal demands. And only a democratic republic, they believe, can enable the workers and peasants to take the leadership of the government in a peaceful transition — the Chinese Communists believe in this *'possibility'* — toward socialism."

In this period, Snow even met many young intellectuals, men and women, who had given up their comfortable metropolitan life and walked long distances to join Maoist forces in the jungle of Yenan. In the same book, Snow cited China's famous writer Lu Xun (1881-1936): "The road to Yenan is for China's youth the road to life." In fact, Snow could not conceal his astonishment over the eager city youths who dreamed of joining Maoist guerrillas in Yenan. "Wherever I went after the war began young people would appear in the most unexpected places, with a copy of *Red Star Over China* (in the pirated Chinese edition) tucked under their arms, to ask me how they could enter one of the schools at Yenan. In one city the commissioner of education came to me like a conspirator wanting me to 'introduce' his son, so that he could enter the Yenan Political and Military Academy. In Hong Kong a prosperous banker astonished me by making the same request." Snow was impressed that there were so many youths who dreamed of joining the Communists to defeat the Japanese invaders. "If I had set up a recruiting station in Shanghai or Hankow or Chunking I could have enlisted several battalions; and it might have been the best service one could render China, at that. Unfortunately I had no commission as a recruiting sergeant and my 'inside connections' with Yenan went no further than the scars left on my kidneys by the war diet. I could not help these would-be bachelors of guerrilla arts much. As far as I knew, the easiest way to 'get into' North Shensi was to walk in. And thousands of young people did walk — from distances of hundreds of miles. They were still coming in, from all over China, when I returned to Sianfu; but it now seemed to amount almost to a crime against the state, in the eyes of General Hu Tsung-na, whose troops controlled most of the roads leading into the ex–Soviet districts, for a young man or woman to join the Eighth Route Army or study at Yenan."

Even Mao's third wife, Jaing Qing, gave up her soap opera stardom in Shanghai and walked to Yenan in those days. Otherwise, China's recent history might have been a little bit different.

Gathering these impressions, Snow, among many others, announced to the outside world that China's mandate of history, if not the Mandate of Heaven, had been transferred to the shoulders of Mao and his guerrilla forces. Of course, neither Snow, nor tens of millions of Chinese, could have dreamed that the Maoist democratic slogans would become grave obstacles to Communist rule once Mao entered the Beijing palace in 1949. These beautiful slogans could help Communists win over all China, but they would also block the Communist authority from ruling China effectively. Indeed, the biggest impediment to Communist rule since 1949 has been the people's memory of the ideal the early Communist slogans promised, which provides a dramatic contrast to the reality the Communist authority has created.

The attitude of the people, especially the intellectuals, determines which political party upholds China's mandate. It was devastating to the Kuomintang authority that most intellectuals began to side with Mao and his party during the war with Japan. Even those intellectuals who could not give up their comfortable lives in the cities could not stop dreaming about Communist guerrilla life.

However, in the late 1970s and 1980s it is the Communist power holders, not the Kuomintang who have lost the support of the intellectuals. Many intellectuals and students show strong interest in and admiration for the democratic and economic progress in Taiwan. Many intellectuals and students from Communist China want to visit Taiwan. Some of them have had chances to go there from overseas where they are studying now. Even the disgraced former party chief Hu Yaobang's granddaughter, together with her husband, went to see Taiwan in January 1990. There she said that it was regrettable that her grandfather had never had a chance to see Taiwan; her trip was partly to make up for that loss.[1]

Faced with this trend, the Beijing leaders have good reasons to be afraid and to show deep anger. Indeed, one feels that the Beijing leaders would like to invent some magic to prevent China's educated people from turning away from faith in the Communist authority.

It must be said that the significance of the Mandate of Heaven has not faded from Chinese mind during the period of Communist rule. For one thing, Chinese people living in Taiwan and those living in mainland China have found it very difficult to communicate, even at the private level, even today. A love affair involving a mainland Chinese and a girl from Taiwan took place when both were students in Japan in 1982. This simple event filled the Chinese news media for several weeks once it became public.[2] People fall in love all the time, so why was this romance so newsworthy? It involved the grandson of a famous writer, Lu Xun. Lu Xun had been elevated over all other writers by the Communist authority in China for several decades. Many Chinese people were amazed that his grandson could fall in love with somebody from Taiwan when the Beijing authority and the Taipei authority were still bitter enemies. Even today, the authorities in both Taiwan and Beijing hardly encourage such romantic connections among the Chinese separated by the Taiwan seas; this occurs despite the fact that both governments do not oppose Chinese citizens marrying foreigners and the fact that people on the two sides have been allowed to visit each other since 1988.

Mainland Chinese intellectuals and students have shown great interest in Taiwan for many years. However, the first group of such people went to see Taiwan only in 1988 (though thousands and thousands of Chinese from Taiwan have toured mainland China in the last few years). That event made big headlines in Chinese newspapers all over the world. Chinese people were surprised that mainland China's intellectuals would visit Kuomintang's Taiwan though the Kuomintang had not possessed the Mandate of Heaven for several decades.[3] It has indeed been difficult for the Chinese people to discard one of China's most ancient and most powerful beliefs.

Another example of China's political traditions involves a political organization in exile called "China Spring" headquartered in New York. This organization tries to challenge the Beijing authority. However, "China Spring" receives much scorn from Chinese individuals both in China and abroad. "China Spring" is scorned not because it does any kind of damage but because "China Spring" does not possess the Mandate of Heaven. Therefore, this group deserves to be treated as "bandits" in accordance with Chinese tradition. If "China Spring" enters the Beijing palace someday, the same people who scorn the group today would sing its praises tomorrow. The Communist party has gone through this entire process in its fight for supreme power. Before the Communist party took power, it was regarded as a bandit party in the minds of most people. Yet when it took over power in 1949, the name of banditry went to the loser, the Kuomintang in Taiwan. The best source for gaining an understanding of these changes is Mao Zedong's works.[4]

There are other aspects to the essential meaning of the Chinese Mandate of Heaven. China's ruler must always be elevated to the position of god in order to maintain his political supremacy. China's ruler must appear to be the fittest leader. The ruler's fitness to govern is based on ability, but even more on his moral character. To China's people, the rights of the ruler come from Heaven. China's ruler has always tried to convince the people that he is the Son of Heaven and that as a ruler he is merely carrying out the wishes of Heaven. "People decide as Heaven decides" is a long-held Confucian motto. That is, the ruler is the supreme over the people just as Heaven is supreme over nature.

Because of these beliefs China's emperors do not act in an "earthly" manner. This is very different from the political structure in America. Under the American system, power is not concentrated at the top. American presidents love to travel around in open cars, shake hands with as many people as possible, and demonstrate their desire to be everyone's good neighbor. China's centralized power structure demands opposite behavior; the ruler is restricted to the walled palace and meets the public as little as possible. When the emperor left the palace, his bodyguards would make sure that the people on the streets did not see him. When the ruler received guests in the palace, they were reminded not to look at him directly. China's ruler demanded the awe and submission of the ordinary people.

This tradition continues in Communist China today. The Beijing supreme leaders live in heavily guarded palaces, their cars are all heavily curtained, and they love to stand on the Tiananmen Tower to inspect masses parading by. When a supreme leader actually steps into a factory or a village, he is always surrounded by his own staff. Even when the central leaders tour public places such as parks, the parks are closed to the public during their tour. The Beijing leaders still find such practices necessary to command the respect of the ordinary people.

It must be said that the Communist leadership is deeply aware of the damaging effects of such practices, but does not seem to know how to alter these things. Even in the 1980s, though Deng Xiaoping and Chen Yun have been very critical of such practices carried out by the ranking cadres, they still cannot put a stop to them.

Traditionally, the circumstances of the ruler's birth are heavenly. Today's China is still rich in such tales. In the popular mind, even Mao Zedong has a fable attached to the circumstances of his birth: "China gave birth to Mao Zedong when the Eastern sky was red and the sun was rising." That is why Mao Zedong did not blush or feel embarrassed when China's people, from Liu Biao and Zhou Enlai on down to the children, worshipped him as a god. He could comfortably stand on the Tiananmen Tower for several hours to watch the ritual performance in devotion to his personality cult.

China's quasi-religion-based political system has a myth in itself: a few open words of mild criticism may start a process that will topple the regime suddenly. That is why even in this reform era the Communist leaders fear the scholar-dissident Fang Lizhi as if he had an army of a half-million armed men. In truth, Fang's words have been so mild that he would have trouble becoming a successful teacher's union activist in another country, like America. But the Communists fear criticism so much the Chinese officials refused to allow Fang to attend when he was invited to a dinner party by President Bush during Bush's visit to Beijing in March 1989. That decision outraged China's people, for the Chinese tradition has placed a high value on absolute civility to guests for several thousand years.[5]

However, the Beijing leadership has few alternatives to suppressing criticism. A few critical words may indeed transform the leaders from gods into humans and change all the mechanisms of authority. Criticism could even deprive China's leaders of the heavenly magic that makes the population revolve around them. A dissident such as Fang Lizhi must not be allowed to coexist peacefully with the Communist authority. Otherwise, more people would develop the courage to join their voices to the dissent. It was almost a "must" to stop Fang from attending the American president's dinner party, even if such action disgraced the Communist authority.

In general, any kind of free press and free speech would bring a sudden collapse of this self-appointed government. Thus it is imperative for Deng and the other authorities to work around the clock to stop China's people from attempting such "bourgeoisie" activity.

Now, return to the question, why were Deng Xiaoping and the other aging leaders afraid to open a dialogue with the demonstrators in Beijing in 1989? In the minds of these aging rulers, to begin a sincere dialogue with the people would be equivalent to admitting the end of Communist supremacy. Indeed, dialogue would mean that the two counterparts involved are independent, and therefore must treat each other fairly equally. This would mean the end of Communist supremacy. Party chief Zhao Ziyang was accused of "crimes" against the Communist party just for suggesting an open dialogue with the students. Thus, not only were the peaceful demonstrators suppressed by the army, but Zhao and his numerous followers were purged from the Communist leadership.

It is nothing new that the Communist party depends on propaganda to promote its legitimacy: China's rulers have always used propaganda. What is new about Communist propaganda is its intensity. All means of communication in China today are controlled directly by the Communist authority. The party possesses the means to make a dead man believe that he sleeps in the golden age.

However, it is precisely this intensive propaganda that has resulted in endless side effects and even caused backfires against the Communist establishment. In fact, the side effects are not really restricted to the explosive results of the relentless condemnations of the Communist losers in the power struggles, as discussed previously. There are other aspects.

Communist authority has made many big promises but produced few big deeds. Mao Zedong dreamed that his class struggle would bring about a so-called socialist miracle. He dreamed that his Great Leap Forward program would make China a modern economic power with a higher living standard than Great Britain within a few years. However, the Great Leap Forward ended in a record-making disaster and resulted in a nationwide famine that killed tens of millions. Following this gigantic failure, the Communist government sent thousands and thousands of officials to the rural areas to stop the farmers from disbanding the Maoist communes.

The Communist authority has spent several decades trying to convince the people that they live in a "golden age"; they have claimed that there are many capitalistic countries whose people have little to eat, little freedom to do what they want, but much unemployment, violence, and repression. Once China's door was opened during the 1980s, the Chinese people discovered that their living standard is lower than the living standard in some 100 countries.

The Communist authority has endlessly stated that "The Communist party consists of the best and the most virtuous elements of the proletarians, and the party is the servant of the people." Mao Zedong's writings repeatedly and proudly assert that "the Chinese Communist party is the core of the leadership of the whole Chinese people." Yet, Communist corruption in the last ten years has gone far beyond the wildest nightmares of the people.

Mao Zedong and his colleagues forced China's farmers to give up their private land and to join "glorious communes" tightly controlled by the Communist bureaucracy. Two decades later, the Beijing leadership abolished this "glorious" system completely. China's farmers have little confidence in the Communist authority today. At the beginning of Communist rule China's poor farmers were the beneficiaries of a land redistribution plan. Land was taken away from the great landowners and given to people who had never owned land. But then a few years later the plots were taken away again and the farmers were forced to work in the tightly controlled collectives and communes. China's farmers want to own their own land, but wonder if the government will first sell them land, then soon take it away again.[6] Zhang Xing reports that China's farmers have great doubts that the present Communist rural reform will last long.[7] Some farmers have carefully planted young trees, which will mature in a few years, on their rental plots. If the Communist authority decides to end the new land rental system, these farmers intend to cut those matured trees down immediately.

One day, the Beijing leadership called the Soviet and the Vietnamese Communist leaders "best friends forever." The next day, those "best friends" became "worst enemies." The Chinese Communist authorities' attitudes concerning the Soviet Union and

Communist Vietnam have created vast confusion in the minds of the Chinese people. After all, China's people hate to make enemies even if they cannot make everybody their friends.

The Communist leadership endlessly states that its government is the people's government, and that "the people's democratic dictatorship is based on the alliance of the working class, the peasantry, and the urban petty bourgeoisie, and mainly based on the alliance of the workers and the peasants, because these two classes comprise 80 to 90 percent of China's population." However, when the people ask for a little democracy, they are met with rifle bullets and rolling tanks, as happened in 1989.

The Communist leadership proudly talks about the army being the people's army, whose chief purpose is to "liberate the people." Chairman Mao asserted that "this army is powerful because all its members have a conscious discipline; they have come together and they fight not for the private interests of a few individuals or a narrow clique, but for the interests of the broad masses and of the whole nation. The sole purpose of this army is to stand firmly with the Chinese people and serve them wholeheartedly." However, "the people's army" used their tanks and guns to kill and wound hundreds of peaceful Chinese people in Beijing in June 1989.

China's people in this reform era are well aware of the progress being made in the outside world, just as they are aware of the tragedies taking place in China. The Maoist "priests" cannot change this new reality with their propaganda. The Maoist ideologues have not learned the proper lessons from previous mistakes. Indeed, the reforms have created new difficulties for these Maoists who cannot come up with new techniques. These men are running around trying to make the people believe that without the Communists, the people in China would only have grass to eat. But the people might well ask, "How come the workers in Taiwan make at least ten times more in wages than their counterparts in China under the Communist party?" Former Communist party chief Hu Yaobang's granddaughter and her husband asked such questions after visiting Taiwan. These two students asked why, in 1989, each person in Taiwan could make an average of about $7,000, while his counterpart in the mainland could make only about $300.[8] The Communist authority can hardly offer reasons that would satisfy China's people today. Maoist doctrinaires would have to rely on coercion to deal with the people.

As long as China's political authority is self-appointed, it will have to live on "absolute truth." Such a political system can hardly coexist with free speech and a free press. To protect the present system from a sudden collapse, Deng Xiaoping, Chen Yun, and the other Communist leaders have no alternatives; they must maintain their efforts to eliminate any tendency that might lead to the so-called bourgeois freedom and liberal ideas. That is the reason why political reform has been difficult, if not impossible, to carry out within the Communist system.

Mao Zedong Versus the Intellectuals

Once a certain political system is established, the ways of communication between the people and the authority, as well as the effectiveness of such communication, is fixed to a great extent. Since China's centralized political system is very different from most political systems in the West, China's population has to use different channels to communicate with the authority than the channels used by Westerners. In particular, under this centralized system, China's people do not have a direct voice, through elections or elected representatives, in their governance, as the modern Western people do. In China, intellectuals and other well-educated people play a crucial role, functioning as the bridge between the people and authority. This situation has remained unchanged throughout China's history.

China's farmers understand this system precisely. One newspaper report indicates this reality: "In a farm shed just outside Chengu [the capital of Sichuan province], an old man with a white beard rolls himself a short thick cigar while he talks about the past 40 years of Communist rule. 'I've been through periods of some pretty mistaken policies,' he says. 'There were mistakes. But they've been corrected. I wouldn't want to go back to that.'⁹ Does he think China's farmers are ready for a direct voice in government? 'We know we can't have a direct voice,' he answers. 'But if the policy is mistaken and our complaining is widespread enough, eventually we get results.'"

As a common practice, the intellectuals and other educated people must carry the voice of the ordinary people through to the authority. The intellectuals have played this special role for several thousand years, and continue to play this role in Communist China today. Intellectuals serve as the intermediary between the people and their rulers.

But even this type of communication does not occur easily. China lacks a free press, a tradition of free expression, a system of public opinion polls—indeed, most forms of making the people's opinions known that are common to modern Western nations. However, educated people in China use literary and artistic forums to present the popular voice. The most popular forms are essays, short stories, films, plays, and lectures. Best-selling books complain about bureaucratic abuses and corruptions. In fact, the quickest way to gain popularity in modern China is to write one or two of such stories. Both Liu Binyan and Wang Meng, two very popular writers in the reform era, gained immediate popularity this way with their youthful stories of this kind in the 1950s.

The educated people of China have always been part of the ruling class. In China's old dynasties, proper governmental function was based on direct involvement of the intellectuals. In traditional Chinese society, the ruling class included two groups. One was the bureaucrats who inherited their positions in one way or another, and the other was the intellectuals who earned positions in the government by successfully demonstrating their ability. In fact, the authority depended on the support of the intellectuals to legitimize their rule; if intellectuals entered government service, they supported the authority by their willingness to serve; if they refused to enter service, or resigned from service, their actions challenged the legitimacy of the ruling power. This was true 1,000 years ago, and remains true today.

This makes the role of China's intellectuals very different from the role of their counterparts in Europe and America. It is very natural that China's intellectuals engage themselves wholeheartedly and persistently in national politics. It is not at all surprising that both the Kuomintang and the Communist party were originally organized by the intellectuals.

Broadly speaking, very close relations between the political authority and the intellectuals have been carefully and delicately maintained throughout China's history. This tradition can be summarized in a single sentence: every successful Chinese government has involved a sharing of power between the rulers and the intellectuals, and has been characterized by a mutual and happy cooperation between the two groups.

Once China's educated people commit themselves to the government, they give up independence of spirit and thoughts. As government servants they live to serve the emperor wholeheartedly.

To hold office is to admit a total willingness to obey the orders of the supreme authority despite personal feelings: a dissenting official is a contradiction in terms.

But smooth government functioning is also based on a tradition of "loyal remonstrance." China's scholar-officials have always believed that loyalty to the government also includes a responsibility to point out its mistakes. Scholar-officials have always believed themselves to be responsible for guarding the interests of the dynasty by speaking their mind directly to the highest ruler freely and whenever necessary — even if they risked punishment and death for their criticism. Thus the scholar-officials have always had a critical role of maintaining "checks and balances" within the bureaucratic establishment, especially between the central power and the provincial power. This particular role has no counterpart in Western bureaucracy.

"Success" stories about the significance of ties between China's ruler and the intellectuals can be illustrated by the impressive progress made by the Kuomintang's Taiwan in the 1980s. Taiwan's rulers and its educated people still believe in a modern version of this traditional system. The Kuomintang encourages individuals who have obtained fine educations at home or abroad to take up government office. Many ministers in high offices are well-trained specialists. In Taiwan today, many high-ranking officials from the present president Li Tenghui (son of a farmer and a Cornell Ph.D.) on down have the best educations. Such well-educated officials add much credibility to the Kuomintang's government. Moreover, their presence increases government quality and guarantees progress. In short, stability and progress in Taiwan have been fundamentally ensured by the employment of scholar-officials.

The Chinese Communist party made a grave mistake: it failed to make intellectuals a part of the ruling class, though it demands their complete obedience. Yet, at the same time, the Communist authority has been unable to create other social forces to replace the role of the intellectuals. In fact, it could not even achieve the kind of stability that has been in existence in the British colony Hong Kong. The British government has painstakingly learned the absolute need of employing Chinese intellectuals as the backbone of the governing body in Hong Kong. The educated Chinese in Hong Kong have been carefully dealt with and made part of the ruling class by the London authority. The British success in Hong Kong reminds us of the success of the Manchu though the Manchus were not native Chinese, they successfully enlisted the aid of Chinese scholars to help them rule, and thereby held on to power for 267 years. The failure of the Communist authority in this respect has cost it dearly in its rule over China. The Chinese Communist authority's failure to employ the intellectual class has been one of its greatest weaknesses.

The nature of the Communist system stands in the way of any genuine cooperation between the Communists and the intellectuals. After all, the Communist party consists of bandits, peddlers, peasants, professional warriors, and purge specialists, among other unproductive social forces. It could never hope to coexist with intellectuals who live on knowledge and talents. The Communist failure somehow reminds us of the failures of the Mongols in the distant past and of the Japanese invaders in the 1930s and 1940s. Neither the Mongols nor the Japanese invaders could pacify China's population in the manner of the British in Hong Kong today. After China's intellectuals refused their cooperation with these invaders, the invaders were reduced to using sheer force to deal with China's population. As a result, both failed to successfully occupy and rule China in the way the Manchus did in the past or the British now succeed in Hong Kong. This is indeed a sad tale for China's Communist power holders, let alone China.

Given China's historical context, once the Communist system was established, there was a little room left for doing things in the best possible way. It must be said that Mao Zedong clearly saw the need for winning the help of intellectuals in running China. Mao's veteran guerrilla warriors all became officials, but they had no knowledge whatsoever about managing factories, banks, schools, hospitals, and businesses. Yet those warriors were most eager to expand their power and put their hands on everything. In fact, as Mao understood, repression seemed to be the only method the cadres knew for dealing with the people, especially the intellectuals. Mao viewed this situation as a grave danger to the Communist party's ability to govern China. That is the only reason why most intellectuals and specialists have been allowed to exist. In many speeches, Mao indicated this point most clearly to his colleagues. In a speech of January 3–4, 1958, Mao said:

> With regard to the treatment of the bourgeoisie, many countries wonder whether China has turned right, in a way unlike the October Revolution. Because instead of doing away with the capitalists,

we are transforming them. In reality, in the end [we] (will transform away) the bourgeoisie: How could that be branded rightist? [It's] still the October Revolution. If [we] do everything like the Soviet Union after the October Revolution, there will be no cloth, no grain, no coal mines, no electricity, no nothing. They [the Soviets] lacked experience, while [we gained] a lot when running our [guerrilla] base areas. [We] have left bureaucratic capital (the system of production) intact, even more so in the case of the national bourgeoisie. But there's a change within nonchange. Nationwide, there are 700,000 households of capitalists and several millions of bourgeois intellectuals; without them [we] can't run newspapers, engage in science, or operate factories. Some people say [you've] turned "right." Such a "right" is necessary, [we] must transform [them] slowly. The correct handling of contradictions among the people is precisely the implementation of this policy. Some are half enemy, half friend; others are one-third or more enemy.

However, the Communist authority has imposed one totally restrictive limit on the intellectuals: whatever an intellectual does — fiction writing, painting, historical studies, scientific research, etc. — he or she must support the absolute power of the Communists. Any thoughts or actions departing from total support will not be allowed. Mao Zedong placed explicit demands on the intellectuals even during the guerrilla period in Yenan. Meanwhile, China's intellectuals have not changed their traditional attitude of dependence on the government authority. Throughout the Maoist period and well into the 1980s, to become an independent social force never really entered the minds of most of the well-educated people in China. But this situation has started to change since 1989.

Nevertheless, the limits set by the Communist party have not forced China's intellectuals into total obedience. Though China's intellectuals and students have yet to achieve that level of determination to become totally independent in spirit, they no longer tolerate Communist misrule. The intellectuals recognize that abuses of power are mainly caused by the absolute power of the Communist authority. The only way to limit these abuses is to limit Communist power. Therefore, Communist mistakes must be constantly criticized so that the Communist authority will rectify its mistakes. The intellectuals clearly understand that only by correcting mistakes can the Communist party maintain its authority over all China. Helping the Communist party to correct its errors was, therefore, deemed a noble task by millions of educated people in China.

By 1956–57, the Communist party had already established its centralized bureaucracy and achieved firm political control over all of China. Now the party decided to focus on an industrialization drive and so-called socialist construction. To do these things, Mao Zedong believed that the Communist authority urgently needed help from the intellectuals. To get that help, China's intellectuals had to be allowed to express their ideas and opinions as freely as possible within their areas of expertise and beyond — but only as long as they stayed within the Communist framework. Most cadres were afraid to let the intellectuals have a little more freedom. Many of Mao's top colleagues openly opposed Mao's effort to woo the intellectuals to the side of the Communist party. However, Mao responded decisively to the popular call for improved relations between the authority and the people and initiated the famous One Hundred Flowers and One Hundred Schools Movement. Communist policies regarding intellectuals were to be relaxed. The intellectuals were encouraged to "freely" express ideas and opinions in their areas of expertise and even to criticize the wrongdoings of the bureaucracy. Mao spent one and a half years trying to convince the cadres and the intellectuals of the coming of a new age, an age in which everyone would be free to speak and join together to help the Communist authority to run China.

To those cadres who were uncomfortable with this new way of thinking, Mao repeatedly offered warnings that the Communists could not run China unless the educated people helped them to govern. Mao asserted repeatedly that it was absolutely necessary to offer the intellectuals some incentives. Mao made numerous speeches that reveal his true motivations on initiating this new policy. This peasant revolutionary leader is among the best orators of all times. He used simple words and earthy expressions to make even illiterate cadres understand precisely what he was trying to get across. Few political leaders have surpassed Mao in his ability to use the spoken word to persuade people. In a four-day period in March 1957 Mao traveled from the north to the south. Like a salesman, he worked to sell his new intellectual policy. In a talk presented in Tianjin to the leading cadres there on March 17, Mao said:

> Today, some people are saying that the Communist party is unfit to run science, that the Communist party can't teach in the universities, can't be a doctor in a hospital, can't run engineering in factories, and doesn't know how to be an engineer or a technician. In

a word, we are inadequate in many respects. How about that kind of talk? Have you heard such comments? Comrades, I have heard such comments, and I say they are correct and correspond with reality. That is to say, we don't have scientists, engineers, technicians, doctors, or university professors. There are also few high school teachers. In literature and art, we have some [strength] but it's still a case of 30/70. That's to say, just like Stalin's mistakes — wasn't Stalin 30 percent wrong, 70 percent right? In our case, it is 30 percent competence, 70 percent incompetence. As far as literature and arts are concerned, superiority still lies outside the Communist party, right? There are two million people in the field of education, in universities, high schools, and primary schools. The "teachers" in the category of government employees and teachers total over two million. What is the Communist party doing? In name it is the leader in the schools; but in reality it is not able to lead, because you don't know how [to lead]. Therefore we must admit that it is one of our weak points.

One day later, Mao went to Shangdong Province and gave another lengthy talk on the same theme to the leading cadres there. Here Mao commented on the greatness of the Communist authority and the magnificence of his personal character:

> Who is more afraid of criticism, the Communist party or the Nationalist party? I think the Nationalist party is. That party is terribly afraid of criticism. They are terrified of such things as "Let a hundred flowers bloom." We alone dare to advocate "Let a hundred flowers bloom, let a hundred schools contend." As for "long-term coexistence," we say we want to coexist with them for a few years, but they absolutely won't do it. Once they set up a so-called National People's Participation Council. The Communist party was represented by several members; I was one of them. What was our status? We were the representatives of the CCP, but we were called worthy and prominent personages. (Laughter) It sounded good but that was all, "worthy" as well as "prominent." (Laughter) They didn't recognize us as representing the CCP. They wouldn't accept short-term coexistence, let alone long-term existence. (Laughter) So we're the only ones who will talk about "Let a hundred flowers bloom, let a hundred schools contend" [and] "Long-term coexistence and mutual supervision." The proletariat is relatively selfless, because its goal is the liberation of all mankind. Only by liberating all mankind will it itself be liberated. The CCP should have the least fear of criticism. No criticism can topple us, and no wind can blow us down.

One day later (March 19), Mao went to Naijing. He immediately met the various provincial cadres in that region. He told them:

As a matter of a fact, criticisms can do much good to the veteran cadres. If we are tainted with bureaucratism and shortcomings, first let people within the party criticize, then let people outside the party criticize us. Let them criticize our shortcomings; let them help us reform our bureaucratism and overcome our shortcomings. Wouldn't that be a good thing? Could [we] be toppled? Of course not. How can the People's Government be blown down? Last year Shanghai was hit by a tornado, and some very huge things were blown away. Houses and petroleum containers were all swept up into the air. But the Shanghai People's Government didn't get swept away. No matter how hard it blows, I believe a typhoon could never bring down the People's Government, the Communist party, Marxism, the veteran cadres, and the new cadres, provided they genuinely and sincerely serve the people. Those who serve the people half-heartedly will get half-blown away, while those who never want to serve but to oppose the people deserve to be blown down.

Mao's tour was not over. The following day, he arrived in Shanghai and gave yet another long speech to the cadres there. With obvious excitement, Mao presented a glorious picture of his future Communist China:

We hope to make ours a lively country, where people dare to criticize, dare to speak, dare to express their opinions. [We] should not make people fearful to speak. People like us must correct our errors and shortcomings whenever we find them. I will not do otherwise because it would be unreasonable. Whether inside or outside the party, we should not practice bureaucracies nor force people to do unreasonable things. If we adopt such a policy, I am sure that the people's political conditions and relations between the people and the government, between the leaders and the led, and among people themselves, will become reasonable and lively. Thus our culture, science, economy, politics, and our whole country will surely develop and prosper more quickly.

However, even Mao found it difficult to arouse the enthusiasm of millions of intellectuals. After all, there had already been 11 political campaigns conducted by the Communist party, as counted by Dai Qing.[10] Also, by this time, Mao had openly acknowledged that more than 700,000 citizens had been executed by the Communist authority. And many times more people had been put in prison and labor camps. These terrorist acts were still fresh in the minds of the people. In particular, in 1955, a group of intellectuals led by a famous literary critic, Hu Fen, were imprisoned for criticizing the party's intellectual policies. But several millions of intellectuals finally yielded to the persuasions of Mao Zedong and opened their mouths in the spring of 1957.

Of those who spoke out, most tried to avoid the big issues and concentrated on the wrongdoings of the "little tigers" — the lesser cadres. Soon, however, some intellectuals began to criticize the root cause of government corruption, the absolute power of the Communist party. Intellectuals and students employed newspapers, magazines, posters, public speeches, and other methods to pour out their disapproval of the Communist authority. Though most of the criticisms were soft and indirect, some courageous people dared to be more outspoken. In the leading Beijing universities, for example, some wall posters and public debates went so far as to totally denounce the role of the Communist party and Mao himself. One poster was put up in May 1957 on the Beijing University campus. This particular poster was very critical of the Communist authority:

> The Constitution says that the people have the right to vote, but all people's representatives are determined within the party alone. The people do not know the representatives and the representatives do not represent the people. / The Constitution says that the people have the right to speak freely, but the newspapers, radio, and broadcasting are the party's monopoly — those who speak not in the same tone as the party have been persecuted as counterrevolutionary criminals. / The Constitution says that the people have the rights to assemble and associate freely, but all the assemblies and associations that take place without the approval of the party and are not headed by party-designated individuals have faced criminal charges for counterrevolution. / The Constitution guarantees the personal safety of the people, but the "Anti-counterrevolution Campaign" shows that party officials at all levels can, in the name of the party, take away the personal freedom of any honest citizen. Chairman Mao says that the nation's authority at this stage is of the nature of dictatorship of the people's democracy, but the party rules and controls all affairs, and the non–Communist parties are nothing more than puppets — democracy is only the label, one-party-monopoly is the thing. / The party's Central Committee is chosen only by twelve million party members, but this Central Committee gives orders to 600 million countrymen who have no way to refuse. The Constitution says that the government at all levels is responsible to the democratic agencies and people's representatives, but all government affairs are run by the party, and the People's Congress is nothing more than a label.[11]

This protester concluded: "We do want the leadership of the party, but must refuse the dictatorship and tyranny of the party. We do not oppose that 'the party can make decisions (for, the party has the rights to do so), but we oppose that "the party's rule" replaces the people's rule.' Let the democratic rights go to the people and let the people enjoy the rights that are guaranteed by the Constitution."

Some intellectuals still remembered the many killings by the Communist party even since its Yenan guerrilla period. Many individuals felt that Mao's new intellectual policies were just another deadly trap. One poster, that was put up on June 1957 at another Beijing university campus, Qihua University, expressed fear:

> When the Communists want to change our mind, they want to dig into our roots, look at our history, check our family background, check our class status, but why can we not check their roots? . . . I oppose what Chairman Mao taught recently at the Youth League Central Committee, "the party is the core for all things, and any deviation from the socialist line is wrong." The truth of this statement is really this: the party's dictatorship must be obeyed; any different ideas from the supreme rulership are wrong and should be punished by death without argument . . . put the questioners in the 18th hell. Oh Emperor, your single statement has wasted how many lives! . . . From 1949 to this day, you have killed more than 700,000 people (not including those who committed suicide)! So, you should go on and kill all the Chinese people![12]

This protester concluded: "Tyrant, killing has become your nature — even in the Yenan era, when the clock struck midnight, how many people did you kill under the name of suspicion? You carried out all these killings under the so-called inner purity movement — the Three-Check-Campaign and the Rectification Movement! Shame! in the so-called sacred Yenan, Wang Shaowei[13] suffered humiliation and imprisonment for nothing other than some soft-spoken criticism. What has happened to him now?"

By this time, Mao Zedong could no longer smile at the intellectuals and students. He no longer remembered his beautiful speeches about "Who is more afraid of criticism, the Communist party or the Nationalist party?" This 64-year-old guerrilla hero panicked like an eight-year-old. He faced ironic choices: either yield some power or put all the discontented intellectuals in prison. Naturally, Mao chose the latter course. After all, he had not spent three decades in the jungles in order to give up his supreme power. What would he become if he yielded the rulership? A Beijing university library clerk as he was once as a young man or a guerrilla warrior in the jungle once more? Instead, Mao soon stopped the criticism movement by purging several million writers, musicians, painters, publishers, engineers, professors, students, and other intellectuals. Both Liu Binyan and Wang Meng were among those imprisoned. In fact, thousands and thousands of lesser figures were put to death immediately. Mao acknowledged (November 21, 1958) that in his home province of Hunan alone, within a few months, 100,000 people became purge targets, 10,000 people were arrested, and 1,000 were executed immediately: "That is why [after] the Qingdao conference [of July 1957] we started making arrests and executions. In Hunan a hundred thousand people were struggled against, ten thousand were arrested, one thousand executed; in other provinces it was the same, and thus the problem was solved."

From that time until his death, Mao never again allowed even a tiny space to the intellectuals for criticism. In fact, the courage of the intellectuals confirmed Mao in his belief that the intellectuals were no longer half-enemy or two-thirds enemy. Rather, the intellectuals were the worst enemy to his absolute power. In 1966 he initiated the Cultural Revolution that persecuted all the intellectuals, from the elementary school teachers to the university presidents. What was more, even many of the top cadres, such as Zhou Yang who had sent countless numbers of intellectuals to labor camps, were themselves sent to labor camps.

Mao's method of stopping all criticism in 1957 and thereafter put a heavy brake on the communications between the people and the authority. China's great civilization was driven rapidly toward total ruin. Now China was solely in the control of millions of ambitious cadres. As a direct consequence, several record-making disasters befell China. Mao's Great Leap Forward resulted in a grand failure. Engineers, researchers, professors, managers, and other specialists were too terrorized by the Communists to offer their help. Thereafter, the cadres at all levels could do anything as they pleased. Even the cadres reported that one mou (one-sixth of an acre) produced 55,000 kilograms of grain a year.[14]

More Communist disasters were bound to follow. Government corruption accelerated. Mao himself went on to create his personality cult, the most extensive yet seen in Chinese history. The people thought that they could rely on Mao's personality cult to handle official corruption and abuse of power. Of course, things did not turn out that way. Many cadres found a short-cut to power abuse and corruption. As Deng Xiaoping revealed (August 18, 1980), many luxurious houses were built for Mao Zedong and other senior leaders. Once the big Communists began to cheat the people, the small cadres followed suit naturally. But the common people could not find a place to register their anger when they saw bureaucratic wrongdoings.

Only by understanding these extraordinary events, among other things, can we comprehend why tens of millions of people were so destructive during the turmoil and chaos of the Maoist Cultural Revolution. That is why within a few months, the Communist bureaucratic establishment, from the state presidency to factory directorships, was destroyed by the masses. Millions of bureaucrats suffered at the hands of the outraged people. Of course, Mao also skillfully utilized this popular anger to get rid of his power-contenders, thereby solidifying his supreme rulership over China.

However, Mao soon stepped into his own trap. By the mid-1970s, China's people finally grew tired of Mao's cult of personality and his regime. Numerous demonstrations took place in cities and in rural areas. The biggest demonstration took place in April 1976 when thousands and thousands of people gathered in Tiananmen Square and denounced Mao's regime. Mao and his arms, the Gang of Four, called in thousands of militiamen and crushed the movement. Deng Xiaoping, a popular reformer, was ousted for the second time from the leadership. However, only a few months later, Mao died in disgrace. Soon, the Gang of Four were put in prison and Deng rose to power again. Then and only then, was China able to enter this reform era and Chinese civilization to get a chance to cure her serious wounds.

Deng Xiaoping Versus Democratic Movements

In this reform era, relations between the people, especially the intellectuals, and the Communist authority have indeed taken on a new face. The new Beijing leadership understands now more than ever that it cannot possibly carry out its new economic reconstruction without help from the intellectuals. However, its relations with the intellectuals have failed to change in a fundamental way. That is, in the minds of the authority, the intellectuals are useful, but they must not be allowed any kind of political independence. Rather, the intellectuals must be treated as the "servants" of the authority.

Throughout the 1980s, the intellectuals have been effectively barred from the leadership in the same way as in Mao's era, although they have enjoyed the most relaxed atmosphere since 1958. But the struggles between the Communist authority and the intellectuals have not stopped for a single day. Rather, it has intensified as the reform developed. These conflicts and confrontations are perhaps the most important reason that the Communist reform effort is doomed.

The Beijing leadership under Deng Xiaoping, as pointed out by Liu Xiaobo,[15] has tried to offer incentives to the intellectuals in order to woo them in the direction of the Communist reform. Such efforts on the part of the Beijing leadership were partially successful, especially in the early stages of reform.

Many chances for reconciliation between the authority and the intellectuals were available in this reform era. Many people had great expectations concerning Deng Xiaoping and his new administration. In fact, Deng was in a much better position than any previous Communist leader to understand the true situation in China. He understood the needs of intellectuals much more acutely than Mao Zedong. Mao had been brought up in a shabby, remote rural region in Hunan. Mao did not know what a newspaper looked like until he was 18 years old.[16] Mao spent much of his life either as a villager or a guerrilla warrior fighting in the jungles.

Deng Xiaoping is different. Deng is one of the most enlightened of the first-generation Communist guerrilla warriors. He spent part of his youth in France and in the Soviet Union. In the 1970s he visited America and there he saw the American highways and toured factories. He knows much more about what modernization really means than the Hunan peasant Mao Zedong. In fact, Deng Xiaoping is one of the most talented members of the Communist party. This short politician does have star quality. He can write well, speak eloquently and with a metropolitan air, knows how to please men and women, and has the courage to do things that other people are too timid to do. He deeply feels the rapid progress of the rest of the world. The idea of dumping the central plan has been discussed since the mid-1950s when the system was new, but no leader had the courage to do something about it until Deng became the supreme ruler in the late 1970s. Deng twice survived persecution by Mao during the Cultural Revolution. No other Communist leader except Deng had the courage to open China to the outside world. China's confused intellectuals really have had a reason to attribute what happiness they enjoy to this short politician.

On the other hand, the long-suffering, very confused people, especially the intellectuals, can no longer tolerate a Communist authority that rules in the Maoist fashion. But the intellectuals have not yet found any sound alternatives for China's future.

Throughout the 1980s the mentality of the intellectuals has remained fundamentally unchanged from previous decades. One crucial fact for understanding this era is that China's intellectuals have not reached that level of determination to become completely independent in thinking and spirit. Rather, the intellectuals desperately sought some new Communist strongman to look after their lives. The intellectuals had been looking around for a superman to save them from the Maoist bitter seas. By the late 1970s they had placed this hope firmly in Deng Xiaoping. This mentality of China's intellectuals was recognized and fully utilized by the Communist authority throughout the late 1970s and 1980s.

"The key to the four modernizations is the modernization of science and technology," Deng said at the National Conference on Science on March 18, 1978. "Without modern science and technology, it is impossible to build modern agriculture, modern industry, or modern defense. Without the rapid development of science and technology, there can be no rapid development of the economy. The party's Central Committee decided to call this national science conference in order to bring home to the party and country the importance of science, to map out a program, to commend advanced units and individuals, and to discuss measures for speeding up the development of science and technology in China."

Deng has tried to offer as much help as possible to the intellectuals. He wants to improve the living standards of the teachers, researchers, and technical specialists; he wants to allow the universities to admit only competent students through a national examination system; he sends thousands of students and scholars to study overseas; he generously rewards those scholars and specialists who offer their knowledge and skills to the authority. He most generously asserts to the people that "getting rich is glorious" rather than a crime in Mao's sense, and he goes so far as to say that Chinese citizens may marry foreigners. In short, Deng has done much to improve relations between the Communist authority and the people, especially the intellectuals. Of course, without doing these things, Deng could not have built up his supreme rulership over China.

Things worked marvelously for Deng for years. In the National Day Celebration on October 1, 1984, the students from Beijing University paraded through Tiananmen Square to wave at the great leader Deng Xiaoping standing high in the Tiananmen Tower: "Long Live Xiaoping" they chanted, in striking contrast to the scenes of 1989.

Most importantly, Deng understands that only free minds can accomplish the "Communist modernization" that he has been so anxious to push ahead. After all, without such a reform, the Communist establishment would be in grave danger. For some 30 years, Mao Zedong had been the only person who had a free mind and almost all other people had become the slaves of Mao's slogans. This had to stop now, Deng Xiaoping asserted. "Once people's thinking becomes rigid, book worship, divorced from reality, becomes a grave malady," he stated. In December 13, 1978, Deng stressed the urgent need to free the mind from the thought prisons of Mao's era: "Those who suffer from it dare not say a word or take a step that is not mentioned in books, documents, or speeches of leaders: everything has to be copied. Thus responsibility to the higher authorities is set in opposition to responsibility to the people. . . . Our driving for the four modernizations will get nowhere unless rigid thinking is broken down and the minds of cadres and of the masses are completely emancipated."

Like Mao Zedong in 1956–57 Deng promised to allow more intellectual freedom. On October 30, 1979, he told the writers and artists: "At the time of the founding of our People's Republic, Comrade Mao Zedong pointed out that 'an upsurge in economic construction is bound to be followed by an upsurge of construction in the cultural sphere.' After waging bitter struggles and overcoming many difficulties, we have smashed the Gang of Four and thus removed our biggest stumbling block. We can now say with full assurance that this upsurge will not take long to appear and that the conditions are daily ripening that will enable us genuinely to put into practice the Marxist policy 'Let one hundred flowers bloom, and let one hundred schools of thought contend.' Thanks to the hard work of the masses of writers and artists, a new age of flourishing literature and art will unfold before us."

Naturally, Deng expected to receive something in return for this new policy. He could not escape the Communist system, consciously or otherwise. After all, his reform is meant to strengthen the Communist authority. His reform effort is limited because all the changes must, above all, guarantee continuing Communist supremacy over China. This limitation indicates that the intellectuals will not really receive true freedom. Whenever an intellectual takes one step outside the pronounced limit, he chances losing his foot if not his life. In fact, the Communist authority could not even offer a little academic freedom such as free academic speech and writing. Yet, reform requires knowledge and knowledge requires free thinking. Without this little freedom, no true knowledge can come into life. Therefore, the Communist authority itself has doomed its great reform programs.

In the late 1970s and 1980s most people in China could not stop congratulating themselves for having found a new savior — Deng Xiaoping, who would save them from three decades of Maoist hell. Even Deng's wrongdoings during Mao's era were forgiven by the Chinese people. Deng's call for China's modernization was to the people what water and compass are to travelers lost in the desert. While most people grew drunk with the Communist authority's beautiful promises, a few brave individuals kept their heads clear. These men asked a few questions, and some even tried to form an opposition party to challenge the Communist domination. Of course, these attempts were not taken lightly by the authority.

"Does Deng Xiaoping really deserve the people's trust?" asked Wei Jingsheng in March 1979, stating,

> No political leaders have a right to expect the people's unconditional trust. If they carry out policies beneficial to the people along the road to peace and prosperity, then we should trust them. Our trust in them is for their policies and the means to apply these policies. Should they carry out policies harmful to the people's interests, the path they are treading is a dictator's path and should be opposed. The people are as much opposed to this path as they are to measures harmful to their interests and to policies undermining their legitimate rights. According to the principles of democracy, any authority must give way to opposition from the people.[17]

Wei believed that Deng played games as Mao Zedong did previously for many decades. Therefore, to assure that China would not repeat her mistakes, organized political opposition must be introduced. Only in this way could China avoid another Mao Zedong. Wei dared to warn the nation: "But Deng Xiaoping does not give way. When the people are demanding a widespread inquiry into the reasons for China's backwardness over the last 30 years and into Mao Zedong's crimes, Deng is the first to declare: 'Without Mao Zedong there would be no new China.' In his speech he even flattered Mao Zedong's ghost when he called him 'the banner of the

Chinese people' and claimed Mao's weaknesses and mistakes were so insignificant as to be unworthy of mention."

Wei went on to dig more deeply into Deng's motives and, at the same time, he talked like the political opposition. Wei stressed the need to establish a system of checks and balances to counter the Beijing authority, so that China would not repeat her old mistakes. Wei continued his questioning:

> Is he afraid that an investigation into Mao's mistakes would lead to an investigation into Mao's collaborators? Or is Deng simply preparing to continue the Mao Zedong brand of dictatorial socialist government? If the former, then Deng has nothing to fear, since the tolerance of the Chinese people is great enough to forgive him his past mistakes provided that he now leads the country toward democracy and prosperity. But if the latter, we will never forgive him, even if he has been the best of leaders. If his aim is to continue the Mao Zedong style of dictatorship, his course of action can only lead to economic ruin and the abuse of the people's interests. Anyone forgiving such a crime would be indirectly guilty of crimes against the people.

Naturally, the new Communist authority did not appreciate the efforts of Wei and the other brave young people like him. Deng Xiaoping could no longer remember that Wei and the other young democratic activists had just helped Deng rise to power against Mao, his arms the Gang of Four, and the Maoists led by Hua Guofeng. Of course, by now, the center of gravity had changed – Deng had defeated Mao's followers in the top leadership and had successfully consolidated his power. He no longer needed help from Wei and the other democratic activists in the way he did previously. Moreover, he had established himself as the sole reform leader in the eyes of the masses. By this time, China's people had grown impatient to get with the job of reform under Deng's slogan "Getting rich is glorious." Most people felt that China had finally found a great politician to lead them to prosperity. Not many people were concerned about establishing some kind of opposition to check and balance the new Communist authority. As a result, Deng simply put Wei and few hundred young democratic activists in prison. Wei was forgotten until 1989 when numerous intellectuals and scholars stepped forward to petition the Beijing leadership to free Wei and his like from the prison.

In the reform decade of the 1980s China's intellectuals and technically trained people devoted themselves to helping with

Deng's reform. Of course, Deng has generously offered many government positions to the thousands of young and able cadres and intellectuals. Numerous think-tanks and research organizations have been created. Thousands of students and scholars are sent to study overseas. Reform leaders such as Hu Yaobang and Zhao Ziyang increasingly depended on those think-tanks, research institutions, and foreign-trained intellectuals to map out new policies.

Yet all was not as good as it seemed. The Communist authority gave government positions to the young reformers and researchers. But the Communist authority did not give them the right to speak and write freely. No free debates on the various government policies are allowed. Most policy studies and ideas come forth like toothpaste squeezed out of the tube. Many of China's intellectuals have developed a habit most distasteful to their counterparts in Western countries: they always speak and write in the same manner as everybody else. They read the editorial comments in the *People's Daily*, and stay in step with the Communist authority.

In reality, even the millions of officials cannot speak their minds freely. The various mayors, provincial heads, and productive enterprise directors are not granted the right to speak freely. Even party chiefs such as Hu Yaobang and Zhao Ziyang cannot speak as freely as they would wish to. Therefore, as in Mao's era when Mao was the only person who had freedom of speech, Deng Xiaoping is the only person in this reform age who can speak freely. The only obvious improvement over Mao's era is that the second most powerful Communist, Chen Yun, can speak as freely as Deng does.

The most abnormal thing about the Communist system is that it cannot utilize the creative energy and the loyalty of China's people. Mao Zedong feared that all his friends, admirers, and worshippers were really foes. Deng has not learned the proper lesson from Mao's behavior. Rather, he has pushed the Maoist tradition to the extreme. Deng depends too much on the Maoist doctrinaires such as Hu Qiaomu and Deng Liqin. These men work around the clock to make sure that the millions of cadres are working effectively to "promote" Communist legitimacy by stopping free speech and free thoughts by the masses. No wonder that this Communist hero, Deng Liqin, feels that he should have been the party chief instead of Hu Yaobang or Zhao Ziyang.

The numerous political campaigns against so-called bourgeois pollution conducted throughout the 1980s have been successful. The people have been terrorized to such a degree that they hardly opened their mouths for a long time after each campaign. These campaigns took place in 1983, 1984, and again in 1986–87.

However, making China mute and deaf did not mean that China's problems have disappeared. Rather, old problems and new ones have accumulated to push China into chaos and violence. China's reform has expanded old conflicts and confrontations between the autocratic central government and the local governments, between the central government and the enterprises, between the authority and the people. The lack of free discussions and debates has hidden these crises; unnoticed, they have worsened rapidly. The crisis of inflation, the crisis of government corruption, the crisis of grain shortage, the crisis of productive enterprise management, the crisis of overpopulation, the ethnic crisis, the education crisis — among many others — have rapidly become explosive. These mounting crises could destroy China's unity and peace.

By 1986, for example, government corruption had reached a level that would make Mao Zedong turn over in his grave. Yet in 1986–87, the Communist authority led another campaign aimed at so-called spiritual pollution. The reform-minded party chief Hu Yaobang was disgraced for showing sympathy with students who had demanded greater political reform. A number of student activists were arrested, and many intellectuals such as Fang Lizhi and Liu Binyan were harassed by the Communist authority. The courageous but weak voice these intellectuals raised against government corruption could not really stop widespread official corruption. But even this little voice had to be silenced by the Communist leaders. Liu Binyan, a leading journalist in China, offers a striking example of the tyranny of the Communist authority. His youthful critical reports of Communist corruption in 1957 were punished with more than 20 years of forced labor camp and internal exile. He was finally rehabilitated in 1979 at the beginning of Deng's era. Immediately he assumed his old duty of reporting the corruptions and wrongdoings of the cadres. One of his most popular works, "A Second Kind of Loyalty," praises the supreme loyalty and the purity of those individuals who dare to criticize the party when it does wrong.

The Communist authority does not recognize the worth of the loyalty of Liu Binyan and his kind. Rather, the Communist authority views Liu Binyan and others like him as the most dangerous social element that threatens Communist power. It is natural, though disturbing, that the Communist authority spends day and night formulating new schemes to "establish" the authority of the

Communist government. Although the stability of any society demands a strong government authority, Deng's administration has failed in every way to make strong government possible. Deng's schemes are to stop the people from speaking freely with whatever means he can use. On July 17, 1981, Deng offered explicit instructions to those cadres in charge of watching over the people:

> Recently, I read some materials that shocked me. Some young poet went to speak a great deal at Beijing Normal University with no restraint. Some students said: what the party organizations have taught them is blown away by just one speech. The University Party Organization noticed that but did nothing to stop it.... Some official in some culture-education bureau in the city of Urumchi recently opened his mouth freely—many of his words are much beyond the wrongs of the average Rightist criticism in 1957. In reflection, the Anti-Rightist Campaign went too far—this was a mistake; however, the campaign was certainly needed. You fellows must still remember how deadly the Rightists were! Now some people are as horrible as before.... After we imposed the Four Principles, our minds are more clear; what is more, following our acts to strictly ban illegal organizations and publications, now the situation is better....

Here, we should point out that it may be quite unreasonable to use the words "good" or "bad" to describe the Communist authority. The party's fear of the people, fear of free speech, fear of criticism is a product of the Communist system. This centralized system depends on maintaining absolute authority over the population. Such authority must be established and maintained by whatever means necessary, including terror. Free expression might undermine or even destroy the authority. The number-one job for the authority is to make sure that China has only one mouth: the Communist authority. China's history for the past four decades shows this fact: the Communist system has great difficulty creating wealth for the Chinese people, it has no trouble producing "great Communist heroes" such as Mao Zedong, the Gang of Four, Lin Biao, Deng Xiaoping, and Chen Yun. As long as this system continues, China's people will be poor in wealth, but rich in Communist heroes.

The fundamental task for the Beijing authority has been to achieve absolute government authority and make the population revolve around the Communist authority. Throughout the 1980s, the Communist authority has failed terribly. Moreover, the Communist authority has been unable to find alternatives to establish its authority. This failure has been so bitter to the Beijing authorities, especially when the governments in Taiwan and South Korea could easily establish their authoritarian ruler over the same period.

Some reform-minded leaders such as Hu Yaobang understand the urgent need for a more relaxed political atmosphere in order to reestablish the Communist authority over China. But by recognizing this need, Hu and his like have departed from Communist tradition, thereby angering the Communist doctrinaires. Thus, Hu and others like him are purged.

From 1988 to the death of Hu Yaobang in April 1989, the Communist authority made even more dreadful mistakes. In particular, it successfully drove away many of its own cadres. Communist corruptions have shaken the trust even between Communist superiors and their inferiors. The centralized bureaucracy reached a total failure stage. The mad pursuits of the Communist leadership have destroyed the interests of tens of millions people. In 1988 alone, the Communist government wrote $7 billion yuan in "IOU" notes instead of paying cash to the farmers.[18] Inflation has become painful for tens of millions of urban residents.

However, the Beijing authority has continued to use terror and intimidation not only against the mainland Chinese, but also against overseas Chinese students. In 1987, one overseas student, Yang Wei, was imprisoned for two years after he returned home to visit for the "crime" of being a member of a democratic organization.[19] Moreover, in the winter of 1989 the Communist authority blandly refused requests by leading intellectuals and scientists, many of whom had served the Communist party for several decades, to free political prisoners.[20]

Deng Xiaoping was absolutely right in his repeated assertions that China's modernization would fail if people rushed into the streets to demand this or that new program. However, it was the Communist authority under his leadership that constantly closed all the normal channels for the people to communicate with the government. It was Deng and his aging colleagues who piled up enough dry wood to cause a fire that could turn the Communist sky red. Finally, tens of millions of people gathered enough strength to say that they were tired of life under the Communist system. China's people wanted to live a different life, a life free of the handcuffs of Communist authority. The death of Hu Yaobang triggered an explosion — the 1989 democratic movement throughout China.

However, the foundation of the 1989 democratic movement was a desire to promote a workable and reasonable relation between the people and the Communist authority. In particular, the people demanded their rights for free expression of thoughts and feelings. They demanded that the Communist leaders understand the life of the people. But even these simple and reasonable wishes by the tens of millions of people were crushed by tanks and rifles. Since June 4, 1989, the Beijing authority has claimed that it has achieved a "glorious victory."

What kind of victory is this? The Communist authority has buried its own power over the people. Ironically, with help from the Communist authority itself, the modern history of the Chinese people's search for supermen, from Jiang Kaishek on to Mao Zedong, Zhou Enlai and Deng Xiaoping, is finally over. China entered a new era after June 4, 1989. Numerous intellectuals and students have tried to flee overseas following the bloody crackdown, and some have succeeded in getting out. The flight of China's intellectuals is a striking proof of the failings of the Communist authority.

For the first time, intellectuals have taken the initiative to escape mad state persecution, though they have been persecuted throughout the last forty years. Hardly any intellectuals fled in the Anti-Rightist Campaign in 1957 when more than half a million intellectuals were sent to labor camps and many were even put to death. Hardly any intellectuals fled during the Maoist Cultural Revolution when practically all intellectuals were humiliated spiritually and physically. Even ten years ago, numerous democratic activists remained at home, only to be taken away by the Communist police during the Anti-Beijing Spring Campaign. However, this time, the intellectuals have tried every means available to flee Communist persecution and killing. Most strikingly, several leading intellectuals and citizens have taken refuge at the foreign embassies in Beijing. The Communist authority has thus pushed itself into another deadly trap.

Notes for Chapter 4

1. *World Journal*, January 11–16, 1990.
2. *Cheng Ming Magazine* 61 (1982).
3. This story started when three overseas mainland Chinese graduate students studying in the U.S. applied for visas to visit Taiwan; see *World*

Journal, March 5, 1988. Finally, five mainland Chinese graduate students in America went to visit Taiwan in December 1988. Their trip received extensive coverage in the global Chinese media. See, for example, *China Times Weekly*, December 1988 and January 1989 issues.

4. See, for example, Mao Zedong's secret speeches given on March 17–20, 1957.

5. This incident received much global attention. See the cover story in *Time* magazine, March 13, 1989, "The Man Who Did Not Come to Dinner — Chinese Dissident Fang Lizhi."

6. This phenomenon was discussed in a reform conference held in early April 1989, in Beijing, as reported by Hong Chuanjing. "How to Help Reform Walk Out of the Trap: A Report from a Beijing Reform Conference," *Wide Angle Monthly*, May 1989.

7. Zhang Xing, "Touring Mainland China — Home Visit Group's Report of the Overseas Chinese Student Economic Association in America," *China Times Weekly*, June 9, 1990.

8. *World Journal*, March 30–31, 1990.

9. *Wall Street Journal*, December 20, 1989.

10. Dai Qing, *Liang Shumin, Chu Anping, and Wang Shiwei* (Jiangsu: Jiangsu Literature and Arts Press, 1989).

11. This is taken from Liming Editors, *How the Chinese Communist Party Treats Intellectuals: A Collection of Original Materials*, 3 vols. (Taiwan: Liming Cultural Enterprise Co., 1983).

12. This is taken from the same source mentioned in note 11.

13. Wang Shaowei was a Communist intellectual who joined the Communist guerrilla forces in Yenan in the late 1930s. Later, in 1942, he led a popular movement critical of Communist bureaucratic ills. Soon he and many other intellectuals were arrested. Wang was killed in 1947, at age 41, by the Communists.

14. Su Xiaokang, Luo Shishu, and Chen Zhen, *A Feast of Utopia — The Summer of 1959 in Lushan* (Beijing: China News Press, 1988).

15. Liu Xiaobo, "Contemporary Chinese Intellectuals Vs. Politics," *Cheng Ming*, April–October issues 1989; continued in 1990.

16. Edgar Snow, *Red Star Over China* (London: Gollancz, 1937).

17. Wei Jingsheng and others, *Say Yes to Yourself, Say Yes to Democracy — A Declaration of Human Rights of the Mainland Youths* (Taipei: Associate Press, 1979). Here we follow the English translation by Gregor Benton, ed., *Wild Lilies, Poisonous Weeds: Dissident Voices from People's Republic of China* (London: Pluto Press, 1982).

18. See note 6 above.

19. See the *New York Times*, January 1, 1987. Also see his wife's article "Save My Husband," as well as other reports on the event in *China Spring*, April and other later issues of 1987.

20. See *Cheng Ming* for March–May 1989 issues. Also see *China Times Weekly*, and *Nineties Monthly Journal*.

5

CHINA BEYOND DENG:
SOURCES OF CHAOS

Deng Xiaoping and the other aging leaders believed that a bloody crackdown on democratic activists would ensure the Communist supremacy for a long time. With this belief, these men masterminded the June 1989 bloodshed. However, killings and terrorist acts have not resolved the various social, political, and economic crises facing Chinese society as a whole and the Communist party in particular. Rather, the bloody killing has pushed China to the point where there can be a sudden volcanic eruption. In short, the Communist authority has effectively burned the bridge, perhaps the last one, for a peaceful evolution in China.

The following chapter examines what social, political, and economic elements could drive China into a volcanic explosion. It is our purpose here to present this picture as realistically as possible. To understand the sources of chaos will help us to minimize or perhaps even avoid approaching disaster.

Political Sources of Chaos

In a country as big and diverse as China, numerous political elements could bring about future chaos and anarchy. However, some of these factors may be more influential and decisive than others. I will consider the most fundamental factors here. I will focus on the role of the Communist authority, for under China's present system, the Communist bureaucracy is the foundation of contemporary Chinese society.

The Communist party is the institution most able, as well as most likely, to cause chaos and anarchy. The Communist power monopoly has created endless troubles for the Communist authority

itself, let alone China in general. These self-made problems endanger the continued existence of the Communist government, and
China's unity and stability. Forty-one years of Communist iron control has left little room for the existence of any independent competing organizations, and left no room at all for any organized political
opposition. The Communist bureaucracy is the source of all social,
economic, and political organization in China. This reality is very
dangerous to the well-being of the Communist government in
China: the Beijing authority lives according to two simple points:
either "long live" or "down with," with nothing in between. So far,
the Beijing authority has made some half-hearted attempts to depart
from this reality. But these halfway attempts have all failed. Today,
most tragically, China's peace and unity hang by a thin thread.

In China today, the Communist bureaucracy owns and controls everything. All decisions, big or small, have to be decided by
this bureaucracy. It controls all aspects of Chinese society and has
all the means for such control. The government is the servant of the
bureaucracy; the army is its "bodyguard";[1] the bank is its financier;
the ministry of the treasury is its accountant; the media, such as
television, radio, and newspapers, are its mouthpieces; the productive enterprises are its "money-tree"; the trade unions, youth
leagues, and women's associations are its fellow travelers. In short,
China belongs to the Communist bureaucracy.

All the troubles in Chinese society, consequently, are the troubles of the Communist party. Economic trouble is a problem of the
party; population pressure is a difficulty for the party; the education
dilemma is a worry for the party; the food supply shortage is a
headache for the party; ethnic trouble is an obstacle for the party;
the intricacies of unemployment are a burden for the party; the
transportation mess is a great handicap for the party; lack of international trade is a handicap for the party. In short, the Communist
bureaucracy has to resolve all troubles that face Chinese society
within the party itself.

Throughout the past forty-plus years during which it has been
in power, the Communist government has been unable to avoid these
troubles. It has put its nose into everybody's business, and refuses
to stop meddling in everything even at this date. Moreover, the
Communist government cannot provide a good life for the Chinese
people, for it is not competent to do so, but it refuses to let anyone
take care of his own life. Communist China has reached such a ter-
minally ill stage that even if the Communist authority peacefully

yielded its stranglehold on power, there is no replacement available as an alternative for governing. The situation in China is very different from the situation prevailing in Communist Poland and other Eastern European Communist states that seem to have managed to end the Communist monopoly of power more or less peacefully since 1989. The Chinese Communist authority has either destroyed or subdued all the traditional social and political organizations that might compete with it. It has created a vacuum for the birth of any independent competing political organization. The birth of independent political organizations, especially during the 1989 democratic movement, was aborted by the tanks of the Communist government. China has no visible organization well organized and strong enough to replace the Communist party when it collapses.

Moreover, the Communist authority has no hope of resolving the complex interwoven problems of the society whose "heights" it pretends to "command." Nonetheless, it still tries to find "solutions" within the party context. Communist "solutions" continue to amount to nothing more than shifts in power caused by power struggles within the Communist bureaucracy itself. All differences on economic issues within the authority have to be resolved by power struggles such as those between Mao Zedong and Peng Dehuai, or between Mao and Li Shaoqi, or between Deng and the Gang of Four, Deng and Hua Guofeng, or Deng and Chen Yun. China has a "government by purge," to use a scholarly term. Never in China's history has a political authority had so many power struggles producing so many destructive results as the Communist authority. Today, the Communist authority continues to possess an unlimited capacity to cause more power struggles, one of which could result in a final deadly split within the bureaucratic system.

The Communist authority has even started to employ massive violence to handle problems within the party. The differences arising between Deng Xiaoping and Zhao Ziyang in the handling of the democratic movements were resolved by the deployment of large contingents of army troops and tanks in 1989. In this way, the Communist party effectively eliminated the leading figures who were emerging in non–Communist political life and thereby cut off its connections with the reform element of the population. The actions of Deng laid the groundwork for a violent split within the Communist authority, for now those seeking moderation and reform have no voice or outlet for expressing these desires within the Communist party.

Once Communism's authoritarian unity is broken and the party split, the whole society will be cast into a state of chaos and anarchy. All social, political, and economic units and organizations will be forced into the chaotic whirlpool because each will be forced to declare whether they support or repudiate the Communists, and which faction within the party they will follow. This will involve all aspects of the government: the military forces, the diplomatic corps, the various provincial and local governments, and productive enterprises. The terrible split will reach down into rural villages, city streets, into every household, and will touch every individual. The chaos and tremendous power struggles of the Cultural Revolution of 1966–76 will seem like a minor upset compared to the disaster that could follow the collapse of the Communist authority.

The top party leadership will be directly responsible for the split of the party. The power of the Communist authority rests in the hands of a few top leaders. Only this top leadership is capable of causing such a catastrophic split within the Communist party. The truth is that the top leadership is the core of the Communist dictatorship. It is also the principle source of man-made disasters over the years of Communist rule. Looking back at the four decades of Communist rule in China, we see that all the troubles and disasters have been initiated by the top leadership. The Cultural Revolution was initiated by Mao Zedong. Mao went as far as to write a wall poster called "My Poster" to denounce the second most powerful Communist, Liu Shaoqi, and other senior colleagues, the so-called revisionists.[2] Only in this way, was he finally able to mobilize tens of millions of youthful Red Guards to carry out his class struggles and mass purges.

Communist power has always been concentrated in the hands of a few strongmen such as Mao Zedong and Deng Xiaoping. These strongmen have been elevated to the level of god-emperors, but, in reality, these men cannot really perform like gods. They can command the blind loyalty of the cadres for a period of years, but never forever. Far from being "supermen," they are in significant ways mediocrities.

Before the Cultural Revolution, Mao Zedong had benefited for several decades from his personality cult and the blind loyalty of the masses as well as the soldiers. Military forces were required to spend a major portion of their training reading Mao's quotations. Every soldier carried Mao's Little Red Book in his pocket. Despite this indoctrination, the military's personal loyalty to Mao turned out to be not very impressive. Every top army commander, the military chief-of-staff, and the navy and air force commanders all joined Lin Piao in the plot to get rid of Mao, according to the official report.[3]

Soldiers who were sent down to the civilian institutions to maintain order instead demonstrated an excessive show of abuse of power. City life and the pleasures of using power proved to be more attractive for many of these soldiers than army life with its strict regulations. Many soldiers violated orders and broke the peace. In fact, many of them became wholeheartedly involved in corruption and power abuse. When Mao Zedong tried to call off the Cultural Revolution in 1968 after his victory over his rivals for power, many in the military would not obey him, would not give up the power they had obtained. That is another reason why the tremendous power struggles of the Cultural Revolution could not be stopped even by Mao Zedong himself. Not until Mao died in 1976 could these power struggles be put to an end.

After the Lin Biao episode Mao Zedong had even greater problems with his Gang of Four, led by his wife, Jiang Qing. During Mao's dying years, the Gang of Four did not try to conceal from Mao's eyes their hunger to become China's supreme rulers, thereby proving what Mao had long believed. Mao Zedong spent his last few years in a state of anxious paranoia, a mental turmoil unmatched except perhaps by such figures as Hitler and Stalin. He could trust nobody, not even his wife, Jiang Qing. He became totally dependent on his nephew, a Red Guard, to communicate with the other leaders. On April 5, 1976, thousands and thousands of people rushed to Tiananmen Square and openly denounced Mao's regime. A few months later, Mao died a mad man.

Deng Xiaoping appears to be cleverer than the Hunan peasant Mao Zedong. Yet he could do no better than Mao as far as the personality cult is concerned. Though Deng's popularity had reached its height by the early 1980s because of his reform movement, it declined even faster than it rose. True, hundreds of thousands of people heroically joined the April 5, 1976, demonstration in Beijing to support Deng's reform programs of that time. That movement, though put down in bloodshed by the Maoists, smoothed the way for Deng's return to power together with the other veteran cadres victimized during the Maoist Cultural Revolution. Many of these same people, who gathered in Tiananmen Square in 1976, together with their sons and daughters, grandsons and granddaughters, joined together again in the 1989 democratic movement. Moreover, the 1989 democratic movement even involved hundreds of thousands of rank-and-file cadres. Most of these demonstrators had worshipped Deng Xiaoping for many years as the savior of the Chinese people. But now the emerging voice in this new history-making movement calls for the removal of that "great reform hero."

Deng Xiaoping has stepped into his own mine-field. He has been defeated badly. He has to rely again on the support of a few aging doctrinaires, such as Chen Yun, to cling to power. Although Deng and these men have been rivals for a long time, Deng now protects their privileges.

Who will become the next Mao Zedong or the next Deng Xiaoping? What will the new leaders do to prevent the split of the whole Communist bureaucracy? What magic will these new leaders employ to make 48 million cadres and 30 million officials continue to revolve around them? A personality cult, smoke and mirrors, or sheer terror?

Mao's personality cult was so overwhelming that his little piece of paper with its six-word message effectively ensured five years of power for his number four heir, Hua Guofeng. Could Deng Xaioping ensure the supremacy of his number three handpicked successor, Jiang Zemin, with a similar deathbed note? Of course not. China is no longer Maoist China and Deng knows this truth better than anyone else. This is why he has come out of his official retirement since November 1989. He had no choice. A nation of 1.1 billion people has revolved around this one man for more than ten years. He had to come out of retirement to ensure the continuation of the Communist system.

The new Beijing leadership has only slim chances to maintain the unity of the Communist party. The death of Deng Xaioping will deprive the new leaders of a symbolic and actual unity figure. There are many political factions in the party. These factions can be traced back to the Communist guerrilla era. They have not stopped fighting with each other for a single day. That is why Communist China has had so many internal struggles and such grave economic failures. That is also why the losers often lose everything in these Communist "games." Factional fighting will not die out after Deng Xaioping. Rather, every cadre will see a chance to grasp for greater power.

The gravest problem with the new third-generation Beijing leadership is the old problem: it may not be allowed to depart from the Communist tradition. One persistent feature of the Chinese Communist party is its total lack of so-called centralized democracy. The top leadership always tries to keep decision-making processes as secretive as possible; even most cadres know little about how and why decisions are made. These secret dealings are very harmful to Communist unity. Top decisions often do not reflect the interests of the cadres who are the "conveyor belts" of communism. The millions of cadres are often outraged by the results of top power struggles.

Deng is unlike his counterpart, the Soviet strongman Gorbachev, who appears to be acutely aware of the danger of an "iron curtain" that hides the decision-making processes and leaves cadres ill-prepared for sudden shifts in policy. A realist, Gorbachev has tried to depart from Soviet Communist tradition by publicizing differences between members of the top leaderships, among other actions. Party opponents, such as Yeltsin, can now openly criticize government policies. Most strikingly, Gorbachev understands that by permitting a more open process, the danger of total disintegration of the party is minimized. Facing a fragmentation within Soviet society, Gorbachev has adopted more open measures to lead the Soviet Union toward more rational solutions. By February 1990 he could see no alternative to continuing to maintain a public facade about the unity of the party in the face of increasing civil strife and national split, except by adopting more features of Western-style democracy. But even these dramatic measures may not be enough to keep the Soviet empire together. However, peaceful change within the Communist Party since July 1990 has shown that the Soviet Communist party has achieved a significant step toward avoiding possible violent conflicts within Soviet society. Though the Soviet Communist party can hardly resolve the Soviet problems, it has at least walked the deadly trap between "long live" and "death with."

The Beijing authority has trouble understanding the shrewdness of Gorbachev's new schemes. Communist supremacy in China is founded on the use of the "iron curtain" to hide the process of making decisions from the people. Only by restricting accessibility to information can the rulers conceal their selfishness and stupidity from the public, thereby keeping the loyalty and obedience of the masses. The skill of the Communist authority in this respect is so great that the Chinese people are often the last people to learn what is going on within China.

The Beijing authority cannot keep its secrets to itself forever. After all, the Beijing authority has to mobilize the Chinese population in order to carry out its policies. Once the split in the Beijing leadership becomes public, the consequences could be explosive. All the cadres, the officials, and eventually the whole society will have to make up their minds as to whom to follow. In this way, there is little room left for negotiation and compromise by the whole society. The entire society will be helplessly drawn into the whirlpool of Communist chaos and anarchy.

Several major issues could precipitate a fundamental split within the Beijing leadership. The first issue is economic policy, the choice between central planning and reform programs based on decentralization. The second issue concerns handling of the popular democratic movement and any political oppositions. The third issue is centered on the power succession and legitimacy beyond Deng. Any one of these issues can cause the split in the top leadership. At this time, it seems that all three issues are linked, one to the other.

China's future chaos and anarchy could lead to violence and last a long time. Should chaos and anarchy beset China, there will be no quick way to end it. What will be the results of this turmoil? All things considered, there are two possible results. China's peace and unity will be restored either by a traditional autocratic government, or by the creation of a democratic government based on a multiparty system. However, either result will take a considerable time to achieve.

The military forces have been touched by the same spirit of political reform as the rest of Chinese society. They too experience all kinds of divisions within. The military has played a crucial role throughout the Communist revolution, and it will surely continue to be involved in all aspects of Chinese society. But the military, like society at large, will be without unity until society has a definite direction in which to turn. However, this definite direction will not manifest itself immediately.

At the present time, both the autocratic and the democratic paths that will determine China's future are wide open. China does not have any experience with democratic institutions. China is the world's biggest country with many thousand years of history during which the few have always ruled over the many. This history troubles those who favor a democratic alternative to Communist rule.

Those who may favor a traditional autocratic government come essentially from the rural population, which comprises about 70 percent of the total population. Chinese farmers are probably prepared to support and carry on their tradition of servitude and unflinching obedience to the central political authority. They have not yet expressed a desire for a direct voice in government. What they want is peace, unity, and prosperity. A working democratic government would demand more time and energy on the part of the citizenry. Moreover, democratic government in its early stages might not be particularly effective or stable. For these reasons, democracy might not seem attractive to China's rural population. The last ten years of reform has not transformed the traditional rural mentality. A dictatorship can offer peace and unity to the rural population without demanding their social involvement in the way that a democracy would. Many powerful autocratic governments have come and gone in China's long history. Modern Communist supremacy is based on the agrarian population and its support of traditional autocratic rule. Those soldiers who performed the June 1989 killing in Beijing were the sons of the largely illiterate peasantry. During the height of the 1989 democratic movement, the peasant population was essentially unaffected, little informed, and nearly totally disinterested by what was going on in the cities.

On the other hand, China's peasants hardly favor the record of the Communist dictatorship. The worst memory for hundreds of millions of farmers is the record-making famine that was caused by Mao's failed Great Leap Forward. The farmers are among the biggest victims of Communist corruption and abuse of power in today's China. Yet China's farmers are bothered by two questions: after the collapse of the Communist authority, will life become better? Will democracy provide peace for all?

The efficiency of an autocratic government is also very attractive to some well-educated people in China. China has not had any significant experience with democratic institutions. The lack of a strongman firmly guiding a central government has traditionally been associated with chaos and civil war. That is the reason why the experiment with a parliamentary system following the Manchu government collapse in the 1910s had such tragic consequences. China was soon thrown into civil war, and was preyed upon by numerous warlords. The Japanese invaders took advantage of the chaos to invade Chinese soil. Thereafter, popular feelings immediately switched to the creation of another autocratic government. The failure of this first democratic experiment smoothed the path for the rise of both Kuomintang and the Communists.

In China today, support for another kind of non–Communist,

autocratic government is intensified by hard reality. China faces an economic crisis and must feed her people. Economic progress can only take place under an umbrella of national unity and peace. Therefore, those who must fear China's economic collapse believe that only a dictatorship can protect the people from famine. For the last few years in China, many voices have called for another strong-man to replace the declining Communist power. These voices have been raised not only within the government and the army, but also in intellectual and cultural circles.

Unfortunately, there may be little room left for any compromise and a peaceful settlement among the various competing political groups. National reconciliation and compromise suffered a great blow in June 1989. There are many other grave problems. Widespread government corruption and abuse of power could inspire a bloody revolution. The murderers of the 1989 democratic demonstrators might have a hard time escaping a similar bloody end.

Naturally, the battle between supporters of democracy and the supporters of a dictatorship is likely to be lengthy. Those who want to make democracy a reality in China must first prove to China's people, by deeds rather than by words, the advantages of democracy. In a society where the rights of the people are an unknown concept, ignorance is the biggest obstacle to a democratic alternative.

However, we have no reasons to blame China's rural population for its lack of interest in a democratic alternative. Chinese civilization has created a talent for compromises at the private level, but it has not yet nurtured institutional experience with democratic life. In the last few years, some so-called democratic parties have been organized outside mainland China. The members are made to swear loyalty to the leaders of these parties. The leaders demand blind obedience from their members. And their activities are conducted in secretive ways. Is this true democracy? If this continues, and these parties gain ascendancy in China, no true democracy will enter China.

All things considered, much difficulty lies ahead for another dictatorship. The 1989 democratic movement has marked a turning point: the majority of China's people are finally tired of looking for a "godly" leader such as Mao Zedong and Deng Xiaoping. They are now searching for institutions that can guarantee their rights. This search will be the biggest obstacle for the rise of another Mao or another Deng.

In summary, advocates of dictatorship and supporters of democracy will have to go through direct confrontation, which may not avoid bloodshed. No matter who wins, China may well walk on a winding path, repeating civil war, chaos, and anarchy that no sane man would want to see repeated.

Economic Sources of Chaos

Many economic factors may push China into chaos and anarchy. Here we will only focus on China's present property ownership system in the light of the current economic reform.

The ambiguity and confusion in the ownership of existing state property will be a major source of economic chaos. China's present property ownership will become a major cause for chaos and anarchy. Over the years of Communist rule, all property, including land, factories, shops, and other means of production have become either state-owned or collectively owned. This situation is most confusing to the Chinese people. Everyone supposedly shares as the rightful owner of society's property and wealth. Yet nobody is sure what this sharing really means in reality. This economic confusion is no less serious than the political confusion that arises from contention that everyone is supposedly a master in Communist society, yet only a few politicians make all the decisions for the whole society.

China's present property ownership is not well defined. China does not really have a modern economic system like those established in Western countries. The Chinese have no clear understanding, or law, or system of responsibility concerning public or state-owned properties. In fact, hardly anybody knows precisely who owns this or that factory, this shop or that shop, this or that school, this land or that land.

This vast confusion is relatively new in Chinese society. In the old society, the landowning gentry class, the rich peasants, and the merchants had the desire as well as the rights to protect their land and other property. They could effectively resist the ambition of the royal houses in taking over more lands from the peasants. Moreover, they were the defenders of the social order even when the central government collapsed and disintegration threatened. The property owners have always helped China to survive her numerous chaotic periods and civil wars.

The Communist authority has created a new order, based on state and collective ownership. Yet, odd things have happened with this state ownership throughout the years. Everyone wants to gain advantages from "their" public possessions, but few wish to defend or care for that property. Even those individuals who can extract the most advantages from this system have no ways to secure their privileges. High-ranking cadres may have unlimited access to luxurious housing, cars, hospitals, special shops and resorts—among many other privileges—one day, but they may lose these privileges altogether the next day. This happened with the state head Liu Shaoqi. One day, he, his family, his relatives, and even his friends enjoyed all the privileges China could possibly provide. The next day, he was ousted from power and he lost all those privileges. His wife and children all lost their share of these privileges, and were even sent to labor camps and into internal exile. The only way Liu's family could regain privileges was through the restoration of Liu's political prestige. Liu died in prison, but he was eventually rehabilitated posthumously during Deng's era. His widow and other family members were called back from internal exile and returned to privileged life. After all, Liu should not have been purged in the first place and, therefore, his family members should again be given their due privileges, according to Communist logic.[4]

Those people who enjoy fewer advantages under this Communist system can only struggle to take away some advantages enjoyed by those who take more. The Communist authority has actually destroyed not only the private ownership, but the good husbandry and sense of stewardship that go with it. Every citizen in China today, from the poorest street person to the head of state, is equally without property and has become a proletarian in the strict sense of the word. Though in theory he has a share of all the wealth and property in Chinese society, in reality he does not feel that he has any share. In fact, he may feel that the only way that he can secure his share is through "class struggle"—political struggle. He must join the Communist party, he must become a powerful politician. Only power can make him feel that he does have a share in China's present ownership system, only power can get him what he would not get otherwise.

Needless to say, not everyone can successfully fight and obtain power and its related privileges. If one fails to make positive and reasonable advancement, he may become more than jealous. He may feel that other people have taken away his share. The cars that are possessed by the high ranking cadres should also be his. The luxurious palace life should also belong to him. After all, he is supposed to be the master of all the things in society, as the Communist slogans declare.

Under the Communist system, men only want to fight for more advantages. They do not care about protecting the properties that already supposedly belong to them — as would be the case in a society based on private ownership, such as the United States. Unlike American society, the Chinese society has lost interest in settling disputes through negotiation and compromise. In fact, China's people do not have a tradition of common law to protect the rights of the individuals. The lack of well-defined property ownership has blocked Chinese society from resolving her problems through compromise and negotiation. Instead, power struggles dominate all aspects of social life.

Those who already enjoy numerous benefits would like to impose more regulations and laws to prevent others from obtaining a share of these benefits at their expense. Those who enjoy few benefits in Chinese society would like to gain more benefits by all possible means. After all, China is a poor country and can provide nice cars, large houses, and vacation trips to the very few. The Communist authority has invented many laws to ensure that special privileges are secured for the few who possess them.

This economic system has created vast internal enemies to China's peace and stability. For most people, the existing regulations and laws have become "chains." Almost everyone feels that he has nothing to lose except the chains around his neck, and yet a whole world to gain by future changes in the economic system. Naturally, the most destructive forces will be spawned from such twisted inspiration and malevolence.

Under the present Beijing authority, property ownership relations have been made more confusing by China's reform efforts during the 1980s. Deng's reform has touched the property ownership system at many points. For example, land is supposedly state-owned, though individual farmers are now allowed to rent plots of land for individual use. It has become commonly accepted that plots of land should belong to the individual farmers who till them and who pay rent and taxes to the state. Also, some people have discussed issuing shares in the various state-owned enterprises. In the urban areas, the issue of private housing has been discussed intensely in recent years. In fact, some houses in the big cities along the coast have been put up for sale, although most of the buyers are overseas Chinese returning home.

Meanwhile, state ownership has remained untouched, in essence. It remains a sacred tenet of the Communist system. Accepting private ownership, or more precisely a clearly defined common property law, has been difficult for the Communist government. A clearly defined property law would undermine the foundation of "universal rights" claimed by the Communist authority. But state "ownership" seems to relieve the people of their obligation to protect the property belonging to society. In fact, when chaos and anarchy set in, the state properties usually become the very first targets of destruction. This is what happened during the turmoil and chaos of the Cultural Revolution. Public property became the symbol of repression. Millions of public facilities and factory machines and tools were mindlessly damaged and destroyed.

Either a stagnant economy or a fast-growing economy can throw China into a state of chaos. Everyone can understand that a stagnating, shortage-filled economy will lead to chaos and anarchy. Only a few people understand that a fast-growing economy could also lead to the collapse of China's Communist system, thus leading to chaos and anarchy. In short, either way, the state of China's economy will determine the future of the country.

Everyone can understand that a stagnated economy can lead to chaos and anarchy. China's people have raised their expectations for higher living standards. A stagnating economy can only deprive the people of the chance to improve their lives economically. The government would have to force upon the whole population the hardships associated with a failing economy. To keep functioning properly, the government would have to force the people to buy government bonds and treasury bills, cut wages, take over a greater share of profits from the productive enterprises, and issue more "empty paper money," among other things. In short, it would have to rely more on coercion to make ends meet. These attempts can create large-scale unemployment, rapid inflation, a critical shortage of basic goods, and thus a grave economic, political, and moral crisis. China has had these kinds of experiences before. For example, toward the end of the Kuomintang era in China in the late 1940s, similar economic events led to the collapse of Kuomintang power. Since 1988, the Beijing leadership has promoted coercive economic policies, accelerating in this direction especially since June 1989.

Some people hope that reform-minded leaders such as Zhao Ziyang and his like will take over the leadership and pursue a more far-reaching economic reform. China could then achieve a more rapid economic growth. However, accelerated growth would not eliminate the danger of chaos and anarchy. On the contrary, faster economic development will only precipitate an immediate transitional crisis during the changeover from the present political-economic system to some emerging future system outside the present Communist framework. Change, even for the better, will lead to economic crisis as the present Communist system accelerates toward collapse. A period of chaos and anarchy may well accompany the fundamental structural changes needed to shift China to a free, market-based economy.

It troubles some people that popular dissatisfaction has been on the increase even while China's living standards have been improving dramatically. In fact, over the decade of the 1980s, China's people have enjoyed the highest living standard since 1949. However, in the same period, China's people have expressed greater discontent with the present political authority than ever before.

Deng Xiaoping feels that he has been "ill-treated" by the Chinese people. In his view, Mao Zedong was most responsible for increasing poverty and misery for the Chinese people. Despite Mao's mishandling of the economy, the people did not openly demand his removal from power. Deng sees himself as being most responsible for ending the Maoist era and as deserving the most credit for correcting Mao's mistakes and initiating true reform. His reform immediately encouraged the people. China's wealth has doubled over the last ten years. Nonetheless, China's people now rush to the streets demanding the immediate removal of Deng Xiaoping. Deng was dismayed by the millions of demonstrators in Beijing and in dozens of cities throughout China. He could not understand why increased prosperity has met with increased criticism of his regime.

In truth, it is precisely Deng's reform that has opened new dreams for the Chinese people. Improved living standards only make the people feel confident about their strength, and they accordingly demand more progress, more private initiatives, more self-determination. They are demanding far more than Deng Xiaoping and the Beijing authority are willing to provide. The new social forces developing from the reform demand greater power sharing and more responsibility for each segment in society. But these reforms can only be achieved when the end of the Communist supremacy comes. Of course, that would be the end of the Beijing authority. Alas!

China's people are absolutely tired of taking orders from a few palace gods whom they now fully understand to have clay feet. The cadres are tired of taking orders from the top bosses; the officials are tired of listening to the Maoist doctrinaires; the people are tired of being pushed around by the cadres. In short, China's people want to follow their personal interests, rather than those of the Beijing leaders.

This phenomenon is occurring in many other countries. The Polish people demanded the end of the Communist system when their economy reached a point of collapse, but the East Germans demanded reforms when they enjoyed the highest living standard in the Eastern European bloc. In the Soviet Union, ethnic conflicts, though always present just under the surface, showed up not during the tightly controlled periods, but during the reform under Gorbachev.

Such observances would also apply to the democratic movements in Taiwan, the Philippines, and South Korea, among others. When economic advancement creates a larger, more powerful professional class, that class begins to demand more participation in the affairs of society. Thus the old order based on rulership by the few must either change to meet the demands of its critics, or suppress the critics to hold onto power.

In China, some aging Beijing leaders are well aware of the danger a fast economic development poses as far as Communist domination is concerned. Chen Yun, the second most powerful Communist, stands for this position. He recognizes that fast development in the rural areas could mean weakening of the Communist order. Rural industrial and trade activities have already caused millions of peasants to leave the fields to seek work in new enterprises. To Deng Xiaoping, this movement is very encouraging: "without industrial workers, China can never be prosperous." But it is very disturbing to Chen Yun: "without peasants, China can never be stable." To save the Communist regime, Deng believes, the party must achieve a high economic growth rate. This can only be accomplished by letting the lower bureaucrats, the productive enterprises, and even the individual businessmen take more decision-making authority. But Chen Yun asks, "If the bird [the people] escapes the cage [the party], what is left to the cage?" Therefore, Chen Yun advocates an all-out effort to make the bird stay in the cage. Chen Yun believes that the central government must take away most decision-making authority from the local and provincial officials; the productive enterprises must again take orders from the Beijing leadership; and the private businessmen must be watched like criminal suspects. To Chen Yun, any relaxation means potential chaos to the Communist power: the 1989 democratic movement is such a result and therefore Deng Xiaoping, not Zhao Ziyang, must be fully responsible for it.

The old debates between Deng and Chen Yun have gone full circle by now. The reform momentum gained by Deng's men, especially by Hu Yaobang and Zhao Ziyang, lasted only a few years. It had already started to decline by 1987. Chen Yun and his followers used reform-related problems such as rising inflation and even the democratic movement to demand a return to Communist economic monopoly and tight political control. In 1988 Zhao Ziyang lost his premiership to Li Peng, and a retrenchment program was immediately set in motion to undo the reform. Hard-liner Communist power holders tried to force the bird to return to the cage. This attempt peaked with the June 1989 crackdown.

The central planners have adopted severe measures to regain their lost power. Tightened credit lines and harsh taxation policies have crushed small individual businesses by the millions, and closed down factories, resulting in large-scale unemployment. Many central planners want to recollectivize the rural areas. Such a policy would deprive millions more of their jobs.

Since the end of 1989, the government has tried to buy stability. To curb the urban democratic movement, the Beijing government used a variety of means to pacify the urban people: it has had to supply urban dwellers with huge quantities of subsidized agricultural products, call back the unemployed workers to the factories, pay them with the same wages as before, and raise wages for state employees such as teachers and office workers.

The government is trapped now. It does not have the money to continue all these practices. It does not have enough money to purchase agricultural products from the farmers. It does not have enough money to subsidize the state-owned enterprises that still run at a loss. In 1988 the government food collectors paid no cash to the farmers for their agricultural products. Instead they wrote "IOU" notes, totaling about $7 billion yuan. Some food collectors were severely beaten by the outraged farmers, who were angry that they had worked so hard and would receive little cash from the government. Now the government has to deal with the outrage of tens of millions of farmers. With little cash in hand, the Beijing leaders must look around for alternatives. One alternative: in the state-owned enterprises, employees are forced to surrender as much as one-third of their wages to buy government-issued bonds. But this policy brings even more dissatisfaction. It has been reported that many millions of workers openly demand food and wages from the government.

China stands at a chaotic point: the retrenchment programs will block all ways for economic progress. The lack of all the means to resolve China's grave economic crisis will make a peaceful transition to a new system practically impossible. A fast economic development would definitely be better than a stagnating one. A fast-growing economy will offer new chances for the people to break out of their deadly trap, leading to a less painful, less tragic transition to a better future. But a stagnant economy will only push the Chinese people into the bitter sea once again. Also, it will shut down all possible paths to a peaceful evolution. The policies put in force by the Communist government in 1988–90 will only result in a stagnating economy. With a failing economy, the government will not be able to feed the people. The disasters in the years of 1959–62 should serve as a grim reminder to China.

Communist Corruption in Light of History

The most dramatic consequence of China's Communist reform is that it has led to a drastic decline of Communist power. In particular, the sanctioned decentralization has ushered in widespread government corruption. The number one reason for the 1989 democracy movement was this official corruption. Government corruption has reached an unprecedented extent, and reaches all the way from the top leadership down to the grassroots bureaucrats. The Communist system seems to be completely powerless to stop this ubiquitous official corruption.

How can we understand this trend? Perhaps by setting it in an historical context. Each old dynasty had its share of corrupt officials. Some corruption has always been inevitable in a country as large and populous as China. But when corruption spreads itself throughout the government, from inside the palace all the way down to tax collectors and other party officials, this is a sign that the central authority has lost the capacity to rule.

The source of government corruption is the government itself. But in the Chinese context, official corruption has very different features. Historically, widespread corruption usually takes place at the end of each dynasty. In general, the demise of the old dynastic governments resulted from the overexpansion of bureaucratic power at every level, especially at the provincial and local levels. The erosion of central government power and the growth of local government power was a deadly cancer for the old dynasties.

Beginning around 2,200 years ago, imperial China was ruled by a succession of powerful autocratic governments. Each government had much power as well as much responsibility. However, the tight control of society by the centralized bureaucracy severely limited the longevity of the old governments. There were no independent forces to provide "checks" and "balances" against the centralized bureaucracy. Economically, China's royal houses had virtually unlimited power over the rest of society. The royal houses could easily swallow more land from the peasants, impose more regulations, call for more forced labor, change the economic rules in the middle of the game, because the central authority stood above the entire society.

In general, each dynasty was founded after a period of national chaos and anarchy. Such national chaos and anarchy could last from a few years to several hundred years.[5] The problems facing Chinese society were easy to identify at the beginning of each dynasty: restore peace and order, repress bandits, appoint good officials, collect taxes, fill the government granaries as a protection against famine. In the dynasty's early stages, the government would adopt harsh methods to deal with the corrupt officials of the previous dynasty. The first emperor of the Ming Dynasty (1368–1644) went so far as to use his special agents to offer bribes to his ministers. Ministers who did not refuse temptation were executed. China's Communist government put to death many powerful but corrupt cadres in the early 1950s. Two Communist provincial heads of the greatest seaport city of northern China, Tianjin, were the victims of such ruthless punishment in the early 1950s.

Once peace and order was restored, the new dynasty would usually enjoy a prosperous and progressive period. The bureaucratic establishment would be painstakingly regulated and restrained by the central government. This prosperous period would provide needed legitimacy and strength to the imperial ruling court. All went well as long as a diligent Son of Heaven surrounded himself with an equally diligent circle of aides, who served in the high court, gave orders, appointed good officials, and maintained bureaucratic efficiency.

Throughout China's long history, there have been no independent forces to counterbalance the government's bureaucratic power. The imperial court itself had to maintain a checks and balances system within its establishment to oversee the whole bureaucratic apparatus. The officials were under the close watch of the imperial court. All the officials, from the prime minister on down to the lowest level of official were directly appointed by the emperor. A new magistrate would be interviewed by the emperor before he took up his office. To prevent local officials from establishing their own little kingdoms, they were rotated to new posts every few years. Before the local officials moved to their new posts, they were again called to the capital to renew their personal ties with the emperor. In this way, local officials were reminded that they represented the interests of the emperor and nothing more. They would have to perform their jobs diligently with integrity.

In today's China, the Beijing government continues to conduct its business in this traditional fashion. The Beijing authority switches the provincial heads and military regional commanders to different regions. In doing so, the central authority hopes to prevent the making of local kingdoms and thus to avoid erosion of the central power. After June 1989 the Beijing government instituted a massive transfer program for the leading provincial officials and regional military commanders.

Interestingly, the Chinese invented one large body of bureaucrats whose main job was to watch over other bureaucrats — a Chinese system of "checks and balances." At every level, some officials were responsible for reporting the wrongdoings and misconduct of other officials. Their reports could eventually pass into the emperor's hands. If these reports never reached the emperor, if they fell into the hands of some powerful eunuch or high court official, then corruption had reached into the high court itself. By such ingenious methods, the high court maintained a close watch over the performance of the various local officials. In fact, this practice could work for centuries to prevent the growth of corruption at the local level and the erosion of central government power.

It was inevitable that the longer a dynasty ruled, the more its vigilance about corruption declined. At its beginning, a new dynasty focused on major problems, particularly restoring and maintaining order. But as the dynasty succeeded, the high court had fewer calls for dealing with chaos, war, and natural disaster – the well-defined targets of government. After a long period of peace the high court became more and more the arbitrator on daily livelihood, businesses, food collection and distributions, racial and religious problems, army conscripts, and millions of other affairs in a vast empire. These small daily problems could not be resolved by the Son of Heaven with a few tough directives. Rather, the situation would usually require more trained hands and soft handling. That meant more direct involvement by the bureaucrats at the lower levels. So, gradually, the high court lost some of its tight central control. As decision-making power slowly shifted from the central government to the local level, more opportunities would arise for the local bureaucrats. Then, once the local officials obtained some independent power, they always wanted to extend it. As the lower bureaucrats gained the power to handle more affairs, they also gained more opportunities to abuse their power. Thus official corruption was a by-product of the growth of local power.

It is not difficult to understand the root causes of the widespread corruption at this stage. Local officials would gradually begin to control all aspects of life at the local level. As a result, every citizen would try to use all the means possible to gain favors from the officials in order to get anything done. This would provide endless opportunities for the bureaucrats to put pressure on the people, especially when the bureaucrats were not watched by the high court.

One noticeable result of increased local bureaucratic power was that the local officials would no longer regard themselves as servants of the Son of Heaven who sat in the distant capital. Moreover, the lower bureaucrats would lose interest in the higher bureaucrats. Now the lower bureaucrats had more advantages. Gradually, the lower bureaucrats would depend less and less on the higher bureaucrats. Of course, the higher bureaucrats would try every means to pressure and control the lower bureaucrats. In addition, there was no clear-cut definition in the bureaucracy as to who would be responsible for what. As a result, each bureaucrat would try harder to feather his own nest. As selfishness and corruption increased, the whole bureaucratic system rapidly disintegrated.

The disintegration of the bureaucracy and the increase in official corruption always had deadly consequences. Indeed, the lives of millions of the people, especially the peasants, would be seriously damaged. But the demands of the peasant population for improvement would meet only brutal repression. Repression often next led to a series of peasant uprisings. As so often happened in China's long history, spreading rebellion and chaos would signal the end of the old dynasty. China's dynasties, from the Qin of more than 2,000 years ago to the Manchu government that ended in this century, have all followed this pattern of rise and fall.

Each of China's old dynastic governments was toppled by these same inner conflicts and corruption. The erosion of the local government would become irreversible. The dynastic government could not cure its problems. Each old government would die out not because of the people, but rather because of themselves. It is important to understand that the fall of a dynastic government was essentially caused by flaws within its own system, not by outside forces. In a sense, it was almost impossible for the vast imperial bureaucracy to be destroyed by an external force alone. After all, China's old bureaucratic system included almost all aspects of the society. It required internal conflicts arising from corruption and power struggle to lead the way to chaos and civil war.

One example of a dynastic government destroyed through internal conflict was the Han Dynasty (202 B.C.–A.D. 220). There were massive peasant uprisings at the end of the Han Dynasty, to be sure. But all of them were crushed by the central government with decisive help from the various local powers. However, intensive palace struggles promoted the rapid growth of the local powers that in turn accelerated the decay of the central power. Very soon, the various local powers, coupled with the regional military forces, took control of their regions and began to prey on each other. The weak ones were swallowed by the strong ones. Finally China was divided among three independent regional powers. Each of them tried to swallow the other two, but a stalement existed for few decades. That age is vividly described, with a romantic tone, by a famous Chinese novel, *The Three Kingdoms*.

The most recent example was the fall of the Manchu government in 1911. The Manchu government survived its grave challenges from the Taiping Uprising (1851–64) involving several million armed peasant warriors. Furthermore, the challenge from Sun Yatsen and his fellow revolutionaries did not affect the Manchu authority in a decisive way. These revolutionaries failed to rally the Chinese people, in general, and the provincial and local powers, in particular. In fact, the Manchu government was able to put an end to the peasant uprisings and the later revolutionary forces by relying decisively on the local powers based on the gentry class. In fact, it was the gentry class from Hunan Province and the other provinces that produced a huge army to offer a death blow to the Taiping Uprisings. Again, it was these same local forces that stopped Sun Yatsen and his fellow revolutionaries. However, once these local powers completely lost their confidence in the central government, the Manchu government was doomed. In reality, the ruin of the Manchu government in 1911 was chiefly caused not by Sun Yatsen and his few revolutionary comrades, but by the local powers. Sun was in America, giving public speeches and collecting donations from the various Chinese communities in America, when he heard the news. He returned to China only a few months later by way of Europe. Naturally, Sun Yatsen and his fellow revolutionaries could not have stopped the intense warlordism that followed for few decades. Actually, Sun Yatsen tried to rally one warlord against another, but he became hopelessly a victim in warlordism until his death in 1925.

Today, the Communist government is not any different than the old autocratic governments. If there is a difference, it is only that the Communist government has pushed China's autocratic tradition to the extreme. That is why we see that many similar historical events have been repeated within the last four decades of the Communist rule.

The Communist power was also established after nearly 30 years of war: civil war as well as the anti–Japanese war. In the early stages of the Communist establishment in 1949, the Communist leaders built a new and powerful autocratic government based on a set of strict rules. In particular, like China's successful old dynasties, the Communist government used harsh means to deal with corruption and power abuse. In the early 1950s, many cadres (including some senior cadres) were executed on charges of corruption or regionalism. The Beijing leaders even encouraged the people, especially the intellectuals, to keep a "check and balance" on the Communist bureaucracy.

The first five or six years were a "golden age," according to the Communist authority as well as the masses. Life returned to normal after a long time of chaos and war. Inflation was stemmed, and living standards were improved. It was during this period that the Communist legitimacy was firmly established over China's populace. This period is well remembered today by the living Chinese as well as the Communist authority.

However, the Communist government had failed to establish an independent force to check on its responsible use of power. In fact, the Communist authority did much less than China's many old dynasties to supervise the centralized bureaucracy. Therefore, all the inner conflicts of the old governments happened again, and within the short time span of just a few decades. What is more, Communist iron control has only caused many problems for the Beijing leadership. Explosive bureaucratic centralization forced the Beijing leadership to dump many of these problems upon the lower bureaucrats.

Today, the Communist government has reached the point that usually would take a well-balanced dynastic government two or three hundred years to reach. The government has become the main force behind its own destruction. Indeed, government corruption has reached a level that is far beyond the wildest imagination of even the Beijing leaders.

This situation should not come as a complete surprise. The Communist government has had a much stronger power grip than any of the old governments. Therefore, the Communists have had many more troubles more rapidly than any of the old governments. Since the late 1950s the Beijing leaders have thought about starting decentralization. But they did not reach that final determination until Deng's era. After all, Deng is the most determined and is perhaps the ablest among the first-generation of Communist warriors. In this reform era, in order to dump their troubles, the Communist leadership has pushed for quick decentralization. This action alone was sufficient to bring volcano-like consequences.

Once the provincial and local officials succeed in getting decision-making authority, they want to expand their power. Nothing can stop them now, just as nothing stopped the old government corruption throughout China's history. The current corruption has reached a level never before seen in all of China's history. But this is no surprise. For one thing, the old governments had officials numbering in the thousands, but the Communist government employs tens of millions of officials. For another thing, the officials in the old society could not comfortably penetrate into the rural villages. But the Communist officials control every village, every street, every household, every individual.

What is more, the Communist cadres have many privileges in Chinese society. They have special houses, cars, shops, resorts, hospitals, schools – among other things. Their relatives and friends can share those privileges with them. The cadres' special privileges have enabled them to take special advantage of Deng's reform movement. For example, now that the central government allows a private sector to do business on its own, hundreds and thousands of enterprises have been established by the sons and daughters of the senior cadres. These sons and daughters of the cadres use their fathers' and mothers' power and influence to attract money and to secure a variety of advantages.

Needless to say, the Communist authority understands the reasons for widespread official corruption. But it does not wish, or — more precisely — it is powerless, to get rid of it. The second most powerful Communist, Chen Yun, has made astonishing observations about some of the institutional wrongdoings in comments to his colleagues (December 20, 1984):

> lavish dining and drinking, exchanging expensive gifts [all with public and state funds], and other private gains at the cost of the nation are negative things. Some of our enterprises claim that "No business can be done if only two dishes and a soup are on the table; an ordinary business can be done if only four dishes and a soup are on the table; a good business can be done only if six dishes and a soup are on the table; a superb business can be done only if eight dishes and a soup are on the table." Even this is no longer working. In some factories, the beautiful girls in their twenties are chosen as acquisitions people to buy factory raw materials and sell goods — they can get what their male counterparts have failed to get. Regarding these things, do not be shocked, because, on the one hand, many enterprises have to aquire needed raw materials on their own; on the other hand, the overwhelming community and collectively-owned enterprises are not within the central plan and on the allocation list — they have to look for raw materials themselves. When these two aspects come together, the above things must happen and therefore there is no surprise.

How precise! Chen Yun has revealed some of the causes of the so-called negative things. Most interestingly, Chen Yun recognizes that China's official corruption is built into the bureaucratic system. Officials who cannot accomplish the things they want using legal channels find holes within the system and use "negative means" to get ahead. In fact, if government enterprises do not use the lure of big dinners and even beautiful girls, they might not be able to get enough raw materials and other necessary things to run their enterprises.

China's official corruption is built into the bureaucratic system. Corruption has had a long history in China. Since the Communist bureaucratic system is similar to the system of the old centralized governments, the same types of official corruptions were bound to show up eventually. But under the Communist authority corruption appeared much earlier and in a much more powerful form than under the old dynasties.

Rather than getting rid of the source of government corruption — the overwhelming power of the government and the lack of a modern political-economic system — the Communist authority shies away from these problems, though it still talks continuously about the need to stop the corruption. Of course, to resolve these troubles, the whole Communist system has to be reformed radically and even dumped. Naturally, this is not the goal of Chen Yun and his like.

Chen Yun and the other Beijing supermen can only offer political and ideological ways to resolve their problems. Following the above analysis, Chen Yun continued, "However, if we do not pay attention to these problems, and offer no necessary administrative measures and education, these things will get out of control, thus damaging the spirit of our party and society. Therefore, it is imperative, while we push for material construction, to push for spiritual construction. Both aspects must be handled equally. As long as we have a clear conscience, recognize these problems, and push for the spiritual construction, these things will be limited. We are a socialist country, we want a high material life, and also a high socialist spirit, which is what we must uphold forever."

But Chen Yun has offered the wrong prescription for the symptom he correctly identified. That is why, since his speech, nothing has really improved. Indeed, ever-growing, ever-spreading corruption will soon topple the Communist system altogether.

Following the June 1989 massacre, Deng Xiaoping offered to punish a couple of dozen corrupt high-ranking officials, the "big tigers," in order to curb popular outrage. But such punishment, if enacted, will do very little to end government corruption. Indeed, it is already well-beyond the ability of the existing system to cure corruption. Each old government ended up in a similar mess and could find no way out. After all, this system has always created these problems. Since official corruption toppled almost all the previous Chinese governments, it will not be a surprise if it happens again with the Communist authority.

The people are tired of the Communist authority and can hardly wait to get rid of government corruption. The 1989 democratic movement took aim at government corruption. Even ordinary people understand as much as the philosophers do regarding the need to rid the country of official corruption. Dozens and dozens of peasant uprisings stimulated by government corruption have occurred in China's history. There is an old saying in China: "It is not the people who want to overthrow the authority; rather it is the authority who is tired of governing." This saying applies to China today. However, China's people have now added a new goal to their desire of getting rid of government corruption: the democratic movement. The 1989 democratic movement went far beyond old China's peasant uprisings against government corruption. Democracy offers a bright chance for China to depart completely from her imprisonment within historical cycles. Increasingly, informed and educated Chinese realize this fact. Once a new political-economic system based on well-defined ownership law takes root, China will have a bright chance of rapidly becoming a truly progressive modern society.

Notes for Chapter 5

1. This terminology is also used by a Liberation Army officer interviewed in Beijing by Ren Mianfu, "Interviews in Beijing: The Views of People from All Walks of Life on the 1989 Democratic Movement," *China Spring,* June 1990.

2. Yan Jaiqi and Gao Gao, *The Ten Year Cultural Revolution* (Hong Kong: Dagongbao Press, 1987).

3. Qun Zhong Press Editors, *The Judgment of History* (Beijing: Qun Zhong Press, 1981). This book reports on the trial of the Gang of Four and Lin Biao's followers.

4. Read Liu Shaoqi's three children's account of their family's ill fate during the Maoist Cultural Revolution in the book edited by Zhou Ming, *History Stops Here to Think: A Record of the Cultural Revolution,* 3 vols. (Beijing: Hua Xia Press, 1986). This book also contains numerous articles on the similar fate of many other leading Communists written by their relatives and others. Also see Liu Aiqin (Liu Shaoqi's daughter), *A Daughter's Remembrance — In Memory of My Father Liu Shaoqi* (Shijiazhoang, Hebai: Hebai People's Press, 1980).

5. Ray Huang, *China: A Macro History* (New York and London: M. E. Sharpe, 1988).

6

A FEW WORDS ON CHINA'S PEACEFUL EVOLUTION

Modernization remains the ultimate goal for China. Modernization is not really a question of whether China should adopt this or that "ism," support this or that political party, elect this or that politician. Rather, China's modernization demands the rapid creation of institutions and laws that can effectively guarantee the rise of various independent social forces. China needs a modern pluralistic and progressive society. More and more people understand that modernization is the only way to free China of her historical pattern of a deadly cycle of unity followed by disintegration, chaos, and civil war. Only true modernization will enable this oldest of all civilized nations to stand on her own feet and truly join the world community.

The sad lesson of China's long revolution during the past 100 years, is that China has yet to create modern economic and political institutions. Instead, the various parties involved in China's revolution have sought this or that "ism," this or that political party, this or that "people's savior." As a result, time has passed but China has not been able to decisively depart from her dynastic past. All the great Communist disasters were caused by the lack of modern political and economic institutions in China. Today, due to the lack of these modern institutions, China confronts the grave danger of another period of chaos and anarchy.

China's modernization will require a peaceful evolution. Chaos and anarchy will only deprive China of many years if not decades of time for progress. However, crisis also brings new opportunities. China now possesses fresh opportunities to achieve this urgent transition. I feel that there are numerous new social forces in Chinese society today. These new social forces could push China in a completely new direction. In this chapter, I want to identify many of these new opportunities.

Who Will Bring China Peace?

Does China possess social and political forces powerful enough to stop or limit the chaos and anarchy that will follow the collapse of the Communist system? Once chaos and anarchy set in, can they be stopped?

Many Chinese believe that today's China does possess the forces that may prevent future disasters, or at least limit disasters once they occur. The biggest force that can prevent disaster is the urgent desire of China's people for peace.

China's reform during the 1980s led to improve living standards. China's people have already moved some distance away from the "pure proletarian life" of Mao's era. Tens of millions of households now contain such modern consumer goods as television sets, cameras, washing machines, and expensive furniture. Many people now possess some savings for the first time in their lives. Millions of farmers have been able to build new houses or to repair and expand their old ones. Millions of individual businessmen are able to make a good living independently for the first time in four decades. In short, Chinese life has departed fundamentally from the poverty-stricken proletarian life of the Maoist era. One may go so far as to say that a new love of a "good life" by millions of people weighs significantly over the hate of a "bad life." China's people do not want a return to chaos and anarchy.

A new life-style has given birth to a new mentality for millions of Chinese. Peace is now prized above all things. Chaos and anarchy would destroy the dreams of hundreds of millions of people. Living standards can only continue to improve if peace is maintained. China has endured 100 years of revolution. Tens of millions of her people perished. The people fear another period of chaos and anarchy. That China must not fall into another disaster is the hope of all the Chinese.

In the decade of the 1980s, much intellectual education has been achieved and much popular enlightenment has been brought to the masses in China. Disastrous events such as the Anti-Rightist Campaign, the Great Leap Forward, and the Cultural Revolution have been publicly condemned and examined in some depth. The very painful and overwhelming "wounded literature" of the 1980s has focused attention upon China's recent man-made tragedies. Today the people see their dark past more clearly. Today, they keep the failures of the past in mind as they look to the future.

Actually, the people in China are acquiring a passion to understand their past. Curiously, many of the new generation writers, poets, and thinkers are former ardent Red Guards. Today, few people consciously want to be exploited by the politicians for the politicians' own ends. Naturally, college students are the group most affected by this new enlightenment sweeping through China in the 1980s. This was why students led the 1989 democratic movement and dominated it. To the surprise of many Chinese elders, today's 20-year-old college students know more about democratic ideas than their elders. Some student leaders have shown rather impressive skills in the organization of demonstrations and in dealing with the Beijing authority. The order and peace maintained by the demonstrators during the 1989 democratic movement for two months impressed all of China's people. China's people themselves have the ability to manage China's reforms and changes in as peaceful a way as possible. In fact, the Communist aging leaders were panicked by the overwhelming but peaceful demonstrations. In contrast, many young demonstrators remained calm and orderly even when confronted by large assemblies of martial-law troops and their tanks. Most gratifyingly, the great achievement of the ancient Chinese is now partly reflected in and carried forward by the actions of China's educated youths today. Undoubtedly, the continued enlightenment of China's youth will be the best investment for China's future. Most realistically, it will help with China's peaceful evolution.

China's new enlightenment in the 1980s is also indicated by the fact that Communist authority has lost its magic power to move the masses, to command them to do this and that, now and then, as it pleased them. China's masses used to be the playthings of the Beijing authority, but now the people have become a source of nightmares for the authority. Hardly anyone would rush to Tiananmen Square to show blind loyalty to the Communist authority in China today. In Mao's era, the Communist strongmen only needed to stand on the Tiananmen Tower to wave for a few minutes, then tens of millions of people would rush from all corners of China to march in front of them. In Mao's era, the Communist authority had no need to call the 27th Army to the capital to destroy so-called counterrevolutionaries. They could have easily mobilized the Red Guards, the worker-militiamen, and most of the Chinese civilian population to achieve that goal. However, sadly for the Communist ideologues, that age is gone forever. In May 1989 the hunger-striking students in Beijing, not the Communist authority, drew the attention and admiration of Beijing residents and caused thousands of students from distant corners of China to rush to join them in Tiananmen Square. Even numerous overseas Chinese flew to Beijing to show support for the democratic movement.

All these events have opened a new chapter in China's history. China's people have awakened, especially since 1989. The last thing that the Communist authority wanted to happen has happened: the Chinese people want to think for themselves. All Chinese, be they farmers, factory workers, office workers, or teachers, students, and managers, have started to express their thoughts and desires in a way that has never occurred in China's long history. This new determination of China's people to win a better life for themselves will be the strongest force to promote a better alternative for China.

Modern electronic media may help China's people to stop the drift into chaos and anarchy. Previous periods of chaos and anarchy were strengthened and prolonged by ignorance caused by the lack of communications among the people. This situation is improving now. Though the Communist authority still controls all the media and tries desperately to block information from circulating, alternatives to state-controlled forms of communication already exist. The heroic efforts of some members of the news media were most helpful in unifying China's people during the 1989 democratic movement. In addition, many overseas and international media organizations provided urgently needed information to a considerable portion of China. The worst thing for China's people is for them to be completely unaware of events that are taking place within China and in the outside world. All efforts to provide truthful news to China's people will help unify them and thus help to stop the spread of chaos and anarchy. The Communist authority cannot block news completely anymore.

In the economic field, the numerous economic trades and exchanges among China's different regions, and between China and the outside world, will help promote China's peace. These joint ventures have become a new way of life for China, definitely helping to prevent future chaos and anarchy. Numerous joint ventures between China and overseas partners, between the central government and the various regional governments, and between different regional governments have been begun. By the end of the 1980s almost every region had been effected by the proliferation of joint economic ventures. These economic links and exchanges have greatly strengthened ties between various Chinese regions. Chaos and anarchy would endanger these profit-making activities; therefore, all the parties involved in these joint ventures will definitely try to avoid the disruption of mutually beneficial arrangements.

Even since June 1989 new joint ventures have been started. These activities have taken place not only within China, but also with help from overseas. Though China has suffered serious setbacks in her investment opportunities with Western nations due to the 1989 bloodshed, some other overseas channels have been opened up or widened. In particular, especially since the end of 1989, more and more Taiwan Chinese have been very active in making investments on the mainland. This has had an immediate effect on the stability of China. Also, it opens new roads for China's peaceful transition towards a better future.

China is undergoing fundamental changes. A new economic life based on commerce and trade is gaining ground. Maoist rural life is being replaced by urban commercial life. China is becoming much more forward-oriented, dynamic, and progress-minded. All of these achievements occur within a worldwide context, for China has established many new links with the world beyond its borders.

Even millions of officials in the various regions have been putting energy into the new investment activities. After all, nobody can solve the big issues in Chinese society today. A citizen today feels that he should do what he can do to bring immediate benefits to himself and all the parties involved. Despite the power struggles and palace intrigues that are going on in Beijing now, China's people are making the best out of the worst situations. Significantly, other centers of power are in competition competing with Beijing today. Most noticeably, the various provincial and local governments are now a very active force in maintaining China's investment environment. This trend will continue and even grow.

In all regions of China, a wide variety of investment activities are still taking place despite the fact that the doctrinaire central planners have been tightening their control over new economic programs and trying desperately to put China's economic life back into the Communist cage. Indeed, many inland regions' economic activity has risen in the last few years. Also, though the farmers may not fully understand the democratic alternative to the Communist authority, many are participating wholeheartedly in the new economic experiments. Tens of millions of farmers have increased their efforts to enlarge their incomes by renting plots of land, raising special crops to sell in the free markets, and becoming entrepreneurs.

In a sense, even if the split in the Communist party occurs, China's rural population may stand on the sidelines during the resulting struggle. Many farmers, like more educated Chinese people in the urban areas, want to move forward, not backward.

In the political realm, the various government officials would find it advantageous to open more channels to communicate with the people in their regions. The popular democratic movement in 1989 has shown the strength and latent power of the people. Millions of officials were surprised and terribly shaken by the strength of the people. Even those aging Communist ideologues could not recover from the terrible shock they received from the 1989 democratic movement. Countless officials have finally recognized that the people themselves have sufficient power to determine the fate of the Communist government. Since June 1989 more and more officials have started to think seriously about how to truly "serve" the people for the first time in the last four decades. This new mentality in officialdom will strengthen possibilities for national reconciliation and compromise. More and more peaceful channels are beginning to open between the people and the government officials. This trend should continue in the future, especially at the local and regional levels. After all, all local and provincial officials, except those of Chengdu, had no blood on their hands after the events of June 1989.

In opposition to entrenched ideologues, various democratic and noncommunist organizations, underground and public, have started to improve their tactics and strategies to promote peaceful change through dealings with various political authorities in their regions. Although today these actions take place only on a small scale, they may gain strength in the near future.

China has now gained its widest contact with the outside world since 1949. Thousands and thousands of students and scholars have gone abroad for study in foreign nations. This door is still open. In addition, businesspeople, officials, and enterprise directors and managers have traveled to other countries and have gained much information about progress and the realities of dealing with the outside world. This information can be used to show China's people that there may be peaceful solutions to China's problems. The Chinese people now have greater hope of building a better China with their own hands than at any previous time.

All these factors combine to improve chances for bringing about a peaceful transition. In fact, when the Communist party splits and the resulting factional divisions become involved in civil unrest or in a civil war, China's people may well resist being drawn into the chaos. The collapse of the Communist power may lead to civil war, but this civil war may be limited to some regions rather than the whole nation.

Even if the potential warlords start to fight with each other, the civil war may not last long. The faction leaders may not be able to advance their interests as much in war as by other means. They may even engage in peaceful dealings under the table while the war is being fought. In the 1910s and 1920s China sank into a period of complete chaos. Various powerful warlords began to fight one another. However, the civil war was limited in scope and intensity. Dealings under the table were much more intensive than the actual fighting in the battleground. After all, these warlords had two basic goals. On the one hand, the warlords wanted to secure their economic strength. The quickest way to do this was to wage wars to take over the rich agricultural and industrial and trading regions such as the lower Yangtze Valley. On the other hand, each warlord had to maintain his leadership position within the group he controlled. Though the first goal could be achieved through military means, achieving the second goal was more complicated. Indeed, the latter goal required intense political dealings, in the open or otherwise. In fact, a military hero with constant victories on the battleground could still turn out to be a big loser unless he could win at the bargaining table too. Moreover, as is common in Chinese history, those who play political games with the greatest skill can get far ahead even if they are big losers on the battlefields.

Jaing Kaishek was such an example. He won few military victories against his foes and power contenders, but he triumphed overwhelmingly in his under-the-table dealings. Even his military victories were ensured by his political maneuvers. Even his terrible defeats by the Communists did not weaken his supremacy over the Kuomintang in Taiwan. In fact, he was the unchallenged ruler in Taiwan until his death in 1975, and after his death his power was still strong enough to ensure his son's rule in Taiwan.

Of course, both Mao Zedong and Deng Xiaoping have outshone Jiang Kaishek. It is a miracle that Deng Xiaoping is still able to maintain his leadership position within the Communist bureaucracy, despite the June 1989 bloodshed and its terrible consequences for China's political and economic well-being. Within the Communist hierarchy, many secret dealings have been carried out within the walled palaces since June 1989. Outside, the Communist authorities try to make the population at large believe that nothing significant happened in 1989, neither the massive demonstrations in support of the democratic movement, nor the brutal repression carried out by the Communist authority.

Once these things are understood, one can comprehend why European political and economic conflicts have resulted in wars lasting for decades, while similar Chinese conflicts may be resolved within one or two years. Peaceful dealings under the table are a favorite game in Chinese political life.

Unlike the China of the past, today's China possesses many industrial and commercial bases. These have changed the nature of military adventures for the regional powers. Resort to military means may be the least suitable tactic for securing economic strength. Rather, economic growth in a region is the quickest way for making profits. Therefore, future warlords may find themselves more interested in commerce and industry than in war. Thus China may suffer disunity but not a total war for some time to come. China's economy in the warring period of the 1910s and 1920s was not jeopardized as much as imagined in many regions. Rather, in many regions, such as the lower Yangtze Valley, due to the collapse of the burdensome centralized bureaucracy, business and economic activities actually thrived.

The most effective way to avoid the impending chaos is to foster the emerging unity of all the social and political forces independent of Communist power. These forces include students and intellectuals, individual businessmen, the productive enterprises, and the provincial and local governments. In particular, provincial and local governments may become a positive force in China's unity and peace in the future. At this point, it is not yet clear how soon and in what manner this emerging unity might happen. Once this happens, however, China's future will no longer be determined by palace politics. The unification of these forces would enable China to embrace a bright alternative.

Now, the Chinese people realize that they must take back the power they surrendered to the Communist authority several decades ago. They need to learn to depend on themselves to make a happy life a reality. The 1989 democratic movement in China showed the determination of the people. One of the great achievements of the 1989 democratic movement was its call for the unity of the people. It also isolated and identified China's biggest obstacle: the Communist authority.

Finally, China has become a true member of the international community. China's engagement with the outside world had reached a historical point by 1990. The international community will not want to see China suffer chaos and anarchy. This issue will be addressed in the next two sections.

The survival of the Chinese people through the chaos of this century and their unquenchable hopes for the future, this author believes, should assure the people of the outside world: China will survive the collapse of the Communist system. China will turn her attention to reconstruction in a way that is most suitable for her culture. The Communist power should be allowed to collapse of its own weight. China has survived countless disasters in the past. The Chinese people have the strength to overcome these current crises and stand on their own feet again. If China's people can survive the Communist power for forty years, they will certainly survive its disappearance.

Keep China's Door Open to the Outside World

Many people wonder how the bridge of transition will be built between today's China and the China of the future. It is clear that this bridge will have to be built partly by increasing China's engagement with the outside world.

To make a better future for China, independent social, economic, and political forces must grow that are strong enough to challenge Communist rule and thus lead to a new order. Only in this way can a democratic, pluralistic society take root in Chinese soil. All this depends on China being open to the outside world.

China has created wealth, enriched philosophy and the arts, and contributed much to the world's store of science and technology over the course of her long history, but China has never had a pluralistic and democratic society. China's central political authority has been the only real source of social and economic organization in the entire society. The unorganized people could not escape the heavy hand of the vast centralized bureaucracy. Independent social, economic, and political forces were almost completely absent throughout China's long history. To eliminate the conditions for the birth of such independent organizations in China's past was the most important task for China's old rulers. In this way, China's population was made to revolve around a single ruler, who alone would decide all the affairs of the society. The rulers, old and new, always managed to suppress any social forces that could potentially provide checks and balances to the authority. The old rulers could easily achieve this as long as China was kept in isolation and China's people had no way to escape the heavy hand of the bureaucracy.

To protect the ruler's interests, old China gave up her chance to develop a modern industrial-commercial and entrepreneurial society. The Industrial Revolution took place in Europe, not China, despite the fact that China created vast wealth long before Europe did, because China's dynastic rulers succeeded in limiting the growth of independence of the people. The state power had a monopoly on all important commercial activities. The government controlled staple articles such as salt, iron, tea, silk, tobacco, and matches. Intense state control over all the affairs of the whole society prevented the growth of free enterprise and independent social forces. Bureaucratic dealings dominated market dealings.

Under centralized bureaucratic control, businesspeople and intellectuals were forced to deal within the framework of the bureaucratic establishment to advance their interests. The traditional dependence of the educated and the businesspeople on the bureaucracy prevented them from taking part in the modern industrial and commercial revolutions. As a result, a rather backward Europe suddenly blossomed during the Renaissance and rapidly gained the "keys" to open the modern era. The Western nations first built up modern political and economic institutions and thus expanded the sphere of human activities.

The Communist power holders kept China isolated for thirty years. In fact, the Communist dictatorship pushed China's isolation to the extreme. By 1966, at the beginning of the chaotic Cultural Revolution, China had only one ambassador, stationed in Cairo, because all the other ambassadors had been called back home to participate in the Maoist power struggles. By isolating China the Communist authority found a power means to maintain its dictatorship. China's people have had very little power to refuse the servitude that the Communist authority demands. The students could be kicked out of school for any signs of independence. The professors, writers, and artists could be deprived of their jobs, if nothing more, if they advocated any liberal ideas. The entrepreneurs could be forced to close their enterprises if their business made them more independent of the authority. That is the reason why Mao spent his life trying to cut the "tails of capitalism." Under such tight control, China could only be pushed into endless civil chaos as its people fought over its very limited wealth. Expanding the sphere of human activities was the least possible thing in China throughout the Maoist era.

It was precisely due to this isolation that the Communist authority could tell China's people that they were enjoying a "golden age," though Mao's China faced grave shortages of staples. That was why the Communist authority found it so essential to isolate China from the rest of the world in order to maintain its supremacy. This isolation deprived the Chinese people of knowledge and of experience of the modern world. The evil practices of Communist authority under Mao Zedong for three decades were only possible when China's door was completely shut.

In this reform era, one significant sign of progress is that China's door is open to the world. Though still a narrow opening, it has already created many positive results. In fact, the 1989 democratic movement in China was a direct result of this new openness. It is worth more than ten thousand books for China's people to see and experience directly the progress in modern political and economic institutions that have taken place throughout the world and to realize what they must do to make China into a truly modern society. To understand this point, the Westerner only needs to recall the effect Marco Polo's tales of "golden Cathay" had on the West: his reports of lavish dining, paper money, frequent hot baths using coal as fuel, golden-roofed palaces, etc., stimulated the minds of the Europeans. Tales of China's wonders helped to stimulate the great voyages of discovery in the fifteenth and sixteenth centuries. Columbus was a product of this new European mentality.

The new knowledge of the progress of the outside world is a most powerful inspiration for China's people in their struggle to create a progressive and pluralistic Chinese society. It has added a new dimension to the lives of China's millions. China's people have gained the choice, though still very limited, to live in China or in the outside world, and to pursue other interests than those imposed by the Communist authority. China's productive enterprises have begun to do business with overseas partners. China's intellectuals can communicate with and visit other intellectuals in other countries. China's ambitious and bright students can study at almost any university in the world. All of these developments have accelerated the disintegration of the Communist dictatorship and promoted a movement for a better China.

China now stands on the threshold of great events. Just a

decade of openness has brought very striking changes in the mentality of the Chinese people. The most important result is that now there are multiple choices for the Chinese people. Instead of just seeing Chinese ways of life, the Chinese can now study the whole outside world. The Chinese experience will be enriched by study of other cultures. This new and growing knowledge was a root cause for the 1989 democratic movement in China. In turn, the heroic struggle of China's people for a better life has also inspired the people of the outside world. In particular, peaceful evolution in the Eastern European Communist states has been influenced by the Chinese struggles for progress.

Greater China's engagement with the outside world will be the shortest way for China to become a truly modern society. China has had tremendous experience with the art of compromise at the private level, but she has inadequate democratic experience at the public level. The Chinese people are eager to learn about the democratic and economic institutions of other nations. Greater contact with the outside world will hopefully help China shorten the time she needs to build truly modern political and economic institutions. The new democracy that is beginning in Taiwan was actually influenced by Western democracy. In China, the new enthusiasm for democracy manifested over the last ten years has been stimulated by educated Chinese who have studied abroad. The Communist authority has carried out numerous political campaigns to end China's "pollution" by Western liberal ideas, but these campaigns are doomed to fail.

China's new generations need to seek knowledge of the outside world. China's intellectuals and students can find a unique environment in which to pursue their work when they have the chance to go abroad. In time, China's intellectuals will help to create economy, a new government, and a new social structure for China, with some elements borrowed from Western models. Already, a number of leading intellectuals are living outside mainland China. Most of them have had extensive experiences with China's economy, politics, and social life. Many of them have been directly involved in China's reform. Outside China they will learn new thinking and new theory that will help China enter the modern world.

The growth of a sizable private sector in China will require greater connection with the outside world. The Communist government could easily destroy any such private force before it gains ground in China. But it can't destroy China's new private business with foreign trading partners looking on. Joint business ventures between Chinese and overseas partners are one important reason why China's door cannot be shut.

Taiwan's democratic process has been boosted by the growth of its private business sector. Taiwan's business sector could grow into an important social force because private individuals were allowed to do business directly with Western counterparts. In this way, private businessmen escaped the heavy hand of the Kuomintang authority. The Kuomintang authority could not restrict Taiwan's businessmen for fear of losing the economic benefits they provided. As a result, the private sector has grown into a force strong enough to challenge the Kuomintang dictatorship. Democratic progress in Taiwan since 1987 is a fruit of this tree of openness. A better future for mainland China will depend on similar progress.

China's new entrepreneurs and productive enterprises have been working diligently and have taken dramatic steps to engage the outside world. This trend will continue despite the setback of 1989. In the future, China's new entrepreneurs will become an important engine for China's modernization. In short, future economic development will increasingly turn China, today primarily a society of farmers, into a modern commercial and industrial society, dynamic and progress-oriented. When that happens, the Communist authority, whose monopoly of power is primarily based on rural backwardness and insularity, will have to make itself one equal member among the many in the Chinese society.

A Message for the International Community

Many American friends ask what America should do to help China. Without hesitation I say the best service Americans and other friends in the world can render China is this: have more contacts with China's people, culturally, economically, and socially.

Today's world faces a decisive turning point. Ongoing worldwide reform movements may direct our world toward peace and progress in all corners of the globe. The sphere of human activities can be extended beyond anything yet imagined. Conversely, the failure of these reform movements may cause the Four Horsemen of the Apocalypse to strike around the globe. Should the latter happen, the sphere of human life will be reduced to such a degree that the population explosion and modern military technology, among other grave dangers, will cast a gigantic shadow of terror over mankind. Today's extraordinary circumstances demand extraordinary thinking and action. The "China Question" must be placed in a global context.

What things must the world community do to make this world more peaceful to live in? Let us ask ourselves what kind of world we would like to live in ten or twenty years ahead. We may then work backward and, hopefully, find out what we need to do now to produce such a world.

No countries can be left isolated in this world. Eastern Europe, the Soviet Union, the Middle East, South Africa, and Latin America cannot be left in isolation, nor can China. This world is already too small to leave any nation isolated—especially China, with almost a quarter of the world's population. Modern technology, the global economic structure, world ecology, and modern military capability will not allow countries to retreat into isolation. The peoples in this world must share this planet together, its natural and human resources, its historical developments, and all the other things that make up this world. Indeed, even cutting some trees down in one corner of the world may have serious effects on the peoples at the other corners ten thousand miles away. Therefore, we feel that it is dangerous to international peace and progress when some countries use China or the Soviet Union or any other nation as a "card" to play with in the international "game" of diplomacy. The people of the world must demand that those card lovers stop playing games.

It is most important to understand that the worldwide reform movement did not stem from the so-called cold war. Rather, it was directly due to increasing exchanges on a global scale. The "cold war" only caused confusion and tension regionally and globally. The extraordinary challenges facing our world demand new skills in dealing with such global challenges. In short, our understanding and arts must increase at least in the same proportion as the increased challenges facing the world in general and China in particular. It is my view that the current debate on the China issue in America and in many other countries is very helpful as well as necessary. It offers an ample opportunity for the people of the world to examine the basic needs of the world: who we are, how long it has taken us to reach this stage of history, and what kind of world we prefer to live in ahead. In this way, we may hope to create better living conditions for all the people on this planet.

To promote a peaceful transition in China, I believe that greater economic, social, and political exchanges between China and the outside world must continue and even accelerate. Such exchanges will also help the world move in a positive direction toward peace and progress. The isolation of China during Mao's era was the biggest obstacle to China's progress. Now, I feel that the isolationist policies of the present Beijing authority may slow, but cannot block, peaceful evolution in China.

China stands at a decisive crossroad and must choose the path that will lead to a better society. More bridges must be built to promote such a peaceful transition. The outside world has the capacity to create a significant portion of the bridge China needs to become an equal partner in the international community.

It is my view that the further isolation of China will only hurt her journey to progress. The Beijing authority has retreated into semi-isolation from the outside world since the June 1989 killings. Its brutal actions were condemned by all save a few Communist dictators such as the Romania's Ceausescu and the East Germany's Erich Honecker. These dictators are now dead or in prison. Many liberal, democratic nations have taken various actions to protest the Beijing leadership's brutal repression of the democracy movement.

But China's continued peaceful evolution must also include the present Beijing authority. The outside world may help to prevent further mistakes by the Beijing leadership. China's new isolation may push the Beijing leadership in the direction of taking actions against its own people. The stormy end of the Eastern European Communist dictatorships, and especially the bloody end of Ceausescu's regime, have shown the Beijing hard-line leaders what their fate could be. These men could try to use greater terror and violence to try to escape a Ceausescu-like end. If this mentality persists, blood will soak the streets of China again. In this way, China will rush into greater anarchy and violence.

China's peaceful evolution depends on the continued reform. At this stage, nobody within China can stop it completely. Greater contact with the international community will help China's continuing reform, and promote a peaceful transition toward a better future.

The "open door" policy of Deng's reform has offered much information to China's people about progress outside China. This progress, in turn, offers inspiration to Hu Yaobang, Zhao Ziyang, and millions of cadres to seek greater reform in China. This information also inspires the Chinese people in general. Knowledge of the outside world will promote positive changes within the Communist party. In particular, it will help China to move in the direction of reconciliation and compromise at the national level. Only through increased compromise and reconciliation can China resolve her transitional crisis in a peaceful manner.

It could be very damaging to focus only on the end of Communist domination in China. The end of the Communist authority would not necessarily give birth to a better China. A better China will have to come from the gradual rise and development of numerous independent social, economic, and political forces. To promote the growth of these independent forces is to promote a more progressive and open China.

Many people believe that the international community has much to contribute to China's reform movement. Foreign powers have already taken many positive steps to aid the Chinese people.

In my opinion, Richard Nixon's trip to Beijing in the fall of 1989 was a good thing. He achieved a positive result by letting the Beijing leadership know what the world thought about the June 1989 brutal crackdown: no country wanted to be friends with Deng and the other leaders. This result alone would have made Mr. Nixon's trip a worthy one. Mr. Nixon himself was even reluctant to shake hands with Li Peng in front of the camera. Nixon carried an impressive message about the reaction of the world community to the brutal crackdown. It is much more effective when such messages are conveyed by proven friends of the Beijing leadership such as Richard Nixon.

I am very pleased by the world's new understanding of China. More and more people have realized that there are two Chinas, as a *New York Times* editorial article, "Don't Punish the Wrong China" (April 27, 1990), indicated. One is the Maoist, peasant-based, rural China. This Maoist China is backward and stubborn, but is losing ground rapidly to the other China, a new China that is urban, progress-minded, and dynamic. It is this new China that increasingly wants to engage the outside world. This new China has made gigantic progress during the 1980s. The 1989 democratic movement represented a showdown between this new China and the Maoist China. In this showdown the forces of the new China were defeated by the forces of Maoist China, but there will be other battles: the new China *will* eventually overcome the old China.

If the international community understands the significance of the two Chinas, it can help to promote the atmosphere of reconciliation and coexistence within China that China needs to move forward into a prosperous democratic future. The world nations do have sufficient means and skills to accomplish this. In short, the opening of China's door to the world must be ensured.

Close contacts and direct dialogues between Beijing and other capitals of the world should continue and increase. Of course, this does not mean that the leaders of other nations should make concessions to the Beijing authority that is responsible for the bloody crackdown on the democratic movement. On the contrary, the leaders of the outside world should make the Beijing leaders know the depth of world anger and outrage over the bloody repression. It is our belief that many leaders in the world have the wisdom as well as the skills to achieve these goals. Also, more direct contacts between Chinese and people of other nations should be most helpful. In particular, the local and provincial officials in China must have more direct contact with the outside world so that they are prepared to share more responsibility in China's future.

More business activities are absolutely necessary between China and the rest of the world. We welcome the latest effort of the international business community to create joint ventures with their Chinese counterparts. Closer relations between China and world markets will make China's transition to a market economy more smooth and peaceful. I feel that increased business activities at the level of enterprises and institutions are very desirable for all parties involved.

More social, cultural, and educational exchanges are worth pursuing. Educators, community leaders, union officials, and students from the outside world are welcome to visit China. Wider educational and cultural programs for Chinese students and intellectuals are the most direct method for the rapid training of the leaders of the future China. During the 1980s overseas Chinese students and scholars have become an active force outside China to promote the Chinese reforms. Intelligent Chinese appreciate the fact that more foreign institutions are working to expand educational opportunities for mainland Chinese. After all, there is no better way for China and the outside world to work together in the promotion of world wealth and peace than to know one another and to understand the richness that such contacts can bring to the lives of each participating nation.

New Opportunities and Society's Choices

China's reform in the 1980s created many new opportunities for Chinese society as a whole. What political and economic systems the future China embraces will depend upon these new elements. The present author believes that most of these opportunities have never shown up previously in China's history. It is my view that China may already possess enough strength to depart decisively from its historical pattern of chaos, dictatorship, and a return to disintegration. China's new elements demand a new form of society. This final section is devoted to a brief discussion of these new elements.

Ring out the old "rich help poor" practices; ring in the new "mutual collaboration and fair competition" practices. First of all, Chinese society faces a new economic environment. The traditional economic foundation of China's powerful autocratic government rests upon the so-called "rich help poor" policy: the central government can freely take away money and material, among other things, from the rich regions, without any compensation, and grant them to the poor regions, without future payback. The Communist authority adopted this tradition. In Mao's era, about half of China's provinces needed and received aid from Beijing. Economic dependent on the central government had been a decisive factor in China's political unity throughout history. The central government has always used its powers to redistribute wealth to maintain its supremacy over the provincial powers, especially the poorer regions.

However, in the 1980s, this situation changed dramatically. The central government began to experience grave economic trouble. It could no longer increase its aid to the poor regions. Indeed, in the last few years, the Beijing government has tried desperately to reduce its loads of this kind.

Keen observation of China's economic order reveals that the foundation of China's unity has changed over this period. In fact, the practice of transferring "free" aid from the rich regions to the poor regions no longer dominates Chinese society. New practices based on mutual and direct trade and exchanges among the various regions have come into being.

Over the course of the 1980s, the inland provinces, especially the northwestern regions, have no longer called for help in the form of "free" economic aid from the rich eastern provinces, especially the coastal regions. The central government has stopped the old practice of transferring food, money, and materials from the rich regions to the poor regions. Things have turned the other way around. The coastal provinces have tried every means to exploit the cheap raw materials and relatively cheap labor available in the inland regions. Also, the poor regions have successfully managed to become equal business partners with the coastal regions.

Meanwhile, the prospering coastal regions have tried to reduce their money contribution to the central government. These regions have found methods, sound or otherwise, to transfer less money to Beijing. They have also tried various means to attract more investment to their regions from all around in China. The rich city of Shanghai provides an instructive example. Shanghai had handed over to the central government as much as $20 billion yuan annually prior to the reform. But by the 1980s the annual amount had declined to no more than $10.5 billion yuan, about half of the old contribution.[1] If one takes into consideration the high inflation of recent years, Shanghai's contributions have been far less. From the consumption point of view, Shanghai spent only 17 percent of its income within Shanghai, but this figure climbed above 80 percent in 1987.[2] In short, today's Shanghai makes a much smaller contribution to the other regions in China.

In addition, due to the "open door" policy in this reform era, China has gradually entered world markets. This engagement with the outside world has changed the dynamics of Chinese society. The rich coastal provinces and the poor inland regions have enjoyed many new opportunities. The coastal provinces have attracted huge investments from all over the world and have witnessed dramatic growth in their local enterprises. Although growth in the inland provinces has been less dramatic, they have also gained many benefits from the new economic situation.

Over the decade of the 1980s, and especially since 1984, the inland provinces have developed many locally owned factories and other productive enterprises. These inland provinces have attracted attention from the international markets. These inland provinces have used their resources, specifically abundant raw materials and cheap labor, to trade with the coastal provinces. These mutual and direct exchanges between the coastal regions and the inland provinces have greatly increased the wealth of all the regions.

In reality, the biggest benefit the inland provinces have received from the central government is the abolition of numerous restrictions and regulations formerly enforced by the Beijing government. In fact, these regulations and restrictions imposed by the central government had been the biggest obstacle for the development of the inland regions' economy. Every human being can become rich and prosperous unless he is kept in a cage. The Beijing government put the inland people in a tight cage for thirty years. Since the reform, the people in the inland regions have escaped this cage. Therefore, it is no surprise to us that they have made impressive progress in just a few years.

The economic foundation of China's unity based on the "rich help poor" practice is no longer in existence. The new practices based on mutual dealings and competitions among China's various regions are gaining strength and becoming a new way of national life. This represents remarkable progress for China. This new economic environment demands that China's people redesign their country's political structure for the benefit of China's unity and progress. After the collapse of the present system, it will be difficult to establish another autocratic government centered on the economic "cage."

A failing bureaucratic body demands a new type of administration. The political foundation of China's traditional autocratic government rests upon a highly centralized bureaucratic system. In reality, the Communist government has been unable to create any kind of new political form. Rather, it has pushed China's highly centralized bureaucratic tradition to the extreme. Over the last few years, however, this centralized bureaucratic system has declined nearly to the point of collapse. Millions of cadres and officials are tired of the problems associated with the Communist hierarchy. These cadres are among the new social forces favoring an end to the present system. This is a strikingly new phenomenon.

China's centralized bureaucratic system is now confronted by deadly foes within the system itself. Inner conflicts have become so explosive that they might destroy the Communist authority itself. The Communist bureaucratic system in China has evolved directly from more than 2,000 years of imperial tradition in China. As noted earlier, the essential feature of this system is that all the bureaucrats are directly appointed by the ruler in the high court. The Son of Heaven represents the highest interest of the nation. All of the officials are treated as servants of the Son of Heaven. They receive wages from the high court, and whatever they do is done for the interest of the Son of Heaven. This has become the standard moral criterion for judging officials. The Communist leaders have pushed this tradition to the extreme. But, the Communist leaders, like all the old rulers, have to suffer the pains that attend this system.

The essential trouble with this system is that the high court cannot handle all affairs effectively by itself and eventually must allow the lower officials to have some decision-making power. Decentralization must be sanctioned from the top leadership. But, when the bureaucrats, especially those at the lower levels, expand their power, the central government has less power left for itself.

Every bureaucratic organization, at either the high or low level, tends to become an independent interest group involved in the endless conflicts within the system. Although the lower officeholders have to be appointed by the higher bureaucrats, the higher-ranking bureaucrats have to rely on the decisions made by the lower bureaucrats to make ends meet. In the Communist political system there are no clearly defined rules or regulations to follow. Each bureaucrat has to rely on administrative regulations imposed from the top down. Over the years since 1949, old dynastic regulations have been replaced by Communist party directives. These directives usually have a red letterhead. The lower bureaucrats fondly refer to them as the "Redhead Directives." But this redhead business is hardly workable, especially in the last few years. This system offers tremendous headaches to all the higher bureaucrats all the way up to men like Mao Zedong and Deng Xiaoping. When the higher bureaucrats do not have good relations with the lower bureaucrats, their directives will be buried under a mountain of other directives. Now, a common practice of millions of officials is this: when the lower officials receive a particular directive they do not wish to follow, they search for the dozens of other, earlier directives that contradict it. Every office contains hundreds and hundreds of directives piled up, so it is easy to find contradicting ones. In today's China, hardly anyone can make the bureaucratic system work. Starting from the party chief and the premier downward to the productive enterprise branch cadre, director, manager — everyone has bitter experiences with the lower bureaucrats who handle the details.

In the last few years, bureaucratic matters have gotten completely out of hand. As a common rule, since the Communist central authority controls appointments to lower office, it therefore hopes to make the lower bureaucrats loyal and obedient. But this is no longer the case. New officials bow to the central leadership, but they may suddenly stop bowing after they secure office. Once the lower officials step into their office, they turn their backs on the top bosses. Today every office has become a temple with a special god to serve. Higher officials have to smile often, make big promises, and try hard to please the lower officials in order to get anything done. As a result, the officials in each bureaucratic establishment become both the spokesmen and defenders of that particular unit. Many harbor bitter feelings for the top bosses. Very often, the lower bureaucrats make tough demands on their superiors. But the higher-ranking bureaucrats have to be soft with their inferiors. Even when the lower ranks are lazy and do not finish assigned tasks, the higher bureaucrats must excuse the lower bureaucrats' poor performance. Nobody loses a penny for bad performance. After all, the higher bureaucrats must always try to make more friends instead of more enemies. The higher bureaucrats have to stand on the layers of lower bureaucrats in order to climb up even higher and faster.

Such troubles as these with the centralized bureaucracy are very negative and even disastrous. Countless great opportunities for the Chinese people are lost as a result of this system. China's wealth cannot stretch far enough under this rigid system. In fact, under this failing Communist system, Communist China cannot gain even a fraction of the glory achieved in the old China by the Han, Tang, and Song dynasties. The Communist authority cannot accomplish as much as the Manchu government did regarding prosperity, and has failed to create a dynamic, progressive, modern China.

However, let us give the Communist bureaucracy its due. Sometimes, the Communist system may accidentally work in favor of the people, contrary to the intention of the central authority. For example, in the 1980s, numerous political campaigns against liberal ideas were largely defeated by millions of "lazy" officials. Also, millions of hardworking officials finally got "tired" of dealing with China's farmers, so now the farmers can make rapid progress in the traditional way as small independent cultivators. Numerous student leaders, badly "wanted" by the Beijing authority after June 1989, have successfully escaped the Communist iron hands and gone overseas with the indifference of many bureaucrats among others.

The Communist system has little strength left to resolve its many inner conflicts. One may even wonder if Mao Zedong and Deng Xiaoping had to start their careers again, would they favor the same centralized bureaucratic system that caused them so many difficulties? After more than 2,000 years of endless inner troubles with this centralized system, more and more people, especially the bureaucrats, are ready for something different.

Possible bridges to a better China. China's new political and economic system will have to come in large measure from new economic and political elements. These elements will involve changes of historical proportions that nobody can ignore. China's future will be determined by a combination of old as well as new elements. Since the economic foundation for another autocratic government based on "rich help poor" practice is no longer in existence, such policies can hardly be instituted again. A new economic foundation has to be found to satisfy all sectors and all regions of the society in order to achieve China's unity and progress. Also, since everyone is tired of the centralized bureaucracy, a new political structure has to be formed — otherwise, there will be only chaos.

Democracy has become a new inspiration for the Chinese people. Democracy will provide new directions for China. China's intellectuals and students have performed diligently in the last few years to make democracy popular in the minds of the people. This trend will continue despite the horrible setback of June 1989. In fact, democracy as a possible alternative for China's future has never had so much popularity.

Actually, as a result of reform, the Communist central authority has much less power in its hands. The Beijing politicians have no real choice except to acknowledge and accept China's new reality.

However, the biggest problem facing the Chinese people is to find good bridges to carry them over from the present China to a hopefully better future China. Even if democracy has become a popular inspiration for China's people, it remains no small task to find appropriate institutions and social structures to implement it. After all, democracy is an abstract concept; each nation has to depend on its own culture, traditions, and social structures to devise workable democratic institutions. In particular, social and political forces must be found that can make democracy happen. What are the forces for democracy in China?

In reality, the local and provincial governments have become an important force for democratic change in today's China. China's peaceful evolution will demand a greater role by the existing local and provincial governments. With the total collapse of the Communist power, there is no other organization strong enough and well-organized enough to maintain order, except, perhaps, for the existing local and provincial governments. Moreover, the local and provincial governments are the governments the people have contact with, even though they have only played the role of agents for the Beijing government and the Communist party for the last 40-some years.

The provincial and local officials have been playing an increasingly important role in the democracy movement. Local and provincial governments adopted different methods than the central government to handle the 1989 democratic movement. Only the local officials in Chengdu reacted in the same way as the central government in Beijing and employed violent repression. All other provincial and local officials in several dozen cities avoided bloody repression. Many local officials achieved and managed to maintain stability in their own areas.

In this era of reform, the local and provincial governments have become a relatively independent and extremely significant economic and political force in moving China toward a better future. Reform progress has been tied to the performance of the local and provincial governments. The local and provincial officials have gained the experience as well as the desire for more independence and authority. This assertion of independence is bound to grow. Millions of provincial and local officials are more interested now in being responsible for the people living in their regions.

Many people clearly see that two forces exist in direct confrontation, the youthful Chinese versus the aging Communist ideologues. Only a few people see other forces that will be important, especially the provincial and local governments, despite the fact that the latter is growing rapidly. This growing provincial and local power also stands in direct confrontation with the Beijing authority. In fact, the local officials are among many coalescing political forces that demand the end of the Beijing autocratic power. China's future will not be determined by palace politics. One should not be surprised if the local and provincial governments rise up to put an end to the existing system. This is what has happened throughout China's history. Today's situation certainly has many similarities with situations from the past.

The future China could move in one of two directions. One is the classical pattern: increasing local power will end the autocratic government and, at the same time, bring China into chaos and disunity. The latest example is what happened with the collapse of the

Manchu government in 1911 and the warlord period that soon followed. The second direction would be something completely new: China may embrace a new government structure, federation. That is, China's political power will be distributed throughout all regions instead of concentrated in Beijing. In particular, China's unity will become federal in character based on regional consent and agreement. China's realities now show that China may turn in this new direction.

This fresh opportunity will soon be presented to China's people in some way or another. The growth in the provincial and local powers could produce a unified China under a federal government. Under a new Chinese republic, each province would manage its own affairs. Would federation help China positively? How should one view this new trend? To answer these questions, we must widen our view.

Dictatorship has rested comfortably on the government's autocratic structure throughout China's history. A powerful autocratic government controls all affairs of the society, but also suffers all the troubles under the sun. When it cannot handle these troubles anymore, unified China is thrown into the state of chaos and disintegration. When one dynasty collapsed, rarely did a complete new government take its place. Usually no other force was powerful enough and organized enough to take over. When the peasants rose in revolt, the rebels could easily chop off the emperor's head, but they did not have the intelligence, training, or wisdom to solve society's problems. The deadly cycle of unity and disintegration in Chinese history is founded on this contradiction: it is far easier to destroy the old than to construct the new. The living Chinese of today can still feel the pain of the ancient poet:

Rise!
You Majestic Dynasty.
Yet How Miserable Are the People!

Fall!
You Pitiful Dynasty.
Yet How Miserable Are the People!

Ending the centralized political system in China is the only way for Chinese society to escape the cycle of unity followed by disunity and civil war. China needs a federal system based on local and provincial powers. Today, all provinces would like to be part of the

Chinese union, but each of them must have its own way. No province wants to be dominated by the Beijing authority. Therefore, the only way to maintain China's future unity is to let the people in each region manage their own affairs and follow their chosen ways.

A Chinese federation is a new concept to China's people. Whether it would be "good" or "bad" is unclear to most Chinese. To Americans, living under a federal system is now taken for granted since this system has been in existence for more than 200 years. Both New York and California want to be part of the American union, though each of these states has its own ways and manages its own affairs independent of Washington. However, it is highly unnatural to the Chinese mind to think about a Chinese federal union. China has never had a federation or anything close to it. A weak central power has always meant chaos and even civil war. Deeply rooted in the Chinese mind is the idea that peace is equivalent to a powerful autocratic government, and that civil war is the result of a weak central government. This traditional belief doomed parliamentary government before it had a chance to take root following the collapse of the autocratic Manchu government in 1911.

The main obstacle to a workable federation in China is really this: are the people ready for self-government? Are the people ready to refuse to have their life managed by god-rulers such as Jiang Kaishek, Mao Zedong, and Deng Xiaoping?

The Chinese people have been searching for an institution where the people's rights can be guaranteed for more than 100 years. They have failed to get anything of this kind. Instead they ended up with a Communist dictatorship whose great power would shock China's old rulers. This fate befell the Chinese people because they were not willing to turn away from tradition and destroy the overextended central government. Since the fall of the Manchus, tens of millions of people have died while China has searched for a wise and powerful leader who can head a powerful yet benevolent government. But strongmen such as Jiang Kaishek, Mao Zedong, and Deng Xiaoping have repeatedly destroyed these popular dreams.

As long as the autocratic central government has all power in its grip, China's people will have few rights for themselves and China's unity will be under constant challenge. If the people want to eliminate the dictators, they must not allow power to be concentrated in the hands of a few individuals. Creating a federation will be a very positive step toward creating a liberal and progressive

China. A federation will also help ultimately to bring about a democratic China.

Really, the whole matter boils down to the ability of the local and provincial governments to manage their own affairs in their own way. Future events in China may still repeat the old formula. Even though the central power will have neither the strength to control nor the prestige to command, the provincial and local governments may let the central government continue to rule until it totally collapses. China will eventually fall into the hands of another Jiang Kaishek, another Mao Zedong, another Deng Xiaoping.

A still vivid example of this kind occurred with the Manchu government. The Taiping Rebels were about to end the Manchu government in the 1850s, but the various provincial and local powers decided to support continuation of the Manchu government. Powerful local armies were organized and financed by the gentry powers. These armies soon destroyed the Taiping Rebellion and restored Manchu authority in 1864. It would take several decades longer for the provincial powers to finally realize the need to overthrow the Manchu authority in order to confront China's twin evils of internal chaos and foreign exploitation. But the goal of the reformers was no more than to replace the Manchu government with a new, more powerful and effective centralized government. China could not depart from her traditional pattern and establish modern political institutions. Following the collapse of the Manchu government in 1911, many intellectuals wanted to establish a parliamentary government. But the Chinese people were not ready for it. Very soon, the concept of a parliamentary system was lost in the midst of civil war and the anti–Japanese war. Now, the Chinese people set on the old course of looking for a strong and powerful government. This was the very foundation for the rise of both the Kuomintang and the Communist party. In essence, China's passion for a godlike leader and a strong central government actually smoothed the way for the misrule of the Communist party during the past four decades.

Underlying the passionate search for an infallible leader and his perfect government is a popular mellow mentality in the Chinese people. This mellow mentality manifests itself in several ways. On the one hand, the Chinese people are more accustomed to believing in the government than in believing in themselves. The people want the government to make rain and sunshine. The people strongly feel that they need to live under an absolute authority or they would not be able to enjoy a single peaceful day. The people have lost their independent spirit and self-determination. Today, such weaknesses remain strong. Even in the 1989 democratic movement, many people demanded only two things. They asked the leaders to try to understand the life of the ordinary people. They asked for the right to speak freely. So far, in the minds of most people in China, this is what democracy is all about. This kind of popular desire is acutely in line with the Confucian tradition. The majority of the people do not understand that China urgently needs to establish modern political and economic institutions in order to create a democratic, progressive, and pluralistic modern China.

Despite the June 1989 massacre, some people in China continue to place their faith for a new future in some new leader, who would enter the capital from some distant province to turn the repressive tide around.

Due to these reasons, establishing a working democracy in China will be very difficult. Chinese culture is strikingly persistent throughout the centuries. The Chinese are a proud people who have had great past glories, but who now are deeply ashamed because they have fallen behind so many other countries in the modern world. They have insufficient experience with democracy. But China may be one step away from a federation. All is ready for a completely new and progressive China, except the merry wind. This merry wind is the independent spirit and great self-determination of the Chinese people.

China's democracy has to start from the grassroots. The various organizations, interest groups, and local assemblies have to be built up from the local level. The people need to learn gradually how to enjoy their rights and freedom in a coherent and harmonious society. Only in this way can a democratic national life become effective and win the support of all sectors of society. There is no shortcut to a working democracy. Through this slow process, the people can gain confidence in their ability to change things for the better.

Finally, mainland China's reunion with Taiwan, Hong Kong, and Macao will be much more credible and realistic under a federal system. The present panic in Hong Kong is caused by the lack of a federal alternative.

Federation will help China's unity. In reality, there are gigantic differences between mainland China and Taiwan, Hong Kong, and Macao. The mainland remains controlled by a powerful autocratic government. But very impressive democratic progress has been made in Taiwan, Hong Kong, and Macao. Also, the people who live on those island outposts of Chinese culture enjoy well-established private property laws. It would be very difficult to put all these new people together under one centralized government. After all, how can the same law be made for all the regions and all the people to follow? But without such a law, how would China be united? Indeed, such a law will not be possible under the centralized power system in force today. A uniform and commanding law can only be produced by the consent of all the independent divisions and people from all regions of China. To create a federation is to make sure that the people of all the regions decide matters based on their own interests. Only in this way is a stable and unified society possible. Only in this way can people from different regions live in harmony. In short, a federal system is definitely a realistic path leading to China's unity and peace.

The Chinese people in Taiwan, Hong Kong, and Macao want to continue to develop in their own chosen directions. No external forces can possibly stop the democratic and market forces in these regions. Also, it is highly beneficial for some of China's regions to advance ahead of other regions and point the way. China needs new ideas, more choices, more kinds of experiences. After all, China's ultimate goal is a pluralistic and progressive society that retains those unique cultural attributes the West has identified with Cathay since the days of Marco Polo, when the empire at the center of the earth was already several thousand years old.

Notes for Chapter 6

1. *Liberation Daily*, April 1988.
2. *Shanghai Statistical Book*, 1988.

WHO'S WHO

Chen Yun (1905–   ). Second most powerful Communist in this reform era and chief opponent of Deng's decentralization-based reform. He is the most important central planner and leads the hard-line Communist group. He insists on Communist political supremacy; at the same time, he stresses that this political supremacy must be guaranteed by economic monopoly. He was victimized during the Maoist Cultural Revolution and rose to power again during the reform era.

Deng Xiaoping (1904–   ). The principal Communist leader in this reform era. He was the second most significant purge target during the Maoist Cultural Revolution. He is the leader in transforming Mao's class struggle into this reform direction. He favors allowing more market elements in the Communist economy, and giving more power to the provincial and local governments and even enterprises. He has won over the hard-line central planners. However, he insists on maintaining Communist political supremacy. For his reform leadership, Deng has been named Man of the Year by *Time* magazine twice since 1978. He betrayed his great reform in 1989 and masterminded the June 1989 repression of the democratic movement.

The Gang of Four. Four Maoists whose power peaked during the Cultural Revolution. The four are Mao's third wife, Jiang Qing (1915–   ), two Maoist propagandists, Zhang Chunqiao (1918–   ) and Yao Wenyuan (1931–   ), and a Red Guard, Wang Huanwen (1935–   ). Wang was Mao's third designated heir. The Gang of Four were Mao's instruments for carrying out his power struggles during the Cultural Revolution. All four were put in prison after a palace coup within a month of Mao's death. Three have since been sentenced by Deng's administration to life imprisonment; Wang received 20 years imprisonment. The four still live in prison today.

Hu Yaobang (1915–89). A reform-minded leader in the 1980s, Deng's first designated heir, and the general secretary of the Communist party from 1981 to 1987. He gradually departed from Deng's ideas and became a liberal reformer. He was purged in early 1987. His death in April 1989 triggered the 1989 democratic movement in China.

Hua Guofeng (1920–   ). Mao's fourth and final designated heir. A provincial cadre for several decades until the early 1970s when he was called

201

to Beijing to become the boss of the secret police. By Mao's arrangement, he became the Communist leader immediately following Mao's death and continued to pursue Maoist policies. He was finally ousted in 1981 by Deng Xiaoping's administration.

Jiang Kaishek (1887–1975). The first generation Kuomintang strongman. He was the bitterest enemy of the Communist party for several decades. Defeated by the Communists in 1949, he was forced to retreat to Taiwan. He died in 1975, one year before Mao. His eldest son, Jiang Jingkuo, became his successor, and led the reform of the Kuomintang in the 1980s.

Jiang Zemin (1926–). Deng's third designated heir. A provincial bureaucrat, he was the party boss in Shanghai in the 1980s. He has revealed no clear line in politics. In May 1989, amidst the democratic demonstrations, he was suddenly called to Beijing to take up his current post. In Communist newspapers, his name is usually listed first, even before Deng Xiaoping.

Li Peng (1928–). A member of Chen Yun's doctrinaire group. He replaced Chao Ziyang as the premier in 1988 and announced martial law in 1989. He has had a close connection with the first generation Communist politicians since his childhood and reportedly was brought up by Zhou Enlai.

Li Tenghui (1923–). A third generation Kuomintang leader in Taiwan; current president of Taiwan. Educated in both Taiwan and the U.S., he holds a Ph.D. from Cornell University.

Lin Biao (1906–71). A leading Red Army general since the 1930s. Mao's number one aide in the Red Army from 1959 until his violent death in 1971. Defense minister from 1959 until his death. He was Mao's second official heir. He was an important instrument for Mao's class struggle during the Cultural Revolution. His plot to overthrow and replace Mao was discovered. The official version of his death is that he was killed in his airplane as he attempted to flee to Moscow.

Liu Shaoqi (1898–1969). Mao's leading, highly loyal aide from 1939 to the late 1950s. He was the first Communist leader to forcefully promote Mao's cult of personality, and he was Mao's first designated heir. He departed from Mao's class struggle line in the late 1950s and thereafter led the "revisionist camp." He was the state head from 1959 until his death in prison in 1969. He was the number one purge target during the Cultural Revolution.

Mao Zedong (1983–1976). First generation leader of the Communist party. Born in Hunan, of peasant origin, he became the de facto leader of the Communist party in the late 1930s and held the chairmanship of the Communist party until his death. He ruled Communist China from 1949 until his death in 1976.

Peng Dehuai (1898–1974). A leading Red Army general and chief commander of the Red Army in Korea. Defense minister in the 1950s. He had been the number one Communist critic of Mao's Great Leap Forward program. For that criticism, he was purged by Mao and met a bad death during the Cultural Revolution.

Zhao Ziyang (1919–   ). A reform-minded leader. Deng's second designated heir in the reform age. He has been a chief executive of the current reform. His sympathy with the 1989 democracy movement got him in trouble with the Communist authority. He was ousted in June 1989.

Zhou Enlai (1898–1976). Mao's most loyal and most powerful aide from the 1940s on. He was premier from 1949 until his death in 1976. He was known as a highly skilled peacemaker, a moderate, and a diligent Communist bureaucrat. He played an indispensable role in maintaining Communist unity, especially during the Cultural Revolution. He called for the four modernization programs for Communist China in his final years. His death triggered a massive movement in April 1976 against Mao's regime that was immediately crushed by Maoist militiamen.

OUTLINE OF
CHINESE DYNASTIES

1. **Pre-Imperial Age** (?–221 B.C.)
   Shang (?–11th century B.C.)
   Zhou (11th century–256 B.C.)
   Age of Confucius (Approximately 6th–5th centuries B.C.)
   Age of the Legalists (Approximately 4th–3rd centuries B.C.)

2. **First Imperial Unification** (221 B.C.–A.D. 220)
   Qin (221–207 B.C.)
   Han (206 B.C.–A.D. 220)

3. **Prolonged Disunity** (A.D. 220–589)
   Chaos and babaric invasion in northern China.
   Age of Six Dynasties in southern China.

4. **Second Imperial Unification** (A.D. 589–907)
   Sui (589–618)
   Tang (618–907)

5. **A Short Disunity** (A.D. 907–960)
   Period of the Five Dynasties and the Ten States

6. **A Weak Imperial Unification** (A.D. 960–1279)
   Song (960–1279)

7. **The Mongol Interlude** (A.D. 1279–1368)
   Yuan (1279–1368)

8. **Last Imperial Unification** (A.D. 1368–1911)
   Ming (1368–1644)
   Ching (1644–1911)

9. **Modern Age** (A.D. 1911–   )
   Republic of China (1912–49)
   People's Republic of China (1949–   )

BIBLIOGRAPHY

This bibliography is divided into eight parts. Most of it consists of books and journal articles in Chinese. It is neither a suggested reading list nor a complete listing of current literature on the subject.

1. Periodicals and Newspapers

Beijing University Journal for Philosophy and Social Science
Central Daily (Taipei)
Cheng Ming Magazine (Hong Kong)
China: Development and Reform (Beijing)
China Spring Magazine (New York)
China Statistical Year (Beijing)
China Times Weekly (Washington, D.C.)
China Tribune Biweekly (Taipei)
China's Agricultural Economy (Beijing)
Chinese Economic Studies: A Journal in Translations (New York: M. E. Sharpe)
Chinese Youth Daily (Beijing)
Christian Science Monitor (Boston)
Commonwealth Magazine (Taipei)
Contemporary Magazine (Taipei)
Dong Xiang Monthly Magazine (Hong Kong)
Economic Management Magazine (Beijing)
Economic Research (Beijing)
Guangming Ribao (Beijing)
Intellectual Magazine (New York)
Journalist Weekly (Taipei)
Liberation Daily (Shanghai)
Ming Pao Monthly (Hong Kong)
Nai Bai Ji Magazine (Hong Kong)
Nan Bai Ji Magazine (Hong Kong)
New York Times
Newsweek (New York)
Nineties Monthly Journal (Hong Kong)

Outlook Weekly, overseas edition (Beijing)
People's Daily (Beijing)
Philosophical Studies (Beijing)
Planned Economy (Beijing)
The Quest Monthly (New York)
Shanghai Economic Research
Social Science (Shanghai)
Studies on Chinese Communism (Taipei)
Tide Monthly (New York)
Time (New York)
Wall Street Journal
Wenhui Bao (Shanghai)
Wide Angle Monthly (Hong Kong)
World Economic Herald Weekly (Shanghai)
World Journal, daily (New York)

2. Books by Communist Leaders

Chen Yun. *Selected Works of Chen Yun, 1926–1949*. Beijing: People's Press, 1984.
————. *Selected Works of Chen Yun, 1956–1985*. Beijing: People's Press, 1986.
Deng Xiaoping. *Fundamental Issues in China, 1982–87*. Beijing: Foreign Language Press, 1987.
————. *Selected Works of Deng Xiaoping, 1975–1982*. Beijing: People's Press, 1983.
————. *Selected Works of Deng Xiaoping, 1938–1965*. Beijing: People's Press, 1989.
Documents of the Chinese Communist 9th National Congress. Beijing: People's Press, 1969.
Documents of the Chinese Communist 10th National Congress. Beijing: People's Press, 1973.
Documents of the Chinese Communist 11th National Congress. Beijing: People's Press, 1977.
Documents of the Chinese Communist 12th National Congress. Beijing: People's Press, 1982.
Documents of the 13th Chinese Communist Party National Congress. Beijing: People's Press, 1987.
Documents Since the "12th Party Congress." Edited by the Chinese Communist Party's Document Research Office. Beijing: People's Press, 1986.
Documents Since the "13th Plenum of the 11th Party Congress." Edited by the Chinese Communist Party's Document Research Office. Beijing: People's Press, 1981.
Jiang Zemin. "A Speech Given at the 40th Anniversary Celebration of the People's Republic of China." *People's Daily*, September 30, 1989.
Lin Biao. *Selected Works of Lin Biao*. Edited by China Problems Research Center. Hong Kong: Chih Luen Press, 1970.

Liu Shaoqi. *Selected Works of Liu Shaoqi.* Beijing: Foreign Language Press, 1981.

_____. *Selected Works of Liu Shaoqi.* Beijing: People's Press, 1981.

Mao Zedong. *Additions to Mao Zedong's Selected Works.* Edited by Ting Wang. Hong Kong: Ming Pao Press, 1971.

_____. *Quotations from Chairman Mao Tze-Tung.* Beijing: Red East Press, 1967.

_____. *The Secret Speeches of Chairman Mao: From the Hundred Flowers to the Great Leap Forward.* Edited by Roderick MacFarquhar, Timothy Cheek, and Eugene Wu. Council on East Asian Studies / Harvard University Press, 1989.

_____. *Selected Works of Mao Zedong.* 5 vols. Beijing: People's Press, 1951–77.

_____. *Selected Works of Mao Zedong.* 5 vols. Peking: Foreign Languages Press, 1965–1977. English translation.

Peng Dehuai. *Autobiography of Peng Dehuai.* Beijing: People's Press, 1981.

_____. *A Special Collection on Peng Dehuai: 3rd Volume of the Material Collections of the Chinese Communist Cultural Revolution.* 2d ed. Edited by Ting Wong. Hong Kong: Ming Pao Monthly Press, 1979.

Zhou Enlai. *Selected Works of Zhou Enlai.* 2 vols. Beijing: People's Press, 1981 and 1984.

_____. *A Selection of Zhou Enlai.* 3 vols. Edited by the Study Group of Chinese Communism. Hong Kong: Yishan Book Co., 1976.

_____. *Selections by Zhou Enlai on the United Front.* Beijing: People's Press, 1984.

3. Official and Semiofficial Versions of the Lives of the Communist Leaders

Chairman Hua Is Our Great Leader: Hunan People Recall the Glorious Revolutionary Experiences of Chairman Hua. People's Press and Hunan People's Press, 1977.

Huang Shenxou and others. *Chairman Hua's Footsteps.* Hunan: Hunan People's Press, 1977.

In Memory of Chairman Mao. Beijing: People's Literature Press, 1977.

In Memory of Comrade Peng Dehuai. Hunan: Hunan People's Press, 1979.

People's Literature Editorial Board and People's Literature Press. *To Remember Our Beloved Premier Zhou.* Beijing: People's Literature Press, 1977.

People's Press Editors. *Chairman Hua Is Closely Linked to the Hearts of Hundreds of Millions of People.* Beijing: People's Press, 1976.

_____. *Comrade Liu Shaoqi Will Live Forever.* Beijing: People's Press, 1980.

_____. *Complete Revelation and Condemnation of the Sky-Filled Crimes of the Gang of Four—A Selection of Newspaper and Magazine Articles.* Beijing: People's Press, 1977.

_____. *Saluting Songs to Chairman Hua.* Beijing: People's Press, 1977.

Qu Zhong and Xing Zhi, eds. *The Life of Deng Xiaoping and Studies on His Thoughts.* Beijing: Chinese Communist Archive Press, 1988. (Contains an extensive bibliography of studies on Deng.)

Qun Zhong Press Editors. *The Judgment of History.* Beijing: Qun Zhong Press, 1981. (Reports of the trial of the Gang of Four and Lin Biao's followers.)

Writing Team of the Communist Party's Hunan Branch. *On the Great Role of the Proletarian Leadership.* Beijing: People's Press, 1977.

Yao Feng. "How Comrade Zhao Ziyang Weakens the Party's Ideological and Political Tasks." *Guangming Ribao,* August 25, 1989.

You Cuhuang and others. *The Historical Development of Mao Zedong's Thoughts.* Beijing: Red Flag Press, 1987.

4. Economic Titles

Anhui Province's Statistical Bureau. *Forty Years of Anhui: 1949–1989.* China Statistics Press, 1990.

Aslund, Anders. *Gorbachev's Struggle for Economic Reform.* Ithaca, N.Y.: Cornell University Press, 1989.

Center for Agriculture Policies of the Agriculture Ministry and Study Group for Economic Growth Problems of the Rural Development Institute, CASS. "Reform and Establish a Land System." *Economic Daily,* January 30, 1988.

Center for Rural Policy Study. "Questionnaires for Ten Thousand Farmers." *People's Daily,* April 12, 1988.

Chao, Kang. *Man and Land in Chinese History: An Economic Analysis.* Stanford: Stanford University Press, 1986.

Chen Guoheng. "On the Dual Constrained Enterprise's Management System." *Economic Research* 11 (1987).

Chen Shenshen. "China's Economic Mechanisms and Comments on the Policies of Zhao Ziyang and Li Peng." *China Times Weekly,* July 1, 1989.

_____. "On China's Property Ownership Revolution." *World Economic Herald,* October 24, 1988.

_____. "On Establishing the Market Order in Today's China." *World Economic Herald,* July 18–August 8, 1988. This article also appears in *China: Reform and Development* 9 (1988).

_____. "On the Evolution of China's Investment System and Its Impact upon the Open Policy," *Social Sciences* 10 (1987).

_____. "Overall Proposition of Opening Further Shanghai's Economy." *Social Sciences* 1 (1987).

_____. "Price Reform in China." *Chinese Economic Studies: A Journal in Translations* (Spring 1989).

_____. "Reviews and Trends of the Investment Reform in China." *Chinese Intellectuals* 3 (1987).

Chen Tong and Jiang Xiaoxuan. "An Analysis of the Shortage of Funds in State-Owned Industrial Enterprises." *Economic Research* 12 (1987).

Chen Xiwen. "The Rural Economy in China Is Transferring from Supra-conventional Growth to Conventional Growth." *Economic Research* 12 (1987).

Comprehensive Study Group of the Development Research Institute. "Farmers, Markets, and New Systems." *Economic Research* 1 (1987).

Dai Yuanchen. "Dual Prices in the Transformation of the Model of the Economic System." *Economic Research* 1 (1986).

Deng Huansong. "On the Duality of Price Subsidies and Ways of Reforming Them." *Economic Research* 10 (1981).

Du Haiyan. "The Contracted System: An Initial Choice in Reforming the State Enterprise System." *Economic Research* 10 (1987).

_____ and others. "Autonomous Rights of State-Owned Enterprises, Market Structure and Incentive Systems – Investigation of 403 State Enterprises." *Economic Research* 1 (1990).

Economic Research Institute of CASS. *The Development of China's Township and Rural Enterprises and Economic System.* Beijing: China's Economy Press, 1987.

Fang Xiaoqiu. *China's Economic Reform and Development of the Special Zones.* Beijing: Economic Science Press, 1988.

Gao Shangquan and others. *Contemporary China's Economic Reform.* Beijing: China's Press for Social Science, 1984. (Contemporary China Book Series.)

General Team for Agriculture Research of the National Statistical Bureau. *Studies on the Incomes of Chinese Farmers.* Shanxi: Shanxi People's Press, 1987.

Group of Macro-Economy Management of the CASS Institute. "Insist on the Direction of Moderate Decentralization and Rebuild the State's Management Pattern." *Economic Research* 6 (1987).

_____. "Rebuilding the Pattern of Main Body of Investment and Cultivating the Financial-Industrial Bloc – More on the Reform of China's Investment System." *Economic Research* 12 (1987).

Gu Shutang and others. *Studies of the Reform of China's Planning System.* Beijing: China's Press for Social Science, 1986.

Guan Mengjue. *Comrade Chen Yun's Economic Thoughts.* Shanghai: Knowledge Press, 1984.

Guangdong Economic Association. *A Study of Guangdong's Economic Reform.* Guangzhou: Zhongshan University Press, 1986.

Han Zhigua. "On the Law-Based Property Ownership System." *Guangming Ribao*, November 11, 1987.

He Wei. "Law of Development of Socialist Public Ownership." *Economic Research* 9 (1986).

Hebai Province's Statistical Bureau. *Forty Years of Hebai: 1949–1989.* China Statistics Press, 1990.

Hu Ruyin. "On the Reasons for Shortage." *Economic Research* 7 (1987).

Hua Sheng. "The Crisis of China's Agriculture." *The Quest* 5 and 6 (1990).

Huang Qinghe, Wang Chengde, and He Daofeng. "Rural-Industrial

Relations in China's Economic Development." *World Economic Herald*, January 11, 1988.

Hunan Province's Statistical Bureau. *Ten Years of Reform in Hunan* (1978–1988). China's Statistics Press, 1988.

Institute of Reform of the Economic System in China. "Change and Choice of Social Environment in China's Economic Reform." *Economic Research* 12 (1987).

Li Hanli. "On Historical Evolution and Reasonable Disposition Toward the Plan Adjustment and the Market Adjustment." *Economic Research* 2 (1990).

Li Jiapeng. "All-Round Contract with Household: An Advance in the Change of Production Relation." *Economic Research* 11 (1983).

Li Yang. "Economic Analysis of Enterprise Subsidy." *Economic Research* 1 (1990).

Li Zhongfeng. *Introduction to China's Economic Reform*. Beijing: Economic Science Press, 1988.

Liang Zhiren and Chen Wenhong. *Chen Yun's Economic Theories*. Hong Kong: Cerd Consultants, 1985.

Lin Jian. "Search for the Model of Rural Development in China." *Economic Research* 8 (1987).

Lin Shuiyuan. "The Theory of Socialist Ownership: Its Change and Development in Practice." *Economic Research* 6 (1987).

Lin Wenyi and Jia Lurang. "On the Law of Supply and Demand and Its Role in Socialist Economy." *Economic Research* 1 (1981).

Liu Suinian and Wu Qungan, eds. *The National Economy during the Period of "Cultural Revolution"* (1966–1976). Heilongjiang People's Press, 1986.

_____. *The National Economy in the First Five Year Plan Period*. Heilongjiang People's Press, 1986.

_____. *The National Economy in the Great Leap and Adjustment Period*. Heilongjiang People's Press, 1986.

_____. *The National Economy in the Period of Recovery*. Heilongjiang People's Press, 1986.

Luo Shouchu and Pan Zhenmin. "On the Enterprise's Goal." *Economic Research* 3 (1987).

Ma Hong, ed. *Dictionary of Contemporary China's Economic Events*. Beijing: China's Press for Social Sciences, 1982.

Peng Min and others, eds. *Contemporary China's Fundamental Constructions*. 2 vols. Beijing: China's Press for Social Science, 1989. (Contemporary China Book Series.)

Qiu Honghui. "The Economic Crisis of Communist China." *Studies on Chinese Communism* 23, no. 7 (1989).

Riskin, Carl. *China's Political Economy*. Oxford: Oxford University Press, 1987.

Shanxi Province's Statistical Bureau. *Forty Years of Shanxi: 1949–1989*. China Statistics Press, 1990.

Shenzhen Party Branch. *Shenzhen in Progress*. Beijing: Red Flag Press, 1984.

Shi Zhengfu. "Transformation of Industrial Organizations and

Reformation of Property Rights Institution." *Economic Research* 10 (1987).

Study Group for Economic Construction and Reform." *Reflections on Economic Construction and Economic Reform in Recent Years." Economic Research* 3 (1987).

Study Group for Price Reform of CASS. "Price: Problems and Thinking for Further Reform." *Economic Research* 4 (1987).

Tan Huozhao. *Shenzhen's Economic Realities.* Shenzhen: He Tien Press, 1987.

Tian Yuan and others, eds. *The Transfer of Ownership of Productive Enterprises.* Beijing: Economic Daily Press, 1988.

Wan Yinien. *Where Will China's Economy Turn To?* Hong Kong: Sang Wu Publishing House, 1989.

Wang Dawei. "The Troublesome Loads in China's Economy." *Ming Pao Monthly,* June 1990.

Wang Jiuying. "A Short Comment on Reasons for the Unequal Distribution System in Our Country." *Guangming Ribao,* October 15, 1988.

Wang Jiye and Chu Yuanzhen, eds. *Dictionary of Economic Reform.* Beijing: Economic Daily Press, 1987.

Wang Jue. "Further Advances in Mao Zedong's Thought about Socialist Economic Construction – Understanding the Selected Works of Deng Xiaoping." *Economic Research* 11 (1983).

Wang Sibin. "Changing Relations in Rural Economic Life." *Beijing University Journal for Philosophy and Social Science* 3 (1987).

Wang Songpei. "Persist in the Principle of Seeking Truth from Facts, Promote China's Socialist Agriculture – Understanding Selected Works of Deng Xiaoping." *Economic Research* 9 (1983).

Wang Xiaochun. "On State-Guided Prices." *Economic Research* 10 (1987).

Wen Zhenfu and Chen Chibo. "On the Deep Reform of China's Grain Purchasing System." *Economic Reform* 10 (1987).

Wu Renhong. "Economic Development and the Transformation of Industrial Structure – On the Current Developing Stage of China's Economy and Its Mission." *Economic Research* 10 (1987).

Xie Ping. "Features of China's Inflation." *Economic Theory and Management* 5 (1988).

Xue Muqiao. "Adjust National Economy, Promote Overall Economy." *Economic Research* 2 (1981).

————. "Evolution of China's Ownership of the Means of Production." *Economic Research* 2 (1987.)

Yan Ruizhen and others. "The Current Situation, Developing Trends, and Countermeasures toward China's Price Scissors in the Exchange of Industrial Products for Agricultural Products." *Economic Research* 2 (1990).

Yang Jianbai and others. *The Contemporary Chinese Economy.* Beijing: China's Press for Social Sciences, 1987. (Contemporary China Book Series.)

Yang Rongshen. "Give Earnest Play to the Fundamental Role of China's Agriculture – Understanding Comrade Chen Yun's Economic Works." *Economic Research* 9 (1983).

Ye Zhenpeng. "Public Finance and Price Reform." *Economic Research* 1 (1986).

Yuan Enzhen and Gu Guangqing. "A Few Thoughts on Economic Reform." *Shanghai Economic Research* 4 (1987).

Zhang Lin. "A Summary of the Discussion on China's Agricultural Development Strategy in Recent Years." *Economic Research* 9 (1983).

Zhang Ping. "On Combining a Planned Economy with Market Adjustment and Perfecting the Regulative Mechanisms of the Macro-Economy." *Economic Research* 2 (1990).

Zhang Zhongfa and Cong Anni. "On Raising Funds to Develop China's Agriculture." *Economic Research* 1 (1990).

Zhao Pengwen and others. *China's Socialist Construction.* Jilin: Jilin University Press, 1985.

Zhao Renwei. "The Dual System Problem in China's Economic Reform." *Economic Research* 9 (1986).

Zhou Xiaochuan and Feng Ailing. "Avoid Repeated Circulation, Making Real Progress of Reform." *Economic Research* 5 (1987).

Zou Shulin. "Six Contradictions Facing the Deepening Agriculture Reform." *China's Agricultural Economy* 5 (1988).

Zu Jianlong. *Studies on the Problems of Property Ownership in Chinese Socialism.* Beijing: People's Press, 1985.

Zuo Mu. "Problems on the Reform of China's Ownership Structure." *Economic Research* 1 (1986).

_____. "On the Goals and Foundations of China's Economic System." *Economic Research* 1 (1990).

5. Titles on 1989 Events in China and Beyond

CCP Central Committee for Discipline Inspection. *The True Face of Fang Lizhi.* Beijing: Law Press, 1989.

Chang Tianyu. "The Crisis of Elderly Politics." *Wide Angle Monthly,* July 1989.

Chen Tianquan. "The Forty Days of the 'Beijing Student Union' — A Shining but Short History." *Ming Pao Monthly,* July 1989.

_____. What Did Mainland China's Newsmedia Do for the Democratic Movement?" *Ming Pao Monthly,* July 1989.

Chen Yizhi. "The Tiananmen Event and the Inner Struggles of the Communist Top Leadership." *Tide Monthly,* June 15, 1990.

Cheng Shi. "The Inner Story of the Rise of Jiang Zemin and the Future Perspective." *Wide Angle Monthly,* July 1989.

Chuan Desai. "The Changing Policies of China's Overseas Studies." *Ming Pao Monthly,* May 1990.

Han Shanbi. *The Wounds of History.* Hong Kong: East and West Culture Co., 1989.

Hong Kong's Sixty-Six Journalists. *People Will Never Forget — Facts about the 1989 Democratic Movement.* Hong Kong: Hong Kong Journalist Association, 1989.

Hu Ping. "On the Future Perspective of the Chinese Communist Leadership Power Struggles." *China Spring* 77 (1989).

Huan Guocang. "Political Exiles and the Overseas Democratic Movement." *China Times Weekly*, November 18–24, 1989.

Jin Zhao. "History Will Remember Them — The Traces of a Few Individuals Involved in the June 4 Event." *China Spring* 6 (1990).

Li Guoqiang and others. *An Analysis on Jiang Zemin.* Hong Kong: Wide Angle Press, 1989.

Li Jianseng. "The Trouble-Making 'Elite' Yan Jiaqi." *People's Daily*, August 3, 1989.

Li Yi. "Return to Face Some Fundamental Questions: A Visit with Chinese Intellectual Su Wei." *Nineties Monthly* 11 (1989).

Luo Bing. "One Year Anniversary of the 'Disturbances' of June 4." *Chengming*, June 1990.

Mao Li. "The Fire in the Hometown of Deng-Li-Yang—1989 Democratic Movement in Chengdu." *China Times Weekly* 275 (1990).

Nineties Monthly Journal editors. "The Intellectual Circle's Views on the 40 Years." *Nineties Monthly Journal*, October 1989.

Pang Pang and others. *Blood Dropping in Beijing—From the Death of Hu Yaobang to the Tiananmen Tragedy.* Taipei: Fengyun Shidai Press, 1989.

Qian Xian. "The Old Brand Trouble-Making Woman 'Elite' Ge Yang." *Guangming Ribao*, October 14, 1989.

Ren Mianfu. "Interviews in Beijing: The Views of People from All Walks of Life on the 1989 Democratic Movement." *China Spring*, June and August 1990.

Ren Zuoren. "Qin Benli and the 'World Economic Herald.' *Cheng Ming*, June 1990.

Shan Haizhi. "A Short Analysis of the Seven Changes in the 'Communist Successors.'" *Cheng Ming*, October 1989.

Su Zhaozhi and Su Xiaoming. "Tanks Can Not Crush the Spread of Democratic Ideas—A Study of Mainland China's 1989 Democratic Movement." *Tide Monthly* 38–40 (1990).

Tan Xia. "Seventy-One Years of History and the Reflections of Four Generations—From May 4th to June 4th." *China Spring*, July 1990.

Xing Tian and Yi Ye. *Two Tiananmen Events.* Hong Kong: Sky River Publishing Co., 1989.

Yang Du and others. "Special Report: From the Tiananmen Event to the Signature Movement." *China Times Weekly* April 8–14, 1989.

Yang Wenyi and others, eds. *The Shocking 71 Days—The Student Movement, Chaos, and Rebellion.* Sichuan: Sichuan People's Press, 1989.

Ye Tai. "The Effects of the 'Tiananmen Event' on Chinese Communist China." *Studies on Chinese Communism* 23, no. 7 (1989).

Yu Guanghua. "Forty Years of Troubles and Disasters." *Cheng Ming*, October 1989.

Zhang Jiefeng and others. *Blood-Soaked Democratic Flowers—Student Movement, Democratic Movement, and National Movement.* Hong Kong: Pai Shing Cultural Enterprise, 1989.

Zhang Xing. "Touring Mainland China — Home Visit Group's Report on the Overseas Chinese Student Economic Association in America." *China Times Weekly,* June 9–22, 1990.

Zhao Zhennan. "The Troublesome Xingjiang — Reflections of 80 Years." *Ming Pao Monthly,* June 1990.

Zhen Yan. "A Trouble-Making 'Salon.'" *People's Daily,* July 25, 1989.

Zhen Zhuyuan. "The Economic Consequences of the Communist Bloodshed in Tiananmen." *Ming Pao Monthly,* July 1989.

————. "Upon the Chinese Communist Fifth Central Meeting: See Its Economic Lines and Tremendous Troubles." *China Times Weekly,* November 18–24, 1989.

6. Taiwan, Hong Kong, and Macao

Chen Kuo, ed. "The Reform of the Kuomintang and Democracy in Taiwan: A Discussion." *China Tribune* 346 (1990).

————. "The Reform of the Democratic Progressive Party and Democracy in Taiwan: A Discussion." *China Tribune* 346 (1990).

Cheng, Joseph. *Hong Kong in Transition.* New York: Oxford University Press, 1987.

Domes, Jurgen, and Yuming Shaw, eds. *Hong Kong: A Chinese and International Concern.* Boulder, Colo.: Westview Press, 1988.

Fei Chengkang. *Four Hundred Years of Macao.* Shanghai: Shanghai People's Press, 1988.

Feng Jiajie. "The 'Hot Waves of Visiting Mainland China' Are Touching the Democratic Progressive Party." *China Times Weekly,* June 9–15, 1990.

Guangdong Province's Social Science Planning Group and Information Institute, ed. *A Collection of Views on "One Country, Two Systems" (1979–86).* 2 vols. Guangdong Province's Social Science Planning Group and Information Institute, 1987.

Ho Jiaju. "The Shock from Wang Yongjian: No Need to Worry about the Conditions and Timing of Investment in the Mainland." *China Tribune* 346 (1990).

Huang Hongzao. *A History of Macao.* Hong Kong: Shang Wu Publishing House, 1987.

Huang Shumin. "Beijing in Bloodshed, Hong Kong in Turmoil: Where Does Taiwan Stand?" *Ming Pao Monthly,* July 1989.

Li Da. *One Country, Two Systems, and Taiwan.* Hong Kong: Wide Angle Press, 1987.

Li Yi. *Hong Kong's Future and Chinese Politics.* Hong Kong: Zhen Shan Cultural Enterprise Co., 1985.

Li Yingming. "The Two Chinese Sides Are Doubling Their Contacts." *China Times Weekly,* June 16–22, 1990.

Lin Jianshan. "The Shock from Wang, Yongjian: Conditions and Timing of Investment on the Mainland." *China Tribune* 346 (1990).

Liu Wei. *History of Dealings over the Sovereignty of Hong Kong.* 2 vols. Hong Kong: Wide Angle Press, 1983.

Peng Huaishi. *Forty Years of Political Transition in Taiwan.* Taipei: Independent Evening News Press, 1987.

Taiwan Province's Archive Committee. *History of Taiwan.* Taipei: Zhong Wei Book Co., 1977.

Wong Xuewen, ed. *A Comparison of Two Systems on the Two Sides of the Taiwan Seas.* Taipei: International Research Center of the National Politics University, 1987.

Yuan Bangjian and Yuan Guixiu. *A History of Macao.* Hong Kong: Zhong Liu Press, 1988.

7. Studies of the Communist and Kuomintang Leaders

Bachman, David. *Chen Yun and the Chinese Political System.* Berkeley: University of California Press, 1985.

Chen Yujin. *A Study of Deng Xiaoping's Thoughts on Promoting New Talents.* Beijing: Liberation Army Press, 1988.

China Shi Pao Editors. *Inner Stories of Deng Xiaoping's Rerise.* Taipei: Shi Pao Cultural Enterprise, 1977.

Fang Chun-kuei, ed. *A Special Collection of Materials on Liu Shaoqi.* Taipei: Institute for Studies of Chinese Communist Problems, 1970.

Fang Xuecun. *Hu Yaobang and Chinese Communist Politics.* Taipei: Overseas Students Press, 1984.

Fen Xuancheng and others. *Studies and Discussions on Mao Zedong's Thoughts.* Shanghai: Shanghai Academy for Social Science Press, 1989.

Gao Yun, ed. *Hu Yaobang's Last Ten Years on China's Political Stage.* Beijing: China's Culture and History Press, 1989.

Han Shanbi. *A Critical Biography of Jiang Jingkuo.* Taipei: Tien Yuan Press, 1988.

Hollingworth, Clare. *Mao and the Men against Him.* London: Jonathan Cape, 1985.

Hong Ming. *The Jiang Dynasty.* Hong Kong: Zhong Yuan Press, 1986.

Huang Dazhi. *Rising Stars in the Chinese Communist Party.* Hong Kong: Po Wen Book Co., 1981.

————. *A Critical Biography of Peng De Huai.* Hong Kong: Po Wen Book Co., 1980.

Jiangxi Academy for Social Sciences. *A Preliminary Study of Deng Xiaoping's Thoughts.* Jiangxi: Jiangxi People's Press, 1985.

Li Ao. *Studies of Jiang Kaishek.* Taipei: Li Ao Publishing Co., 1986.

Li Dongfang. *A Chronicle of His Majesty Jiang Kaishek.* Taipei: Lian Jin Publishing Co., 1976.

Li Tien-Min. *Biography of Lin Biao.* Hong Kong: Ming Pao Monthly, 1978.

Lin Qingshan. *Biography of Lin Biao.* 2 vols. Beijing: Knowledge Press, 1988.

————. *Ten Years of Dramatic Scenes and Deng Xiaoping.* Beijing: Liberation Army Press, 1989.

Liu Xingzhang, ed. *Hu Yaobang.* Beijing: Zhong Wai Cultural Press, 1989.

Luo Bing. "Deng Xiaoping and Chen Yun Allowed Zhao Ziyang Not to Stand a Trial." *Cheng Ming*, October 1989.

_____. "A New Phase of Power Struggles." *Cheng Ming*, May 1987.

_____. "The Secret Stories of the Summer Palace Meeting." *Cheng Ming*, September 1987.

Ma Yuqing and Zhang Wanlu. *In Memory of the Ten Year Anniversary of Mao Zedong's Death — The Growing Path of Mao Zedong*. Shaanxi: Shaanxi People's Press, 1986.

Nan Xinzhou. *The Life of Zhou Enlai*. Beijing: China Youth Press, 1987.

Ren Baijian. "The Inner Stories of the Chinese Communist Campaign against the Five Gentlemen." *Cheng Ming*, September 1987.

Schram, Stuart. *Mao Tse-tung*. Harmondsworth, England: Penguin, 1966.

Song Ping. *Life of Jiang Kaishek*. Jilin: Jilin People's Press, 1987.

Su Yanzhong, ed. *The Late Years of Mao Zedong*. Beijing: Chun Qiu Press, 1989.

Sze Ma Ba-Ping. *The Gang of Four*. Hong Kong: Culture Book House. 1978.

Terrill, Ross. *The White-Boned Demon. A Biography of Madame Mao Zedong*. London: Henemann, 1984.

Ting Wang. *Biographies of Wang Hung-Wen and Chang Chun-Chiao*. Hong Kong: Ming Pao Monthly Press, 1977.

_____. *Biographies of Yao Wan Yung and Mao Yuan Hsin*. Hong Kong: Ming Pao Monthly Press, 1979.

_____. *Hua Kuo-Feng, Chi Teng-Kuai, and a New Generation*. Ming Pao Monthly Press, 1977.

Xu Ce. *A Biography of Li Tenghui*. Taipei: Tian Yuan Press, 1988.

Xu Guanshan and He Junren. *Liu Shaoqi and Liu Shaoqi's Line*. Hong Kong: Chung Tao Publication Company, 1980.

Yang Zhongmei. *A Critical Biography of Hu Yaobang*. Hong Kong: Ben Ma Press, 1989.

Ye Yonglie. *The Rise and Fall of Wang Hongwen*. Chongchun: Contemporary Literature and Arts Press, 1989.

_____. *Yao Pengzhi and Yao Wenyuan*. Hong Kong: South China Press, 1989.

Zhao Wei. *The Biography of Zhao Ziyang*. Translated into English by Chen Shi-Bin. Hong Kong: Educational & Cultural Press, 1989.

Zhen Binnai. *Mao Zedong and Jiang Qing*. Taipei: Dong Zha Press, 1988.

Zhi Ping. *Mao Yuanxin, Chen Baida and Four Giants*. Hong Kong: Ke Hua Book Co., 1982.

Zhou Xun and others. *Deng Xiaoping*. Hong Kong: Wide Angle Press, 1978.

8. Other Titles

Benton, Gregor, ed. *Wild Lilies, Poisonous Weeds: Dissident Voices from People's Republic of China*. London: Pluto Press, 1982.

Braudel, Fernand. *Civilization and Capitalism, 15th–18th Century*. 3 vols. Translated by Sian Reynolds. New York: Harper & Row, 1982.

Chen An. "The Roads to China's Democracy." *The Quest Monthly* 5 (1990).

Chen, Jerome. *China and the West*. London: Hutchinson, 1979.

Chen Wenhong. "The Crisis of Inflation Has Ignited the Power Succession in the Chinese Communist Party — Economic and Political Situations on the Eve of the 17th Party Congress." *Ming Pao Monthly*, October 1987.

Chen Yi. "How the Chinese Communist Party Rules Tibet." *Ming Pao Monthly*, January 1990.

Chen Zhifang, ed. *China Stops Here to Reflect: A Record of Cultural Revolution, 1966–76.* Sichuan: Sichuan Literature and Arts Press, 1989.

Chronological Table of Major Events in Chinese Communist Party History. Beijing: People's Press, 1987.

Chu, T'ung-tsü. *Local Government in China under the Ch'ing.* Cambridge: Harvard University Press, 1962.

Dai Qing. Chu Anping and the Party's Domination." *Min Pao Monthly,* January 1989.

_____. *Liang Shumin, Chu Anping, and Wang Shiwei.* Jiangsu: Jiangsu Literature and Arts Press, 1989.

_____. "Wang Shiwei and the 'Wild Lilies.'" *Min Pao Monthly,* May and June 1988.

Fairbank, John King. *The United States and China.* 4th ed. Cambridge: Harvard University Press, 1983.

Fang Lizhi. *After Saluting My Master — Fang Lizhi's Selection of His Articles.* Singapore: World Scientific Publishing Co., 1988.

Fei Xiaotong. *Small Towns in China.* Beijing: New World Press, 1986.

Goldman, Merle. *China's Intellectuals: Advise and Dissent.* Cambridge: Harvard University Press, 1981.

Gu Zhibin. "Questions on the Nature of China's Reform: A Visit with Chen Shenshen." *Hai Nei Wai* 65 (1989).

Guangdong People's Press Editors. *Firmly Counterattack the Rightist Attacks.* Guangdong People's Press, 1957.

Harding, Harry, ed. *China's Foreign Relations in the 1980s.* New Haven: Yale University Press, 1984.

Hinton, William. *Fanshen.* New York: Random House, 1983.

_____. *Fanshen: A Documentary of Revolution in a Chinese Village.* New York: Vintage, 1966.

Ho Ping-Ti. *The Ladder of Success in Imperial China.* New York: John Wiley and Sons, 1964.

Ho Xianjie. *Life of Yuan Shikai.* Henan: Henan People's Press, 1982.

Hong Chuanjing. "How to Help Reform Walk Out of the Trap: Report from a Beijing Reform Conference." *Wide Angle Monthly,* May 1989.

Huang Jilu and others. *Mr. Sun Yatsen and the Xing Hai Revolution.* 3 vols. Taipei: Center for Historical Collections of ROP, 1981.

Huang, Ray. *China: A Macro History.* New York and London: M. E. Sharpe, 1988.

_____. *1587, A Year of No Significance: Ming Dynasty in Decline.* New Haven: Yale University Press, 1981.

Jen Yunwen. *The Taiping Revolutionary Movement.* New Haven: Yale University Press, 1973.

Jin Chunming. *An Analysis of "Cultural Revolution."* Shanghai: Shanghai People's Press, 1985.

_____ and others. *Ten Lectures on the Complete Negation of "Cultural Revolution."* Beijing: Liberation Army Press, 1985.

Lam, Willy Wo-Lap. *The Era of Zhao Ziyang: Power Struggle in China, 1986–88* (In English) Hong Kong: A. B. Books & Stationery, 1989.

"Law Consultation" Editors. *Records of Ten Years' Shocking Cases of Injustice.* Beijing: Qun Zhong Press, 1986.

Li Honglin. *Science Vs. Superstition.* Tianjin: Tianjin People's Press, 1980.

Li Jiequan. "Three-Feet Deep Ice Must Come from a Long Way — From the Activities of Beijing's Cultural Circles to the Student Movement." *Ming Pao Monthly,* July 1987.

Li Rui. *Promoting a New Generation.* Hunan: Hunan People's Press, 1985.

Li Shengping and Zhang Mingpeng. *1976–1986: Chronicle of Ten Years of Political Events.* Beijing: Guangming Ribao Press, 1988.

Liang Heng and Judith Shapiro. *Son of the Revolution.* London: Chatto and Windus, 1983.

Liang Shumin. *Best Scholarly Writings of Liang Shumin.* Beijing: Beijing Normal University Press, 1988.

Liming Editors. *How the Chinese Communist Party Treats Intellectuals: A Collection of Original Materials.* 3 vols. Taiwan: Liming Cultural Enterprise Co., 1983.

Lin Yu-Sheng. *The Crisis of Chinese Consciousness: Radical Antitraditionalism in the May Fourth Era.* Madison, Wis.: University of Wisconsin Press, 1979.

Lin Yutang. *My Country and My People.* New York: Halcyon House, 1935.

Liu Aiqin. *A Daughter's Remembrance — In Memory of My Father Liu Shaoqi.* Shijiazhoang, Hebai: Hebai People's Press, 1980.

Liu Binyan. *Liu Binyan.* Taipei: Gui Guan Books, 1987.

_____. *A Higher Kind of Loyalty: A Memoir of China's Foremost Journalist.* Translated into English by Zhu Hong. New York: Pantheon Books, 1990.

_____. *A Selection of Liu Binyan's Report Writings.* Beijing: Beijing Press, 1981.

Liu Xiaobo. "Contemporary Chinese Intellectuals Vs. Politics." *Cheng Ming,* April–October issues 1989 and continued in 1990.

Liu Yunzhou. "An Analysis of China's 'Dependent Culture.'" *Hai Nei Wai* 65 (1989).

Lu Keng. *The Dramatic Scenes of Deng Xiaoping's Era.* Hong Kong: Pai Shing Cultural Enterprise, 1988.

Lü Yuan. "Hu Feng and Me." *Hei Nai Wei* 67–68 (1990).

Luo Jicai. *The Wild Waves of the Chinese Communist Rehabilitation Movement.* Taipei: You Shi Cultural Enterprise Co., 1983.

Luo Zi-Ping. *A Generation Lost: China under the Cultural Revolution.* New York: Henry Holt and Company, 1990.

MacFarquhar, Roderick. *The Origins of the Cultural Revolution.* 2 vols. New York: Columbia University Press, 1974 and 1983.

Ming Lei. "The 'Dark Hands' of Democratic Movement Talk on the Chinese Intellectuals — A Visit with the Intellectual Representatives of the 1989 Democratic Movement Wang Runsheng and Zhang Lun." *Cheng Ming* 5 (1990).

Mu Fu. *China in Deng's Times.* Hong Kong: Pioneer Publishers, 1986.

Nathan, Andrew J. *Chinese Democracy.* New York: Alfred A. Knopf, 1985.

Needham, Joseph, and Collaborators. *Science and Civilization in China.* Cambridge, England: Cambridge University Press, 1954.

People's Daily Editors. *The Events of April 5.* Beijing: People's Daily Press, 1980.

People's Press Editors. *Completely Eliminate Counterrevolutionary Activities.* Beijing: People's Press, 1951.

_____. *Materials Concerning the Hu Feng Anti-Party Group.* Beijing: People's Press, 1955.

Pu Yi. *From Emperor to Citizen.* Beijing: Foreign Language Press, 1964, 1965.

Qian Jiaju. "Eighty Years of National Events and Me – Witness to the Four Dynasties." *Ming Pao Monthly,* January 1989.

_____. "Entered the Communist Pirate Boat – Reflections on the People's Political Consultant Conference." *China Times Weekly* 270–72 (1990).

_____. "We Need 'New Enlightenment' to Save China – After the Tiananmen Event, Where Will China Go?" *China Times Weekly,* September 1989.

Schell, Orville. *To Get Rich Is Glorious: China in the Eighties.* New York and Toronto: Pantheon Books/Random House of Canada, 1984.

Schwartz, Benjamin I. *Chinese Communism and the Rise of Mao.* Cambridge: Harvard University Press, 1964.

Shang Xiaoyuan. "The Changing Outlook of the Contemporary Chinese." *Ming Pao Monthly,* May 1988.

Si Maguang. *Lessons of History.* 10 vols. Beijing: Ancient Books Press, 1956.

_____. *Lessons of History (with New Footnotes).* 15 vols. Taipei: Sang Wu Publishing House, 1970.

Snow, Edgar. *The Battle for Asia.* New York: World Publishing Company, 1942.

_____. *The Long Revolution.* London: Hutchinson, 1973.

_____. *Red Star over China.* London: Gollancz, 1937.

Song Shiqi. "The Official Body of Our Nation Has Reached 30 Million." *People's Daily,* September 16, 1989.

Student Association for National Issues at Hong Kong University, eds. *Voice for Reform: A Collection of Articles Contributing to the Liberation of Thoughts.* Hong Kong: Ji Xian Club, 1988.

Su Chaoran and others. *A Concise Dictionary of the Chinese Communist Party's History.* 2 vols. Beijing: Liberation Army Press, 1987.

Su Xiaokang, Luo Shishu, and Chen Zhen. *A Feast of "Utopia" – The Summer of 1959 in Lushan.* Beijing: China News Press, 1988.

Su Zhaozhi and Wang Mianzhou. "Crisis and Thoughts – On Current China's Situation and Next Step Reform." *World Economic Herald,* October 24, 1988.

Tao Zhi. "The Legal System and the Road to a Better Nation." *The Quest Monthly* 6 (1990).

Ting Wang. *The Wall Posters of Li Yizhe.* Hong Kong: Ming Pao Monthly Press, 1976.

Vogel, Ezra F. *One Step Ahead in China: Guangdong under Reform*. Cambridge: Harvard University Press, 1989.

Wang Feixing and others, eds. *The Theories and Practices of the Reform of Political System since the Third Plenum of the 11th Party Congress*. Beijing: Chuan Qiu Press, 1987.

Wang Jue and Lu Congming. "On the Main Contradiction in the Elementary Stage of Socialism in China." *Economic Research* 10 (1987).

Wang Meng. *Selected Works of Wang Meng*. Vol. 1: *The Straw of Meeting*, translated by Denis Mair; Vol. 2: *Snowball*, translated by Cathy Silber and Deirdre. Beijing: Foreign Language Press, 1989.

_____. *A Selection of Wang Meng's Novels and Reporting*. Beijing: Beijing Press, 1981.

Wang Paikun. *We Must Surpass Britain*. Beijing: World Knowledge Press, 1958.

Wang Ruowang. *There Is a Spirit between Earth and Heaven: A Selection of Wang Ruowang's Essays*. Hong Kong: Pai Shing Cultural Enterprise, 1989.

Wang Xiaoqiang and Bai Nanfeng. *Wealth Drawn into Poverty*. Sichuan: Sichuan People's Press, 1986.

Wang Yifang and Chen Mingxian. *The Purification and Rectification Movements of the Chinese Communist Party*. Heilongjiang: Heilongjiang People's Press, 1985.

Wei Chengshi. "Three Cultural Problems for Reform." *World Economic Herald*, August 8, 1988.

Wei Jingsheng and others. *A Selection of Poetry and Essays from the Beijing Spring Movement — The Fate of the "Democratic Wall."* Hong Kong: Ping Ming Press, 1979.

_____. *Say Yes to Yourself, Say Yes to Democracy — A Declaration of Human Rights by the Mainland Youths*. Taipei: Associate Press, 1979.

Wen Yuankai. *The Light of Reform*. Shanxi: Shanxi People's Press, 1984.

_____ and Nie Duan. *The Reform of the Chinese Character*. Hong Kong: Shu Guang Book Co., 1988.

Wong Donglin. *Dialogues with Liang Shumin*. Hunan: Hunan People's Press, 1988.

Wu Yannan. *Sun Yatsen and the Xing Hai Revolution*. Guizhou: Guizhou People's Press, 1986.

Xiao Zhou. *Ten Year Archives*. Hong Kong: Mirror Post Cultural Enterprises Co., 1988.

Xie Benshu. *Yun Shikai and the Northern Warlords*. Shanghai: Shanghai People's Press, 1984.

Xie Tianyou and Jian Xiuwei. *A Brief History of the Chinese Peasant War*. Shanghai: Shanghai People's Press, 1981.

Xinhua News Agency's Domestic Information Office. *Chronicles of Ten Years of Reform: 1978–1987*. Beijing: Xinhau News Agency, 1988.

Xu Xing. *China's Politics in the Reform Era*. Hong Kong: Pioneer Publishers, 1986.

_____. *Deng's Open Policy*. Hong Kong: Pioneer Publishers, 1987.

Yan Jiaqi and Gao Gao. *A Ten Year History of the Cultural Revolution.*
    Hong Kong: Dagongbao Press, 1987.
Yan Jiaqi and others. *The True Face of the April 5th Movement.* Beijing:
    People's Press, 1979.
Yin Hai-Kwong. *Reappraisal of Cultural Change in Modern China.* Taipei:
    Book World Co., 1966.
Yu Chuanjiang, ed. *A Collection of Jokes on the Cultural Revolution.*
    Sichuan: Southwestern Finance and Economics University Press, 1988.
Zheng Ming. *Wei Jingsheng and the Democratic Movement.* Taipei: Liming
    Cultural Enterprise, 1982.
Zhou Ming, ed. *History Stops Here to Reflect.* 3 vols. Beijing: Hua Xia
    Press, 1986.

INDEX